Santa Cruz Public Library

Finding list of books in the Santa Cruz city free public library

Santa Cruz Public Library

Finding list of books in the Santa Cruz city free public library

ISBN/EAN: 9783337284060

Printed in Europe, USA, Canada, Australia, Japan

Cover: Foto ©Andreas Hilbeck / pixelio.de

More available books at **www.hansebooks.com**

Finding List---Santa Cruz City Free Library.

ABBOTT, Charles C
Notes of the night. 9842 E
Upland and meadow. 2741 E
Waste-land wanderings. 1636 E

ABBOTT, Evelyn
History of Greece. 9580 H
Louis XIV. 11183 B
Pericles and the golden age of Athens. 11196 B

ABBOTT. Edwin, Rev
English lessons for English people. 11517 EE

ABBOTT, Jacob
Rollo on the Atlantic. 9265 J
— in Geneva. 9262 J
— In Holland. 9261 J
— in London. 9258 J
— in Paris. 9264 J
— in Rome. 9260 J
— in Scotland. 9259 J
— in Switzerland. 9257 J
Science for the young series.
Heat. 6423 J
Water and land. 6420 J

Light. 6224 J
Force. 6425 J

ABBOTT, Jacob and Abbott, John C
Alexander the Great. 4900 J
Alfred the Great. 4901 J
Cyrus the Great. 4907 J
Cleopatra. 4905 J
Charles I. 4903 J
Charles II. 4904 J
Darius the Great. 4908 J
Genghis Khan. 4910 J
Hannibal. 4911 J
Henry IV. 4912 J
Hernando Cortez. 4906 J
Julius Caesar. 4902 J
Josephine. 4915 J
Joseph Bonaparte. 4914 J
King Philip. 4916 J
Louis XIV. 4918 J
Louis Philippe. 4917 J
Mary Queen of Scotts. 4922 J
Marie Antoinette. 4920 J
Madame Roland. 4919 J
Margaret of Anjou. 4921 J

Nero. 4923 J
Peter the Great. 4924 J
Pyrrhus. 4925 J
Queen Elizabeth. 4909 J
Queen Hortense. 4913 J
Romulus. 4929 J
Richard I. 4926 J
Richard II. 4927 J
Richard III. 4928 J
William the Conqueror. 4930 J
Xerxes. 4931 J
ABBOTT, J S C
"American Pioneers and Patriots.
A series.
Life of Daniel Boone., 247 B
Columbus. 249 B
Kit Carson. 5545 B
David Crockett. 250 B
De Soto. 248 B
Paul Jones. 5604 B
Captain Kidd. 6344 B
La Salle. 252 B
Peter Stuyvesant. 253 B
Miles Standish. 5627 B
George Washington. 251 B
(These biographies throw side lights
on the early history of the United
States).
Civil War, history of, 3 vols. 4007 H
Napoleon Bonaparte. History of, 2
vols. 9822 H
Practical Christianity. 587 RE
Presidents, Lives of the. 8922 B
ABBOTT, Lyman
Life and letters of Paul, the apostle.
12577 B
ABBOTT, Mary
Alexia. 11501 F
Beverleys. 6224 F
(A story of Calcutta).
ABDY, J T
Feudalism: its rise, progress and
consequences. 7451 H
A'BECKET, Gilbert A
The comic Blackstone. 1146 F
ABER, Mary A-Alling
An experiment in education. 10494
EE
ABOUT, Edward
King of the mountains. 6175 F
Saving a daughter's dowry. 6175 F
ADAMS, Brooks
The law of civilization and decay: an
essay on history. 9988 H
ADAMS, Charles Francis Jr
A chapter of Erie. 11657 V
Richard Henry Dana; a biography;
2 vols. 6535 B

ADAMS, Charles Kendall
Representative American orations; 3
vols. 6514 E
Representative British orations; 3
vols. 6511 E
ADAMS, Davenport (ed)
By-ways in book-land. 7604 EE
Golden book of English song. 5789 P
ADAMS, George Burton
Civilization during the middle ages.
9582 H
ADAMS, Henry
Historical essays. 11393 H
History of the United States; 9 vols.
12124 H
John Randolph. Life of. 187 B
ADAMS, Henry C
Public debts. 8834 SS
ADAMS, Herbert B (ed)
Johns Hopkins university series in
historical and political economy.
First series. 10601 H
I—An introduction to American con-
stitutional history. By Edward A.
Freeman; with an account of Mr.
Freeman's visit to Baltimore, by the
editor.
II—The Germanic origin of New En-
gland towns. With notes on co-op-
eration in university work. By Her-
bert B. Adams.
III—Local government in Illinois. By
Albert Shaw, A. B. Local govern-
ment of Pennsylvania. By E. R. L.
Gould.
IV—Saxon tithingmen in America. By
Herbert B. Adams.
V—Local government in Michigan and
the northwest. By Edward W. Bemis.
VI—Parish institutions of Maryland.
With illustrations from parish rec-
ords. By Howard Ingle.
VII—Old Maryland manors. With the
records of a court leet and a court
baron. By John Johnson, A. B.
VIII—Norman constables in America.
By Herbert B. Adams.
IX-X—Village communities of Cape
Anne and Salem. By Herbert B.
Adams.
XI—The Genesis of a New England
state. By Alexander Johnston.
XII—Local government and free
schools in South Carolina. By B. J.
Ramage.
Second series. 10602 H
I-II—Methods of historical study. By
the editor.

III—The past and present of political economy. By Richard T. Ely.

IV—Samuel Adams, the man of the town meeting. By James K. Hosmer.

V-VI—Taxation in the United States. By Henry Carter Adams.

VII—Institutional beginnings in a western state. By Jesse Macy.

VIII-IX— Indian money as a factor in New England civilization. By William B. Weeden.

X—Town and county government in the English colonies of North America. The Toppan essay for 1883. By Edward Channing.

XI—Rudimentary society among boys. By John Johnson.

XII—Land laws of mining districts. By Charles Howard Shinn.

Third series. 11603 H

I—Maryland's influence upon land cessions to the United States. With minor papers on George Washington's interest in western lands. The Potomac company, pp. 79-91; Washington's plan for a national university, pp. 93-95; Origin of the Baltimore and Ohio railroad, pp. 97-102. By the editor.

II-III—Virginia local institutions, pp. 103-229; Virginia and Virginians, pp. 109-102; The land system, pp.123-142; The hundred, pp. 143-149; English parish in America, pp. 152-175; County, pp. 177-199; town, pp. 201-217; conclusion, pp. 217-222; appendix, pp. 223-229. By Edward Ingle.

IV—Recent American socialism, pp. 231-304; Early American communism, pp. 239-246; Henry George and the beginnings of revolutionary socialism, pp. 246-257; International workingmen's association, pp. 257-264; Propaganda of deed and the educational campaign, pp. 264-276; Socialistic labor party, pp. 276-283; ; Strength of revolutionary socialism, pp. 283-294; Remedies, pp. 294-304. By Richard T. Ely.

V-VI-VII—Local institutions of Maryland, pp. 305-433; Land system, pp. 311-342; Hundred, pp. 343-369; County, pp. 368-400; Town, pp. 401-433; By Lewis W. Wilhelm.

VIII—Influence of the proprieties in founding the state of New Jersey, pp. 435-460. By Austin Scott.

IX-X—American constitutions, pp. 461-530; Introduction, pp. 467-472; Revolutionary period, pp. 472-477; Modern state constitutions, pp. 477-482; Federal government, pp. 482-504; Judiciary, pp. 504-523; Tabulated comparison of modern state constitutions, pp. 522-530. By Hon. Horace Davis.

XI-XII—City of Washington, its origin and administration, pp. 531-585. By John Addison Porter.

Fourth series. 10604 H

I—Dutch village communities on the Hudson river. By Irving Elting.

II—Town government in Rhode Island. By Wm. E. Foster.

III—The Narragansett planters. By Edward Channing.

IV—Pennsylvania boroughs. By William P. Holcomb.

V—Introduction to the constitutional and political history of individual states. By J. F. Jameson.

VI—The Puritan colony at Annapolis, Maryland. By Daniel R. Randall.

VII-VIII-IX—History of the land question in the United States. By Shosuke Sato.

X—The town and city government of New Haven. By Charles H. Livermore.

XI-XII—The land system of the New England colonies. By Melville Egleston.

Fifth series. 10605 H

I-II—City government of Philadelphia. By Edward P. Allison.

III—City government of Boston. By James M. Bugbee.

V-VI—Local government in Canada. By George Bourinot.

VII—The influence of the war of 1812 upon the consolidation of the american union. By Nicholas Murray Butler.

VIII—Notes on the literature of charities. By Herbert B. Adams.

IX—The predictions of Hamilton and De Tocqueville. By James Bryce.

X—The study of history in England and Scotland. By Paul Fredericq.

XI—Seminary libraries and university extension. By Herbert B. Adams.

XII—European schools of history and politics. By Andrew D. White.

Sixth series. 10606 H

I-II—Co-operation in New England. By Edward W. Bemis.

III—Co-operation in the middle states. By Edward W. Bemis.
IV-V-VI—Co-operation in the north-west. By Albert Shaw.
VII-VIII—Three phases of co-opera-tion in the west. By Amos G. War-ner.
IX-X—Co-operation on the Pacific coast. By Charles Howard Shinn.
XI-XII—Co-operation in Maryland and the south. By Daniel R. Randall.
Seventh series. 10607 H
I—Arnold Toynbee. By F. C. Mon-tague. With an account of the work of Toynbee Hall in East London, by Phillip Lyttelton Gell. Also an ac-count of the neighborhood guild in New York, by Charles B. Stover.
II-III—The establishment of munici-pal government in San Francisco. By Bernard Moses.
IV—Municipal history of New Or-leans. By William W. Howe.
V-VI—English culture in Virginia. A study of the Gilmer letters, and an account of the English professors ob-tained by Jefferson for the Univer-sity of Virginia. By William P. Trent.
VII-VIII-IX—The river towns of Con-necticut, Wethersfield, Hartford and Winsor. By Charles M. Andrews.
X-XI-XII—Federal government in Canada. By John G. Bourinot.
Eighth series. 10608 H
I-II—The beginnings of American na-tionality. The constitutional rela-tions between the continental con-gress and the colonies and states. By Albion W. Small.
III—Local government in Wisconsin. By David E. Spencer.
IV—Spanish colonization in the south-west. By Frank W. Blackmar.
V-VI—The study of history in Ger-many and France. By Professor Paul Fredericq.
VII-VIII-IX—Progress of the colored people of Maryland since the war. By Jeffrey R. Brackett.
X—The study of history in Belgium and Holland. By Prof. Paul Fred-ericq.
XI-XII—Seminary notes on recent his-torical literature. By Dr. H. B. Adams, Dr. J. M. Vincent, Dr. W. B. Scaife and others.
Ninth series. 10609 H
I-II—Government and administration of the United States. By W. W. Willoughby and W. F. Willoughby.
III-IV—University education in Mary-land. By B. C. Steiner. The Johns Hopkins University (1876-1891. By President D. C. Gilman. With sup-plementary notes on university ex-tension and the university of the fu-ture. By R. G. Moulton.
V-VI—The communes of Lombardy from the VI to the X century. By William Klapp Williams.
VII-VIII—Public lands and agrarian laws of the Roman republic. By An-drew Stephenson.
IX—Constitutional development of Japan (1853-1881). By Toyokichi Iyenaga.

X—A history of Liberia. By J H. McPherson.

XI-XII—The character and influence of the Indian trade in Wisconsin. By Frederick Jackson Turner.

Tenth series. 10610 H

I The Bishop Hill colony; a religious communistic settlement in Henry county, Illinois. By Michael A Mikkelsen.

II-III—Church and state in New England. By Paul E. Lauer.

IV—Church and state in early Maryland. By Professor George Petrie.

V-VI—The religious development in the province of North Carolina. By Prof Stephen B. Weeks.

VII—Maryland's attitude in the struggle for Canada. By Professor John W. Black.

VIII-IX—The Quakers in Pennsylvania, 1622-1776. By Albert Clayton Applegarth.

X-XI—Columbus and his discovery of America. By Professors H. B. Adams and Henry Wood.

XII—Causes of the American revolution. By Prof James A Woodburn.

Eleventh series. 10611 H

I—The social condition of labor. By Dr. R. E. L. Gould.

II—The world's representative assemblies of today; a study in comparative legislation. By Professor Edmund K. Alden.

III-IV—The negro in the District of Columbia. By Professor Stephen B. Weeks.

V-VI—Church and state in North Carolina. By Prof. Stephen B. Weeks.

VII-VIII—The condition of the western farmer as illustrated by the economic history of a Nebraska township. By Arthur Fisher Bentley.

IX-X—History of slavery in Connecticut. By B. C. Steiner.

XI-XII—Local government in the south and the southwest. By Professor Edward W. Bemis and others. Popular election of United States senators. By John Haynes.

Twelfth series. 10612 H

I-II—The Cincinnati southern railway; a study in municipal activity. By J. H. Hollander. With a memorial of Dr. Lucius S. Merriam.

III—The constitutional beginnings of North Carolina (1663-1729). By J. S. Bassett.

IV—The struggle of the Protestant Dissenters for religious toleration in Virginia.

V-VI-VII—The Carolina pirates and colonial commerce, 1670-1740. By S. C. Hughson.

VIII-IX—History of representation and suffrage in Massachusetts (1620-1691). By G. H. Baynes.

X—English institutions and the American Indian. By J. A. James.

XI-XII—The international beginnings of the Congo Free State. By J. S. Reeves.

Thirteenth series. 10613 H

I-II—Government of the colony of South Carolina. By Edson L. Whitney.

III-IV—The early relations between Maryland and Virginia. By John H. Latane.

V—The rise and development of the bicameral system in America. By Thomas Francis Moran.

VI-VII—White servitude in the colony of Virginia. By James Curtis Ballagh.

VIII—The genesis of California's first constitution (1846-49). By Rockwell Dennis Hunt.

IX—Benjamin Franklin as an economist. By W. A. Wetzel.

X—The provisional government of Maryland (1774-1777). By John Archer Silver.

XI-XII—Government and Religion of the Virginia Indians. By S. R. Hendren.

Fourteenth series. 10614 H

I—Constitutional history of Hawaii. By Henry E. Chambers.

II—City government of Baltimore. By Thaddeus P. Thomas.

III—Colonial origins of New England senates. By F. L. Riley.

IV-V—Slavery and servitude in North Carolina. By John S. Bassett.

VI-VII—Representation in Virginia. By J. A. C. Chandler.

VIII—The history of taxation in Connecticut (1636-1776). By F. R. Jones.

IX-X—Slavery in New Jersey. By H. S. Cooley.

XI-XII—Causes of the Maryland revolution of 1689. By F. E. Sparks.

ADAMS, H G
Beautiful shells. 5083 S

Beautiful butterflies. 5084 S
ADAMS, John Coleman
   Christian types of heroism. S754 RE
ADAMS, Oscar Fay
   Dictionary of American authors. 11249 R
   Jane Austen; the story of her life. 12562 B
ADAMS, W H D
   Collection of English epigrams. 4824 L
   Good Queen Anne, 2 vols. 5113 B
   Land of the Incas. 2199 J
   Washington and other great military commanders. 11776 B
ADAMS, W I Lincoln
   Sunlight and shadow; a book for photographers, both amateur and professional. 12514 A
ADAMS, W T (See "Oliver Optic").
ADAMSON, Robert
   Tichte. 7637 B
ADDISON, Joseph
   Miscellaneous prose works. "Spectator, Tattler, etc.," 6 vols. 561 E
   Poetical works of. 560 P
ADELER, Max
   Random shots. 2917 L
A F and R L (edited by)
   Letters of Celia Thaxter. 9356 E
AGASSIZ, Alex
   Three cruises of the Blake, 2 vols. 1424 V
   (A coast survey steamer in Carribean sea, Mexican gulf and along Atlantic coast).)
AGASSIZ, Elizabeth Carey (ed)
   Louis Agassiz, his life and correspondence, 2 vols. 1234 B
AGASSIZ, L and Mrs. Elizabeth Carey

Journey in Brazil. 3390 V
AGUILAR Grace
(English writer of Spanish-Hebrew extraction).
   Days of Bruce. 11331 F
   (Robert, king of Scotland, 13th cen).
   Essays and miscellanies. 375 E
   Home influence (English home life) 2270 F
   Home scenes. 733 F
   Mother's recompense, sequel to Home influence. 2483 F
   Vale of cedars; or, The martyr. 744 F
   (Expulsion of the Jews from Spain, 15th century).
   Woman's friendship. 11497 F
   Women of Israel. 6420 B
AIDE, Hamilton
   Voyage of discovery; a novel of American society. 7337 F
AINGER, Alfred
   Charles Lamb. Life of. 6393 B
AINSWORTH, W Harrison
(Stories founded upon material taken from English history).
   Auriol; or, Elixir of life. 6080 F
   Beau-Nash; or, Bath in the 18th century. 6088 F
   Boscobel. 6091 F
   (England, 1651).
   Cardinal Pole; or, Days of Philip and Mary.
   Constable of the tower.
   Crichton. 6090 F
   Flitch of Bacon. 6093 F
   (Local customs of Dunmow for central plot).
   Guy Fawks; or, The gunpowder plot. 6096 F

(England, 1605).
Jack Sheppard. 6087 F
James II; or, The revolution of 1688.
6082 F
Lancashire witches. 6098 F
(Time of James I (1603-25).
Manchester rebels. 6083 F
Mervyn Clitheroe. 6097 F
Miser s daughter. 6094 F
(Time of George II).
Old Saint Paul's. 6099 F
(Plague and fire of London, 1666)
Ovingdean Grange. 6080 F
Rook-wood. 6095 F
Saint-James's. 6089 F
(Court of Queen Anne).
Spendthrift. 6081 F
Star-chamber. 6085 F
Tower of London. 6092 F
Windsor castle. 6084 F
(Time of Henry VIII).
AIRY, Osmund
English restoration and Louis XIV.
5489 H
AITKEN, Mary Carlyle
Scottish song. 6504 P
ALCOCK, Sir Rutherford
Capital of the Tycoon, 2 vols. 3280 V
ALCOTT, A Bronson
Ralph Waldo Emerson, an estimate
of his character. 6354 E
ALCOTT, Louisa M
Comic Tragedies. 8013 P
Cupid and chow-chow. 6486 J
Eight cousins. 10206 J
Garland for girls. 10199 J
Hospital sketches. 10200 J
Jack and Jill. 10205 J
Jimmy's cruise in the Pinafore, and
other stories. 10298 J
Jo's boys; sequel to Little men.
10331 J
Little men. 7886 J
Little women. 10207 J
Lulu's library. 711 J
Modern Mephistophles. 10210 J
Moods. 10212 F
My boys, and other stories. 6483 J
My girls and other stories. 6485 J
Old-fashioned girl. 7893 J   .
Old-fashioned Thanksgiving and oth-
er stories. 6484 J
Proverb stories. 10202 J
Rose in bloom. 10211 J
Sequel to Eight cousins.
Shawl straps.
Silver pitchers, and other stories.
10208 J
Spinning-wheel stories. 10208 J
Under the lilacs. 10298 J
Work; a story of experience. 10201 F
ALDEN, Mrs I M (See "Pansy")
ALDEN, W L
Christopher Columbus, Life of. 2000B
Jimmy Brown papers. 9983 J
Loss of the Swansea. 10908 J
Moral pirates. 4934 J
New Robinson Crusoe. 8651 J
ALDRICH, Herbert L
Arctic Alaska and Siberia. 4941 J
Flower and thorn. 6192 P
From Ponkapog to Pesth. 1075 V
Marjorie Daw and other people.
1077 F
Mercedes; a drama in two parts.
8245 P
Out of his head. 937 F
Prudence Palfrey. 1078 F
Queen of Sheba. 2130 F
Stillwater tragedy. 1076 F
Story of a bad boy. 8653 J
Two bites of a cherry, with other
tales. 8009 F
ALEXANDER, Archibald
Canon of the old and new testa-
ments. 7382 RE
Evidences of the authenticity, in-
spiration and canonical authority of
the Holy Scriptures. 7385 RE
Theories of the will in the history of
philosophy. 12596 EE
ALEXANDER, James W
Archibald Alexander, Life of. 7384 B
ALEXANDER, Mrs (pseud of Mrs. A
F Hector)
Blind fate. 7475 F
Broken links. 8489 F
Fight with fate. 9590 F
Mrs. Crichten's creditor. 10736 F
Snare of the fowler. 7825 F
Wooing o't. 10822 F
ALEXANDER, W D
Brief history of the Hawaiian peo-
ple. 8222 H
ALGER, Horatio Jr
Errand boy. 11337 J
Facing the world. 7962 J
Helen Ford. 6271 J
The $500 check. 7716 J
Train boy. 11337 J
ALGER, William
Genesis of solitude. 6379 E
ALLARD, Hafix
Nirgis and Bismillah. 5072 F
ALLEN, Alexander
Jonathan Edwards. 6254 B

ALLEN, C B
Man wonderful in the house beauti-
ful. 5405 S
ALLEN, C L
Bulbs and tuberous-rooted plants.
11175 A
ALLEN, Francis H (compiler)
Nature's diary. 10809 E
ALLEN, Grant
Charles Darwin, Life of. 232 B
Common sense science. 289 S
Evolution of the idea of God. 10862
RE
Incidental bishop. 12354 F
Scallyway. 7982 F
Story of the plants. 9378 S
AILLEN, Henry S
Two Americas. 4140 H
ALLEN, James Lane
Aftermath sequel to Kentucky car-
dinal. 10507 F
Blue-grass region of Kentucky.
9587 V
Choir invisible. 10726 F
John Gray. 7744 F
Kentucky cardinal. 10506 F
ALLEN, Joseph
Battles of the British army, 2 vols.
6620 H
ALLEN, Louis F
American farm book. 6728 A
ALLEN ,Paul
Lewis and Clark's expeditions, 2 vols.
1632 V
ALLEN, William Francis
Readers' guide to English history.
6733 R
Essays and monographs. 10597 ͳ
ALLEN, Willis Boyd
Red mountains of Alaska. 6341 V
Pineboro quartette. 11908 J
ALLEN and Myers
Ancient history. 8218 H
ALLIN, Thomas
Universalism asserted as hope of the
gospel. 8866 RE
ALLINGHAM, William
Ballad book. 6508 P

ALLISON, Archibald
Europe, History of (1789-1815).
4099 H
A. L. O. E.
Fairy Frisket; or peeps at insect life.
8123 J
Fairy know-a-bit. 8139 J
ALTON, Edmund (Edmund Bailey)
Among the law-makers. 8155 J
ALZOG
Universal church history, 3 vols.
4275 RE
AMERICAN Poultry Association
American standard of excellence.
1823 A
AMES, Lucia True
Memorial of a millionaire. 7254 B
AMES, Mary Clemmer
Eirene. 702 F
AMICIS, E de
Cuore; an Italian school-boy's jour-
nal. 8128 J
Morocco; its people and places. 8530V
AMMEN, Rear Admiral
Old navy and the new. 11187 H
AMOS, Sheldon
Science of law. 1392 SS
Political and legal remedies of war.
8532 SS
Science of politics. 11364 SS
"AN AMERICAN"
Story of Mary. 11706 F
ANDERSON, Edward Playfair
Best letters of Madame de Sevigne.
7242 E
ANDERSON, Hans Christian
Improvisitore. 7351 F
(Life in Italy contrasted with life in
Denmark. Story of a little Roman
singer).
Fairy tales and stories. 10419 J
Story book. 942 J
Story of my life. 6217 B
ANDERSON, Jerome A
Drifting in dreamland. 10329 P
Karma; a story of the law of cause
and effect. 11788 RE
Reincarnation. 8536 RE

ANDERSON, Mrs A Maskell
Children with the birds. 10986 J
Children with the fishes. 10985 J
ANDERSON, Rasmus B
America not discovered by Columbus. 7275 H
Literature of Scandinavian north. 8095 EE
Norse mythology. 8093 F
ANDERSON, Winslow
Mineral springs and health resorts of California. 8348 R
ANDRAE, Percy
Vanished Emperor. 10458 F
ANDREWS, Byron
William McKinley, Life and speeches of. 11574 B
ANDREWS, Charles M
Historical development of modern Europe. 11286 H
ANDREWS, E Benjamine
History of the last quarter century in the United States, 2 vols. 10080 H
ANDREWS, Israel Ward
Manual of the constitution. 9585 H
ANDREWS, Jane
Seven little sisters. 4936 J
Seven little sisters prove their sisterhood. 10517 J
Stories mother nature told her children. 11177 J
Ten boys who lived on the road from long ago until now. 4937 J
(Good introduction to history for young readers).
ANDREWS, Samuel J
Our Lord upon the earth, Life of. 11842 B
ANGOT, Alfred
Aurora Borealis. 11361 S
ANNANDALE, Charles (ed)
Imperial dictionary, 4 vols. 1654 R
"AN OLD BOY"
Notes for boys. 336 J
"AN OLD Stair Builder"
New system of hand railing. 8280 A
ANSTEY, F (pseud, F. A. Guthrie)
Black poodle. 3059 F
Giant's robe. 8960 F
Statement of Stella Maberly. 9912 F
Tinted Venus. 30660 F
Vice.Versa; a lesson to fathers. 3058F
ANTHON, William
Dictionary of antiquities. 4833 R
APGAR, Austin C
Trees of the northern United States. 7723 S

APPLETON, D
General guide to the United States and Canada (western and southern states). 9050 V
ARBER, Edward
Pilgrim fathers, Story of (1608-1623) 1487 H
ARCHER, T A
Crusades. 9567 H
ARGYLL, Duke of
Primeval man. 1461 S
Reign of Law. 1488 S
Unity of nature. 1467 S
ARISTOTLE, Nicomochean Ethics
Tr. by Rev. R. W. Browne.
Rhetoric and poetics. 8035 EE
"ARKANSAS Traveller" (see O. P. Read).
ARMSTRONG, Annie E
Three bright girls. 11329 J
ARMSTRONG, E
Lorenzzo De Medici and Florence in the 15th century. 10883 B
ARMSTRONG, Eliza
Teacup club. 12012 B
ARMSTRONG, Walter
Wrestling. 7544 A
ARNOLD, Sir Edward
Adzuma and the Japanese wife. 7740 P
Indian idyls. 6734 P
Japonica. 6759 H
Light of Asia. 10651 P
Light of the world. 6055 P
Lotus and jewel. 88 P
Potiphar's wife. 7042 P
ARNOLD, Frederick
Turning points in life. 455 E
ARNOLD, Isaac N
Abraham Lincoln, Life of. 1292 B
ARNOLD, MATTHEW
Culture and anarchy. 465 E
Essays in criticism. 464 E
Estimate of General Grant. 1278 B
Friendship's garland. 465 E
Last essays. 324 E
Literature and dogma. 3047 E
Poetical works of. 7952 P
St. Paul and protestantism. 324 E
Sweetness and light. 527 E
ARNOLD, Sarah L
Waymarks for teachers showing aims, principles and plans of everyday teaching. 12284 EE
ARNOLD, Thomas
Rome, History of. 11174 H
ARNOLD, Thomas Kechever
First Latin book. 8378 EE

Practical introduction to Latin com-
position. 8383 EE
ARNOT, William
Illustrations of the book of Prov-
erbs. 11717 RE
ARTHUR, T S
Bar-room at Brantley. 2115 F
Buds and blossoms. 936 F
Good time coming. 6415 F
Home scenes. 3069 F
Lessons in life. 3075_F
Married life. 3067 F
Off-hand sketches. 3071 F
Six nights with the Washingtonians.
5245 F
Stories for young housekeepers. 3070
F
Words for the wise. 3074 F
ABJORNSEN, P C
Fairy tales from the nor.... 12367 J
ASHMONT (pseud)
Dogs; their management and treat-
ment in disease. 11874 A
ASHMUN, J
Memoir of life and character of Rev
Samuel Bacon. 7383 B
ATHERTON, Gertrude F
American wives and English hus-
bands. 11065 F
Doomswoman. 7841 F
Los Cerritos. 6949 F
Whirl asunder. 9982 F
ATKINS, Frederick A
Moral muscle. 7280 EE
ATKINSON, Edward
Distribution of products. 209 SS
Elementary treatise of physics.
9883 S
Industrial progress of the nation.
7612 SS
Science of nutrition. 5993 S
ATKINSON, James (trans)
Shah Nameh of the Persian poet
Firdausi. 357 P
ATKINSON, Philip
Elements of dynamics, electricity and
magnetism. 7096 S
ATKINSON, Thomas W

Travels on the upper and lower
Amoor. 3289 V
ATWOOD, Daniel T
Atwood's country and suburban
houses. 11660 A
AUBREY, Frank
Devil tree of the El Dorado. 10699 F
AUBREY, W H S
Rise and growth of the English na-
tion, 3 vols. 11349 H
AUDUBON, Mrs Lucy (ed)
John J Audubon, Life of. 5524 B
AUERBACH, Berthold
Aloys. 837 F
Brigitta. 1177 F
Convicts and their children. 1182 F
Joseph in the snow. 7474 F
Lorley and Reinhard. 836 F
On the heights, 2 vols. 6750 F
AUSTEN, **Jane**
(English national and social life).
Emma. 6661 F
Mansfield park. 6453 F
Northanger abbey. 6312 F
Persuasion. 6314 F
Pride and prejudice. 5826 F
Sense and sensibility. 6313 F
AUSTIN, Sir Alfred
English lyrics. 6509 P
Human tragedy. 6773 P
Prince Lucifer. 6772 P
Tower of Babel. 6771 P
AUSTIN, Jane G
(American colonial life).
Betty Alden. 10082 F
(Sequel to Standish of Standish).
David Alden's daughter, and other
stories. 8642 F
Desmond hundred. ?
Dr. Le Baron and his daughters.
8643 F
(Sequel to Nameless nobleman).
Mrs Beauchamp Brown
Nameless nobleman. 5713 F
Nantucket scraps. 2233 F
"A VOLUNTEER SPECIAL"
Volcano under the city. 4358 H

Leibbrandt & Lewis,

Staple and
Fancy Groceries.

Fresh Fruits & Vegetables a specialty.
HAY, WOOD AND GRAIN.
COUNTRY PRODUCE.
10 Pacific Av. Tel. Red 85.
All street cars pass the door.

AVERY, Elroy M
Elements of natural philosophy.
8365 S
AYRE, Rev John
Treasury of Bible knowledge. 16731
AZARIAS, Brother (pseud)
Phases of thought and criticism.
7603 E

BABCOCK, William C
Two lost centuries of Britain. 6552 H
BACKUS, Truman J (ed)
Shaw's English literature. 11762 EE
BACON, Alice Mabel
Japanese girls and women. 7110 H
Japanese interior. 11279 H
BACON, Francis
Essays. 315 E
Essays and counsels. 10157 E
R W Church, Life of. 217 E
BACON, George B (compiler)
Siam, the land of the white elephant.
9059 V
BAGBY, Albert Morris
Miss Fra umerei; a Weimar idyl.
12212 F
BAILEY, Alice Ward
Mark Heffron. 9732 F
BAILEY, J M
They all do it. 8999 F
BAILEY, Philip James
Angel world and other poems. 9763P
Fairy tale,, the mystic, and a spirit-
ual legend. 9 P
Festus; a poem. 8895 P
BAILLE, Joanna
Dramatic works of. 3 vols. 5023 P
BAILEY, William L
Our own birds. 7743 S
BAIN, Alex
Mind and body. 1386 EE
Education as a science. 1405 EE
BAIN, R. Nesbet
Charles XII and the collapse of the
Swedish empire. 11192 B
BAIRD, Charles W
Huguenot emigration, History of, 2
vols. 6385 H
Henry of Navarre and the Hu-
guenots. 4167 H
BAKER, George A
Mrs. Hephaistus and other tales.
3182 F
Bad habits of good society. 7291 EE
BAKER, George M
Handy speaker. 7100 P
Mimic stage. 433 P

Popular speaker. 7101 P
Running to waste. 509 J
BAKER, Gen L C
United States secret service, History
of. 546 H
BAKER, Sir S W
Cast up by the sea. 3005 F
Nile tributaries of Abysinnia.3353 V
Rifle and hound in Ceylon. 3006 V
BAKER, W M
Blessed Saint Certainty. 7959 F
(Connected with His majesty, my-
self).
His majesty, myself. 7960 F
Making of a man. 7961 F
(Sequel to His majesty, myself).
Mose Evans. 1140 F
New Timothy. 794 F
BALCH, William R
James A. Garfield, Life of. 1264 B
James G. Blaine, Life and public
services of. 8925
General Grant, Life and services of.
171 B
BALDWIN, James
Book-lover (a guide to the best read-
ing). 7596 EE
Story of the golden age. 9339 F
BALDWIN, John D
Ancient America. 556 H
Prehistoric nations. 559 H
BALDWIN, Joseph
Art of school management. 8833 EE
Psychology applied to the art of
teaching 7432 EE
BALESTIER, Wolcott
Benefits forgot (joint author. See
Kipling, R)
BALFOUR, M C
White sand. 10457 F
BALL, J Dyer
Things Chinese. 11265 H
BALL, Sir Robert S
Cause of an ice age. 7066 S
In starry realms. 7698 S
Story of the heavens. 1434 S
BALL, W W
Short account of the history of
mathematics. 12202 S
BALLANTYNE, Archibald
Lord Catharet: a political biography,
1690-1763. 12479 B
BALLANTYNE, Robert Michael
Erling the bold. 11790 F
Fire brigade. 11668 F
Freaks on the fells. 6262 F
Gorilla hunters. 4815 J

Shifting winds; a story of the sea. 3119 F

Wild man of the west. 512 F

BALLANTYNE, Sergeant
Experiences of a barrister's life. 244 B

BALLOU, M Maturin
New Eldorado; a summer journey to Alaska. 5843 V
Story of Malta. 7737 H
Under the southern cross. 3131 V

BALMES, Rev J
European civilization. 4278 H

BALZAC, Honore de
Alcahest. 3196 F
Catharine de Medici. 8773 F
C'esar Birotteau. 3194 F
Country doctor. 771 F
Cousin Pons. 3192 F
Daughter of Eve. 9420 F
Duchess de Langeais. 6320 F
Eugenie Grandet. 9045 F
Fame and sorrow. 6318 F
Magic skin. 3195 F
Marriage contract. 9351 F
Pere Goriot. 3191 F
Seraphita. 6321 F
Sons of the soil. 6322 F
Start in life. 9350 F
Terragus, chief of the Devorants. Two young married women. 8184 F
Vendetta. 6952 F
Village rector. 8185 F

BAMFORD, Mary E
Land and water friends. 11287 J
Up and down the brooks. 5439 J

BANCROFT, Charles
Footprints of time. 6363 F

BANCROFT, Geo
United States, History of (to 1789), 9 vols. 4053 H

BANCROFT, Hubert Howe
California interpocula. 4450 H
California pastoral. 4453 H
Essays and miscellany. 5854 H
Alaska, History of (1730-1885). 4448 H

Arizona and New Mexico, History of. 5848 H
British Columbia, History of. 4447H
California, History of, 1542-1890, 7 4435 H
Central America, History of, 3 vols. vols. 4435 H
Literary industries. 5855 II
Mexico, History of (1516-1887), 6 vols, 4428 H
Native races, 5 vols. 4420 H
Nevada, Colorado and Wyoming, History of. 5850 H
New Mexican states and Texas (1531-1789), History of, 2 vols. 4434 H
Northwest coast, History of, 2 vols. 4445 H
Oregon, History of, 2 vols. 4449 H
Popular tribunals. 4451 H
Utah, History of. 4782 H
Washington, Idaho and Montana (1845-1889). 5853 H

BANDELIER, A F
Delight makers. 6451 F
(Pueblo Indians).

BANGS, John Kendrick
Ghosts I have met and some others. 11991 F
Houseboat on the Styx. 9519 F
Idiot. 9287 F
Mr. Bonaparte of Corsica. 9135 F
Pursuit of the houseboat. 10551 F
Toppleton's client. 7806 F
Water ghost and other stories. 8790F

BANKS, Martha Burr
Little comrade mine. 7930 F

BANKS, Mary Ross
Bright days in old plantation time. 9910 F

BANKS, Mattie B
Richard and Robin. 7789 F

BANVARD, Rev John
Daniel Webster, Life and character of. 159 B
Court and times of George IV. 11712B

BARBER, Edward C
Crack shot. 11859 A

BARHAM, R H (Thomas Ingoldsby)
Ingoldsby legends. ?
BARING, Gould S (see Gould, S Baring)
BARKER, Capt A S (U S N)
Deep sea soundings. 7724 S
BARKER, Charles Francis
American checker player. 7937 A
BARKER, Lady
Spring comedies. 765 F
BARNARD, Henry (ed)
Papers on Froebel's kindergarten. 7606 EE
BARNEBY, W Henry
Life and labor in the far, far west. 163 V
BARNES'
Ancient peoples, History of. 8854 H
United States, Popular history of. 8905 H
BARNES, James
For king or country. 8908 J
Midshipman Farragut. 10004 J
Princetonian. 10868 J
BARNES, Josiah
Old inn. 507 F
BARR, Amelia
Bernicia. 9327 F
Between two loves. 5525 F
Border shepherdess. 773 F
Bow of orange ribbon. 4944 F
Cluny McPherson. 8180 F
Christopher and other stories. 9610 F
Daughter of fife. 5945 F
Feet of clay. 9608 F
Friend Olivia. 5957 F
Hallam succession. 8473 F
Household of McNeil. 5958 F
Knight of the nets. 9901 F
Jan Vedder's wife. 5526 F
Last of the Macallisters. 5527 F
Lone house. 8404 F
Lost silver of Briffault. 9797 F
Love for an hour is love forever. 8475 F
Master of his fate. 4946 F
Michael and Theodora. 7689 F
Paul and Christina. 3124 F
Preacher's daughter. 7692 F
Prisoners of conscience. 10371 F
Remember the Alamo. 11477 F
Scottish sketches. 2163 F
She loved a sailor. 8474 F
Singer from the sea. 8181 F
Sister to Esau. 9609 F
Squire of sandal-side. 3165 F

BARR, Robert
In the midst of alarms. 10633 F
Mutable many. 10539 F
Tekla; a romance of love and war. 12574 F
Woman intervenes. 9545 F
BARRETT, Frank
Admirable Lady Biddy Fane. 3229 F
Kit Wyndham. 6962 F
Smuggler's secret. 6984 F
BARRETT, Joseph H
Abraham Lincoln, Life of. 127 B
BARRETT, Mary
William the Silent.. 7312 B
BARRIE, J M
Auld licht idylls. 10425 F
Edinburgh eleven. 7766 E
Little minister. 7768 F
Margaret Ogilvy. 10083 F
Sentimental Tommy. 12348 F
When a man's single. 8637 F
Window in Thrums. 8636 F
BARRITT, Leon (ed)
All the world over. (Selections from famous American authors. 1131 L
BARROW, J
Mutiny of the bounty. 1131 L
BARROWS, Anna (ed)
Eggs; facts and fancies about them. 7117 L
BARROWS, Samuel J and Isabel C
Shaybacks in camp; ten summers under canvas. 3146 J
BARROWS, William
Oregon, History of. 4283 H
BARRY, Fanny
Soap bubble stories. 7577 J
BARRY, J (compiler)
Columbus, Life of. 258 B
BARRY, P
Fruit garden. 9572 A
BARRY, T A
Men and memories of San Francisco. 274 H
BARTH, Henry
Travels and discoveries in north and central Africa. 3376 V
BARTLETT, David W
London by day and night. 5510
BARTLETT, William
Facts I ought to know about the government of my country. 12009 SS
BASKETT, James Newton
Story of the birds. 10333 S
BASTIAT, M Frederic
Sophisms of protection. 11820 SS

BATES, Arlo
In the bundle of time. 7746 F
Lad's love. 3145 F
Pagans. 11819 F
Puritans. 12547 F
Talks on the study of literature. 10849 EE
Talks on writing English. 10084 EE
Told in the gate. 11509 F
Wheel of fire. 2598 F
BATES, Henry Walter
Naturalist on the river Amazon. 7701 V
BATES, Catherine Lee
Hermit island. 6468 F
BAUGHAN, Rosa
Influence of the stars. 11097 S
BAXLEY, H Willis
Spain, History of, 2 vols. 4223 H
BAXTER, W E
America and the Americans. 1226 V
BAYARD, Chevalier and The Cid
Heroes of history. 523 H
BAYARD, James (see Taylor, Bayard)
BAYLISS, Clara Kern
In brook and bayou. 10499 F
BAYLOR, Francis C
Behind the blue ridge. 3152 F
BAYLY Ada Ellen (see Lyall, Edna)
BAYN, George M
Galaski. 2913 F
BAYNE, Peter
Essays in biography and criticism, 2 vols. 5499 E
Martin Luther: his life and work. 7315 B
BAYNES, Herbert
Dante and his ideal. 6830 B
BAZAN. Emilia Pardo
Russia; people and literature. 11428H
BEACONSFIELD. B; Disraeli, Earl of
Coningsby. 2812 F

Contarini Fleming. 2806 F
Count Alarcos. 2805 F
Endymion. 2814 F
Henrietta Temple. 2808 F
Infernal marriage. 2807 F
Ixion in heaven. 2807 F
Lothiar. 2813 F
Miriam Alroy. 2807 F
Rise of Iskander. 2806 F
Sybil. 2810 F
Tancred. 2811 F
Venetia. 2809 F
Vivian Grey. 2804 F
Young Duke. 2805 F
BEADLE, J H
Undeveloped west. 3389 V
BEALE, Lionel S
Protoplasm; physical life and law. 7522 S
BEALE, Stephen
Profitable poultry keeping. 1796 A
BEAMER, A Hume
M. Stambuloff; a biography. 9753 B
BEARD, Dan
Moonlight and six feet of romance. 7127 F
BEARD, J R and C (ed)
Cassell's Latin dictionary. 1670 R
BEARD, D C
American boys' handy book. 8308 J
BEARD, James Carter
Curious homes and their tenants. 10792 S
BEARD, Lena and Adelia B
American girls' handy book. 520 J
BEATH, Robert B
Grand army of the republic, History of. 4762 H
BEAUGRAND, Charles
Walks abroad of two young naturalists. 8143 J

BEAUMONT, and J. Fletcher
Best plays of. 8194 P
BEAUREPAIRE, Guy de
Woodman. 7681 F
BEAZLEY, C. Raymond
Prince Henry, the navigator. 11185B
John and Sebastian Cabot. 11979 B
BECKE, Louis
Wild life in the southern seas. 11091V
Pacific tales. 11982 F
FORD, William
Caliph Vethek. History of the 653 F
BEECHER, Charles
Eden tableau. 8907 RE
BEECHER, C E and Mrs Stowe
American women's home. 4063 A
BEECHER, Henry Ward
Christ. Life of. 222 B
Norwood: or, village life in New England. 2878 F
Star papers 6203 EE
Twelve lectures to young men. 724EE
BEECHER, Mrs Henry Ward
Letters from Florida. 9270 V
BEECHER, Lyman
Autobiography of. 132 B
BEEHLER W H
Cruise of the Brooklyn. 3287 V
BEERS, Henry A
N. P. Willis. Life of. 1237 B
Outline sketch of American literature. 1278 EE
BEESLY, A H
Gracchi, Marius and Sulla. 5473 B
Sir John Franklin. 5354 B
BEESLY, E S
Queen Elizabeth. 6776 B
BEGG, Alex
Wrecks in the sea of life. 2943 F
BEHR, H H
Local flora (San Francisco). 8448 S
BELDEN Franklin Edson
Crown jewels of art. 9673 R
BEL L, Catharine
An orphan at Karnsford. 838 F
Grange: or, home life. 2261 F
BELL, Sir Charles
Hand: its mechanism, etc. 1466 S
BELL, Clarence Clough and Robert
Underwood Johnson (eds)
Battles and leaders of civil war, 4
vols. 6028 H
BELL, Clara (pseud)
Tridolins mystical marriage. 2009 F
Hour will come. 2672 F
Our own set. 2247 F
Trafalgar. 1170 F
BELL, James S

Journal of residence in Circassia.
'37 to '39, 2 vols. 50100 V
BELL, Lilian
From a girl's point of view. 10638 E
Little sister to the wilderness. 10152F
Love affairs of an old maid. 7902 F
Under-side of things. 1031 F
BELL, N R E (N D'anvers)
Elementary history of art, 2 vols.
11156 A
BELL, Robert
Songs of the dramatists. 7o-1 P
BELLAMY, Edward
Blind man's world and other stories.
12547 F
Equality. 10495 F
Looking backward. 2000-1887. 11480F
Miss Ludington's sister. 6281 F
BELLAMY, William
Century of charades. 9528 A
BELT, Thomas
Naturalist in Nicaragua. 7712 V
BELTON, John Devoe
Literary manual of foreign quotations. 6336 R
BENEDICT, E L
Happy time faces in rhyme. 10686 P
Stories of persons and places in
Europe. 8079 J
BENEDICT, Frank Lee
Twixt hammer and anvil. 9452 F
BENJAMINE, Park
Age of electricity. 1537 S
BENJAMINE, S G W
Our American artists. 7266 B
Persia, story of. 533 H
BENNETT, Alfred and G Murray
Cryptogamic botany. 1678 L
BENNETT, Charles
London people. 544 L
BENNETT, Emerson
Phantom of the forest.11769 F
BENNETT, W H M A
Bible stories retold for the young.
12324 J
BENSOW, E W
Boy life; its trial, its strength and
its fulness. 6522 E
BENSON, Luther
Life of. (Called "Fifteen years in
hell"). 1254 B
BENTON, Thomas Hart
Decision in the Dred Scott case. 694H
Thirty years' view, 1820-1850, 2 vols.
434 H
BERDOE, Edward
Browning cyclopedia. 7865 R
Browning studies. 9500 R

BERGER, E (pseud)
Charles Auchester. 1402 S
BERNARD, F and R Whiting
Wonderful escapes
BERNSTEIN, Julius
Five senses of man. 1402 S
BERTRAM, James G
Harvest of the sea. 11663 S
BESANT, Walter
All in a garden fair. 5160 F
All sorts and conditions of men.
5161 F
Armorel of Lyonesse. 10817 F
Beyond the dreams of avarice. 9164F
Changeling. 12551 F
Children of Gibeon. 10818 F
Fountain sealed. 10852 F
In deacon's orders. 9364 F
Master craftsman. 9801 F
Rebel queen. 7905 F
St. Katharine by the tower. 8243 F
Westminster. 9815 H
BESANT and Palmer
Jerusalem the city of Herod and Sa-
ladin.. 8258 H
BESANT and Rice
By Celia's arbour. 5154 F
Case of Mr. Lucraft and other tales.
5154 F
Chaplain of the fleet. 5191 F
Golden butterfly. 5149 F
Lament of Dives. 6954 F
Monk of Thelema. 5151 F
My little girl. 5141 F
Ready money Mortiboy. 5142 F
Seamy side. 5152 F
Son of Vulcan. 5146 F
'Twas in Trafalgar bay. 5153 F
With harp and crown. 6287 F
BESSEY Charles E
Essentials of botany. 10886 S
BIART Lucian
Aztecs, their history manners and
customs. 10512 H
BICKERSTRETH, Edward Henry
Two brothers, and other poems.
11553 P

BICKMORE, Albert S
Travels in the East Indian Archipel-
ago. 3356 V
BIDWELL, Jennie
There's nothing in it. 10181 F
BIERCE, Ambrose
Black beetles in amber. 7423 P
Can such things be? 8210 F
Fantastic tales. 12630 F
In the midst of life. 11922 F
BIERCE, Ambrose and Danziger, G A
Monk and hangman's daughter.7422F
BIGELOW, John
William Cullen Bryant, Life of
BIGELOW, John (ed)
Benjamin Franklin. Life of. 3 vols.
12286 B
BIGELOW, Poultney
German emperor. 7252 B
White man's Africa. ..248 V
BILLINGS, Frank S
Relation of animal diseases to pub-
lic health. 12329 S
BILLINGS, Josh (Henry Shaw)
Works of. 4846 F
BINGHAM, D
Bastile, The. 2 vols. 6562 H
BIRCH B
Egypt, to B C 300 (Ancient history
from the monuments). 12452 H
BIRD, Isabella L (Mrs Isabella L
Bishop)
Golden Chersonese. 5529 V
Hawaiian archipelago; six months
among the Sandwich islands. 3775V
Lady's life in the Rocky mountains.
5530 V
Unbeaten tracks in Japan. 5531 V
BIRNEY, William
James G Burney and his times.
11699 B
BIRRELL, Augustine
Men, women and books. 8097 E
Obiter dicta, 2 vols. 7108 E
BISHOP, Daniel H
Thousand miles' walk across South
America. 3358 V

BISHOP, W H
  Golden justice. 3126 F
  Old Mexico and her lost provinces.
  3391 V
BISSELL, Mary Taylor
  Physical development and exercise
  for women. 7302 S
BJORNSON, Bjornstjerne
  Arne. 2277 F
  Bridal march and other stories. 6879F
  Happy boy. 831 F
  Magnhild. 6878 F
  Sigurd Slembe. 3210 P
  Synnove Solbakken
BLACK William
  Adventures of a house-boat. 6439 F
  Briseis. 10026 F
  Green pastures and Picacd.....y. 938 F
  Handsome Humes. 8208 F
  Highland cousins. 8743 F
  Judith Shakespeare. 8066 F
  Macleod of Dare. 2083 F
  Madcap Violet. 11489 F
  Oliver Goldsmith, Life of. 8462 F
  Princess of Thule. 8462 F
  Stand fast, Craig-Royston. 6078 F
  Sunrise. 6304 F
  That beautiful wretch. 6237 F
  Wolfenberg. 7764 F
BLACKBURN, Henry
  Traveling in Spain. 5181 V
BLACKMORE, Richard D
  Craddock Nowell. 2359 F
  Cripps, the carrier. 2360 F
  Dariel; a romance of Surrey. 11297 F
  Erema. 2360 F
  Kit and Kitty. 5532 F
  Lorna Doone. 9735 F
  Perlycross. 8638 F
  Springhaven. 3215 F
BLAIKIE, William
  How to get strong and how to stay
  so. 6443 S
  Sound bodies for our boys and girls.
  6397 S
BLAINE, James G
  Twenty years of Congress, 2 vols.
  214 H
BLAIR, Thomas S
  Human progress; what can man do
  to further it? 10406 SS
BLAKE, Lillie D
  Woman's place today. 2942 SS
BLAKE, Mary
  Twenty-six hours a day. 2254 A
BLAKE, Mary Elizabeth and Mary F
Sullivan
  Mexico; picturesque, political and

progressive. 5453 H
BLAKELEE, George E
  Industrial cyclopedia. 1548 R
BLANCHARD, Amy E
  Girl of '76. 12310 J
  Taking a stand. 12225 J
BLASERNA, Pietro
  Theory of sound in its relation to
  music. 1401 S
BLAVATSKY, Madame H P
  Isis unveiled, 2 vols. 1216 RE
BLIND, Mathilde
  George Eliot, Life of. 1267 B
  Madame Roland, Life of. 6350 B
BLISS, Frank C
  Our country and government for 100
  years. 8356 H
BLISS, W D (ed)
  Fabian essays and socialism. 8867 SS
BLODGET, Lorin
  Climatology of the United States.
  7869 S
BLOOMER, D C
  Amelia Bloomer, Life and writings
  of. 10706 B
BLOT, Pierre
  Handbook of practical cookery.
  1814 A
BLOUET, Paul (see O'Rell, Max)
BLOXAM, Charles L
  Chemistry, organic and inorganic.
  1521 S
BOAS, Frederick S
  Shakespeare and his predecessors.
  11370 EE
BOCACCIO, G
  Decameron
BODLEY, John Edward
  France, History of, 2 vols. 11976 H
BOGARDUS, Adam H
  Field, cover and trap shooting.
  8932 A
BOISSIER, Gaston
  Cicero and his friends; a study of
  Roman society in the time of
  Caesar. 10379 B
  Madam de Sevigne.
BOLAND, Mary A
  Handbook of invalid cooking. 11170 A
BOLAS, Thomas
  Glass blowing and working. 11970 A
BOLDREWOOD, Rolf (pseud T A
  Browne)
  Colonial reformer. 6065 F
  Crooked stick. 9328 F
  Miner's right. 6459 F
  Nevermore. 6920 F
  Plain living; a bush idyll. 11913 F

Squatter's dream. 6062 F
Sydney-side saxon. 6850 F
BOLLES, Albert S
Financial history of the United States, 3 vols. 10615 R
BOLTON, Sarah K
Famous American authors. 1367 B
Famous English authors. 6047 B
Famous European artists. 6046 B
Famous leaders among men. 9121 B
Famous types of womanhood. 7411 B
How success is won. 10984 B
Poor boys who became famous. 5536 B
Poor girls who became famous. 5537 B
Stories from life. 7187 B
BLOUNDELLE, John Burton
Across the salt seas. 11413 F
Denounced; a romance. 10042 F
BONNER, John
Child's history of Spain. 8237 J
BONNER, Sherwood (pseud Mrs K S McDowell)
Suwanee river tales. 2224 J
BONSAL, Stephen Jr
Morocco as it is. 7619 V
BONTWELL, George
Why I am a Republican. 201 S
BONVALOT, Gabriel
Across Thibet. 7365 V
BOONE, Richard G
Education in the United States. 5423 EE
BOOTH, Maude B
Beneath two flags. 8910 SS
BOOTH, "General" W
In darkest England and the way out. 6050 SS
BOOTHBY, Guy
Beautiful white devil. 11202 F
Bid for fortune. 10714 F
Dr Nikola. 10197 F
Sheilah McLeod, a hero of the back blocks. 10713 F
BORDE, Andrew
Book of the introduction to knowledge. 5279 R

BORROW, George
Bible in Spain. 11171 V
Lavengro, the scholar, the gypsy, the priest. 6174 F
Zincali, The. 12185 V
BOSTON Browning Society Papers
Papers selected to represent the work of the society. 1886-1887. 11436 R
BOSWELL, James
Samuel Johnson, Life of, 2 vols. 167 B
BOURGET, Paul
Tragic Idyl. 10087 F
BOURMOT, J G
Canada, Story of. 10088 H
BOURNE, H R Fox
Sir Philip Sydney, type of English chivalry in the Elizabethian age. 11194 B
BOUSSENARD, Lewis
Crusoes of Guiana. 2467 J
BOUTMY, Emile
English constitution. 11729 H
BOUVET, Marguerite
. Prince Tip-Top; a fairy tale. 7407 J
Sweet William. 10155 J
BOWEN, Benjamine F
America discovered by the Welsh in 1770. 4809 H
BOWES, James L
Japanese marks and seals. 1759 R
BOWLES, Samuel
Across the continent. 3320 V
BOWMAN, Annie
Kangaroo hunters. 2110 J
BOWRING, Edgar Alfred (trans)
Poems of Heine. 9177 P
BOYD, Alfred H
Leisure hours in town. 762 E
BOYD, James A R
Elements of English composition. 11571 EE
BOYD, Robert
World's hope. 9448 R E
BOYESEN, Hjalmar Hjorth
Light of her countenance. 7156 F
Mammon of unrighteousness. 7183 F
Modern Vikings. 8909 F
Norway, Story of. 4346 H

Queen Titania. 508 F
Social struggles. 7847 F
BOYLE, Cornelius B
North American mesosoic inverte-
brata. 8586 S
BOYLE, Frederick
Narrative of an expelled correspond-
ent. 5004 V
BOYLSTON Peter
John Charax es. 5599 F
BRABOURN, Lord
Ferdinand's adventures, etc. 5265 V
BRACKETT, Anna C
Technique of rest. 11282 S
BRACKETT, Anna C (ed)
Education of American girls. 11715EE
BRACKETT, Anna C and Ida M Eliot
(eds)
Poetry for home and school. 4840 P
BRADDON, Mary E
(Mrs M E Maxwell)
Christmas hirelings. 8822 F
Golden calf. 2220 F
Venetians. 7361 F
Vixen. 6973 F
When the world was younger.
11291 F
BRADLEY, Henry
Goths. Story of. 4340 H
BRADY, Cyrus Townsend
For love of country. 11891 F
BRADY, William
Kedge anchor: or, Young sailor's
assistant. 1689 A
BRAINERD, Thomas H (Mrs Jarboe)
Go forth and find. 9188 F
Robert Atterbury. 9596 F
BRAMBLE, Charles A
A B C of mining. 11937 S
BRAMHALL, Mae St John
Wee ones of Japan. 8329 H
BRANCH, Mary L B
Kanter girls, The. 9360 J
BRAND, John
Popular antiquities. 5043 R
BRANDE, W T
Cyclopedia of science, literature and
art. 1604 R
BRASSEY, Lady Annie
Around the world in the yacht Sun-
beam. 5433 V
In the trades, the tropics and the
roaring forties. 5434 V
One year's adventures. 11309 J
BRAY, Claude
King's revenge. 10023 J

BREMER, Charlotte
Frederika Bremer, Life and letters
of. 11591 B
BREMER, Frederika
Home, The: strife and peace. 3112 F
President's daughters: Nina. 3113 F
BREMSTER, George
New philosophy of matter. 432 S
BRENNAN, Richard
Pope Pius the Ninth, Life of. 8395 B
BREWER, E Cobham
Dictionary of miracles. 1675 R
Dictionary of phrase and fable. 1662R
Historic note-book. 6551 R
Readers' hand book. 1664 R
BREWSTER, H. Pomeroy
England and its rulers. 7639 H
BRIDGE, Horatio
Personal recollections of Nathaniel
Hawthorne. 7853 B
BRIDGES, Mrs (see Mrs Forrester)
BRIGGS, Charles Augustus
Higher criticisms of the Hexateuch.
10972 RE
BRIGHT, John
American question. 213 SS
Speeches in England.
BRIGHT, M
Samuel Pepys, Diary of, 5 vols. 349 B
BRIGHT, William
Chapters of early English church
history. 12480 RE
BRIMLEY, George
Essays of. 7439 E
BRINTON, Daniel G
American race. 7722 H
Myths of the new world. 10381 F
Races and peoples. 7720 S
BRISTOL, Augusta C
Poems of. 67 P
BRITTON, Nathaniel Lord, and Hon.
Addison Brown
Illustrated flora of the United States
and Canada. 3 vols. 10779 S
BROCK, Mrs Garey
Sunday echoes in week day hours.
11759 RE
BROCKETT, L. P. and Mrs Mary C
Vaughan
Woman's work in the civil war.
6173 H
BRODHEAD, Eva Wilder (see Mc-
Glasson, Eva W
BRODHEAD, L W
Delaware water gap. 11801 V
BRODRIBB, Grant
Demosthenes, Aristotle, Plato. 622 H

BRONTE, Charlotte (Mrs C Nichols)
Jane Eyre. 10567 F
Professor. 1113 F
Shirley. 9290 F
BROOKE, Stopford A
Tennyson; his art and relation to
modern life. 10086 E
BROOKE, Charles T
Invisible lodge, The. 6731 F
BROOKS, Eldridge G
Universalism in life and doctrine.
8766 RE
BROOKS, Eldridge S
Boy of the first empire. 9433 J
Century work for young Americans.
8776 J
Eldridge G Brooks. Life of. 8755 B
Historic boys. 4200 J
In No-Man's Land. 10998 J
Story of the American Indian. 12170 J
Story of the American sailor. 7207 J
Story of the American soldier. 6900 J
BROOKS, Henry M
Olden time music. 7292 A
BROOKS, Noah
Explorers and travelers. 8017 B
Fairport nine. 2183 J
BROOKS, Phillips
Best methods of promoting spiritual
life. 10748 RE
New starts in life. 10085 RE
BROUGHTON, Rhoda
Dear Faustina. 10540 F
Mrs Bligh. 11766 F
Scylla or charybdis. 9354 F
BROWN, Alice
Fools of nature. 3132 F
BROWN, Anna Robeson.
Sir Mark; a tale of the first empire.
10143 F
BROWN, Edward
Poultry keeping as an industry.
10356 A
BROWN, E E
Estimate of General Grant. 1279 B
Young folks' life of Washington.
5535 J

BROWN, Everit
Dictionary of American politics.
11342 R
BROWN, George Preston
Sewer gas and its dangers. 11533 A
BROWN, Helen Dawes
Petrie estate. 8019 F
Two college girls. 1144 F
BROWN, James Baldwin
Christian policy of life. 11589 RE
BROWN, James Sayles
Partisan politics; the evil and the
remedy. 10753 SS
BROWN, John
Rab and his friends. 7232 F
BROWN, Mary (ed)
Friendship's offering. 11615 L
BROWN, Rebecca Warren
Great events of the world. 8100 H
BROWN, Thomas
Serious and comical amusements.
1532 A
BROWN, Thomas
Taxidermist's manual. 1824 A
BROWN, Thurlow
Temperance tales. 654 F
BROWN, William H
Maryland, History of. 4286 H
Witty sayings of witty people. 540 L
BROWNE, Francis F
Bugle echoes; poems of the civil war.
6442 P
BROWNE, J Ross
Adventures in the Apache country.
2678 V
Crusoe's island. 688 J
Land of Thor. 6213 S
Mineral resources west of the Rocky
mountains. 1754 S
BROWNE, Sir Thomas
Works of. 3 vols. 6651 E
BROWNING, Elizabeth B
Aurora Leigh. 75 P
Poems of the intellect and the affec-
tions. 11566 P
Poetical works, 5 vols. 1370 P
BROWNING, Oscar
Dante; his life and writings. 6829 B

Goethe; his life and writings. 6831B
BROWNING, Robert
Asolando. 5773 P
Blot in the, Scutcheon. 5800 P
Poetical works of. 10643 P
Ring and the book, 3 vols. 5982 P
Selected poems of. 8900 P
BROWNLOW, W G
Sketches of rise and progress of
secession. 686 H
BROWNSON, O A
Christianity and heathenism, 3 vols.
4272 RE
BRUCE, Charles
Selections of poems and songs of the
sea. 5079 P
BRUCE, Philip Alexander
Economic history of Virginia in the
seventeenth century, 2 vols. 12142 H
Plantation negro as a freeman. 7855
SS
BRUNETIERE, Ferdinand
Manual of the history of French lit-
erature. 12560 EE
BRUNNER, Arnold W
Interior decorations. 7727 A
BRUSH, C C
Colonel's opera cloak. F
BRYAN, Michael
Marks and monograms of early en-
gravers. 1092 R
BRYAN, William S
Footprints of the world's history.
10573 H
BRYANT, Jacob
Dessertation on the war of Troy.
5278 H
BRYANT, William C
Letters from the east. 466 V
Letters from a traveler. 3363 V
Poetical works of. 9669 P
Popular history of the United States,
4 vols. 4205 H
BRYCE, James
American commonwealth, 2 vols.
5839 H
Holy Roman empire. 7274 H
Impressions of South America. 11240
H
Persia, History of. 533 H
BUCHANAN, Joseph R
Moral pirates. 681 J
BUCHANAN, Robert
Come live with me. 7146 F
Poems of. 8215 P
BUCK, Albert
Ear disease. 8712 S
BUCKLE, Henry T

History of civilization in England.
4215 H
BUCKLEY, Arabella (Mrs Fisher)
Fairy land of science. 2720 J
Short history of natural science.
11371 S
Thro magic glasses. 6406 J
Winners in life's race. 5539 E
BUCKLEY, C H (compiler)
Plato's best thoughts. 6721 E
BUCKLEY, J M
Faith healing, Christian science and
kindred phenomena. 893 RE
BUCKLEY, Theodore Alois
Great cities of the middle ages.
6421 V
BUEL, J W
Heroes of the dark continent. 6897V
Living world. 10574 S
Manual of self help. 10868 EE
Story of man. 10577 S
BULL, Sara C
Ole Bull, a memoir. 6356 B
BULLFINCH, T .
Age of chivalry (E E Hale, ed)
6334 F
Age of fable. (E E Hale ed). 6335 F
Legends of Charlemagne. 6336 F
BULWER-LYTTON, E G
Alice. 8612 F
(Sequel to Ernest Maltravers).
Calderon, the courtier. 8608 F
(Spain, Philip III).
Caxtons. 8617 F
Coming race. 2946 F
Devereux. 8610 F
(Times of Queen Anne, introducing
Bolingbroke).
Disowned. 8615 F
Dramas and poems. 11281 P
Ernest Maltravers. 8612 F
(Continued in Alice).
Eugene Aram. 8609 F
Falkland. 8608 F
Godolphin. 8619 F
Harold, last of the Saxon kings.
8608 F
Kenelm Chillingly. 8622 F
Last days of Pompeii. 8613 F
Last of the barons. 8621 F
Leila. 8619 F
Lucretia. 8620 F
My novel, 2 vols. 8607 F
(English politics).
Night and morning. 8623 F
Parisians. 8611 F
Paul Clifford. 8618 F

Pausanias, the Spartan (Greece, 5th century, B C). 8619 F
Pelham. 2050 F
Rienzi; the last of the Roman tribunes. 8614 F
Strange story. 8616 F
What will he do with it? 2 vols. 2057 F
Zanoni. 8609 F
(First French revolution. 1792). Zicci. 8617 F
BULWER, Rob.,Earl of Lytton (see Owen Meredith).
BUMSTEAD, S J
Riversons. 6479 F
BUNCE, John Thackeray
Fairy tales; their origin and meaning. 6814 F
BUNCE, Oliver Bell (Censor)
Bachelor Bluff; his opinions, sentiments, etc. 11682 F
BUNNELL, Lafayette Houghton
Discovery of the Yosemite and the Indian war of 1851. 10361 H
BUNNER, H C
Jersey street and Jersey lane. 9817 F
Love in old clothes, and other stories. 10715 F
Made in France. 7839 F
Poems of. 11152 P
Rowen, second crop songs. 7680 P
Short sixes. 7152 F
Zodac pine and other stories. 8173 F
BUNYAN, John
Pilgrim's progress. 10981 F
BURBANK, W H
Photographic printing methods. 12189 A
BURCH, Harriette E
Stella Rae. 7167 F
BURDER, William
History of all religions. 4291 RE
BURDETTE, Robert J
Recitations and readings. 2021 P
William Penn, Life of. 2001 B
BURGESS, Edward (ed)
Spiders of the United States. 7998 S

BURGESS, John W
Middle period 1817-1858. 10322 H
Political science and comparative constitutional law. 10039 SS
BURNETT, Mrs Frances Hodgson
Editha's burglar. 7907 J
Fair barbarian. 2837 F
Giovanni and the other children who have made stories. 7456 J
Haworths
His grace of Osmonde. 11467 F
(Sequel to Lady of quality).
Lady of quality. 9546 F
Little Lord Fauntleroy. 11311 J
Little Saint Elizabeth, etc. 11472 J
Louisiana. 2835 J
Pretty sister of Jose. 8961 F
Sara Crewe. 5451 J
Surly Tim, etc. 2838 J
That lass o' Lowries. 2836 F
Thro one administration. 10561 F
Two little pilgrims' progress. 9361 J
Vagabondia. 2834 F
BURNEY, Frances (Mme F B d'Arblay)
Cecelia, 2 vols. 2849 F
Evelina. 2851 F
BURNHAM, Clara Louise
A great love. 11584 F
Dearly bought. 5717 F
Dr Latimer. 7831 F
Miss Archer Archer. 10505 F
Miss Bagg's secretary. 6745 F
Mistress of Beech-knoll. 6659 F
Next door. 7778 F
No gentleman. 7779 F
Sane lunatic. 9626 F
Sweet clover. 9137 F
Wise woman. 9417 F
Young maids and old. 6460 F
BURNS, Robert
Poetical works of. 39 P
BURR —
Ecce Collum; or, parish astronomy. 2168 S
BURR, Frank A and Richard J Hilton
General Phil Sheridan, Life of. 6901B

BURROUGHS, John
Birds and poets. 5760 E
Fresh fields. 493 E
Indoor studies. 5758 E
Locusts and wild honey. 5757 E
Pepacton. 5759 E
Riverby. 8793 E
Signs and seasons. 5762 E
Wake-robin. 5763 E
Winter sunshine. 5761 E
BURT, Mary E
Literary landmarks. EE
BURTON, Isabel
Captain Sir Richard Burton, Life of 7909 B
BURTON, Robert
Anatomy of melancholy. 6628 EE
BURY, J B
Later Roman empire. History of, 2 vo's. 9583 H
BUSCH, Dr Moritz
Bismarck; some secret pages of his history, 2 vols. 12278 B
BUSCH, William
Nonsense songs. 9978 P
BUSH, Richard J
Reindeer, dogs and snowshoes. 3388 V
BUTCHER, S H
Some aspects of the Greek genius. 6801 EE
BUTTER, Arthur J
Baron Morbot, Memoirs of. 7260 E
BUTLER, Hiram E
Solar biology; a scientific method.
BUTLER, Josephine E
Woman's work and woman's culture. 358 A
BUTLER, Nicholas Murray
Meaning of education. 11960 EE
BUTLER, Samuel
Hudibras. 48 P
Poetical works of, 3 vols. 6627 P
BUTLER, Sir William F
Charles George Gordon, Life of. 6540 B
BUTTERWORTH, Hezekiah
Boys of Greenway court. 8078 J
Great composers. 12492 B
In the boyhood of Lincoln. 7043 J
Log school house on the Columbia. 6236 J
Wampum belt. 10005 J
Zigzag jurneys in Acadia and New France. 2198 J
Zigzag journeys in Australia. 6899 J
Zigzag journeys in India. 1223 J
Zigzag journeys in the Antipodes. 3397 J
Zigzag journeys in the Levant. 2718J
Zigzag journeys on the Mississippi. 7373 J
Zigzag journeys in the White city. 8815 J
BUTTS Edmund L
Manual of physical drill. 11868 S
BYERS, S N M
Switzerland and the Swiss. 6372 H
BYNNER, Edwin L
Agnes Surriage. 5715 F
Zachary Phips. 7584 F
BYRON, George G N
Jacqueline; a tale. 6169 F
Poetical works of, 17 vols. 6597 P
CABLE, George W
Bonaventure. 3413 F
Creoles of Louisiana. 4268 F
Doctor Sevier. 4948 F
Grandissimes. 4951 F
John March, southerner. 8800 F
Old Creole days. 4949 F
Silent south. 200 F
Strange true stories of Louisiana. 4950 F
CABOT, James Elliot
R. W. Emerson, Memoir of, 2 vols. 1268 B
CAHAN, A
Imported bridegroom. 12356 F
Yekl; a tale of the New York ghetto. 9865 F
CAINE, Hall
Blind brother. 8205 F
Bondman. 7001 F
Capt'n Davy's honeymoon. 9807 F
Christian. 10645 F
Deemster. 12435 F
Last confession. 8205 F
Manxman. 9148 F
Shadow of a crime. 5155 F
Son of Hagar. 5156 F
CAIRD. Edward
Hegel. 7634 B
CAIRD, Mona
Romance of the Moors. 7477 H
Wing of Azrael. 6977 F
CAJORI, Florian
Teaching and history of mathematics in the United States. 5946 EE
CALCRAFT, William
(Public hangman in England). Recollections and life of. 4878 B
CALKINE, Alonzo
Opium and the opium appetite. 1544S

CALL, Annie Payson
Power through repose. 11271 S
CALVERLY, C S
Fly-leaves. 4829 F
CAMBRIDGE, Ada
My guardian. 8681 F
Not in vain. 8680 F
Three Miss Kings. 8669 F
CAMERON, Mrs H Lovett
Bachelor's bridal. 10452 F
CAMERON, Vernon Lovett
Across Africa. 3345 V
Cruise of the "Black Prince." 8985 V
CAMPAN, Mme Jeanne L H
Marie Antoinette, Private life of.
1320 B
CAMPBELL, Douglas ,
Puritan in Holland, England and
America. 7362 H
Structure and development of the
mosses and ferns. 10383 S
CAMPBELL, Helen (pseud Mrs Helen
C Weeks)
American girls' book of work and
play. 4939 J
Household economics. 11162 A
In foreign kitchens. 7617 A
Miss Melinda's opportunity. 2887 J
Prisoners of poverty abroad. 6400SS
Under green apple boughs. 1081 F
What-to-do club. 8105 J
CAMPBELL, John
Travels in South Africa. 5104 V
CAMPBELL, Thomas
Poetical works of. 44 P
CANNON, Geo C
Tom. 1163 J
CAPES, W W
Age of Antonines. 5471 H
Early empire. 5472 H
CAREY, Annie
Wonders of common things. 260 J
CAREY, Mrs M (trans and ed)
Duruy's history of France. 5571 H
Fairy legends of the French prov-
inces. 638 J
CAREY, Rosa Nouchette
Aunt Diana. 4954 F

Doctor Luttrell's first patient. 10488F
Esther; a story for girls. 4953 F
Heriot's choice. 10812 F
Lover or friend. 10813 F
Mary St John. 10814
Mistress of Brae farm. 9899 F
Nellie's memories. 10811 F
Our Bessie. 10810 F
Queen's whim. 7326 F
Search for Basil Lyndhurst. 10815 F
Wee wifie. 7128 F
CARLETON, George W
Our artist in Cuba. 5935 V
CARLETON, Will
City ballads. 35 P
City festivals. 7376 P
Farm ballads. 7377 P
Farm festivals. 40 P
Farm legends. 7 P
Rhymes of our planet. 7379 P
Young folks' centennial rhymes.
9063 P
CARLETON, William
Traits and stories of the Irish peas-
antry. 6956 F
Willy Reilly. 3092 F
CARLETON, A B
Wonderlands of the wild west. 9052V
CARLETON, Robert
New purchase, or seven and one-half
years in the far west, 2 vols. 5926 V
CARLYLE, Alex
Autobiography of. 266 B
CARLYLE, Thomas
Crit and misc. essays, 3 vols. 12398 E
French revolution, 2 vols. 12394 H
Frederick II of Prussia, 4 vols.
12386 B
Heroes and hero-worship. 12396 E
John Sterling, Life of. 12397 B
Past and present. 5448 E
Sartor resartus. 5449 E
CARLYLE, Thomas (ed)
Cromwell's letters and speeches, 3
vols. 12391 E
CARLYLE, Thomas, and R W Emerson
Correspondence of, 2 vols. 595 E

CARMARTHEN, Katherine
Lover of the beautiful. 6842 F
CARMICHAEL, Sarah
Poems of. 6 P
CARO, E
George Sand, Life of. 7248 B
CARPENTER, Edward
From Adam's peak to Elephanta.
12203 V
CARPENTER, Esther B
South country neighbors. 3172 F
CARPENTER, Frank G
Travels through North America with
the children. 12632 J
CARPENTER, William B
Mesmerism and spiritualism. 5729 S
Microscope and its revelations. 8701S
CARPENTER, S C
American speeches. 2 vols. 440 E
CARR, Lucien
Missouri, History of. 4281 H
CARRINGTON, Henry
Ab-sa-ra-ka; Wyoming opened. 877V
CARROL, Lewis (pseud C L Dodgson)
Alice's adventures in wonderland.
2924 J
Silvie and Bruno. 6272 J
Through the looking-glass. 4938 J
CARRYL, Charles E
Admiral's caravan. 9647 J
CARTER, R. Kelso
Alpha and Omega. 9095 S
CARTER, N H
Letters from Europe, 2 vols. 11764 V
CARTER, Susan M (compiler)
Art suggestions from the masters.
11408 A
CARTWRIGHT, Peter
Autobiography. 6914 B
CARY, Alice
Clovernook. 2 vols. 6994 F
Clovernook children. 6995 F
From year to year. 6966 J
Snow berries. 7134 F
CARY, Alice and Phoebe
Poetical works of. 87 P
CARY, II F (trans)
Dante's hell, purgatory and paradise.
49 P
CASIN, Achille
Phenomena and laws of heat. 278 S
CASTELAR, Emilio
Old Rome and new Italy. 6370 H
CATHERWOOD, Mary Hartwell
Old Kaskaskia. 8064 F
Romance of Dollard. 4859 F
Tonty, Story of. 5631 F
White islander. 8010 F

CAUGHEY, James
"Arrows from my quiver." 4735 RE
CAVENDISH, Thomas
Voyages of, around the world, 1586-
1591. 3350 V
CELLANI, Benvenuto
Memoirs of. 10349 B
CERVANTES, Saavendra Miguel de
Don Quixote, 2 vols. 11469 F
CHACE, A W
Practical receipts. 11794 R
CHACE, William Henry
Day by day. 8874 RE
CHADBOURNE, P A
Lectures on natural history. 12527 S
CHADWICK, William
Daniel Defoe, Life and times of. 257B
CHAFA, Mrs Sara G
Napoleon Bonaparte and other poems.
3449 P
CHAMBERS, Robert
Cyclopedia of English literatue. 2
vols. 12455 R
Vistages of natural history. 9272 S
CHAMBERS, Robert W
Ashes of empire. 12567 F
Lorraine. 11895 F
Maker of moons. 10089 F
Red republic; a romance of the com-
mune. 9541 F
CHAMBLISS, Rev
David Livingstone, Life and labors
of. 113 B
CHAMBERLAIN, N H
Sphinx in Aubrey parish. 544 F
CHAMBERS, Adalbert von
Peter Schlemihl. 9860 F
CHAMPLIN, John D
Young folks' cyclopaedia of common
things. 4841 R
Young folks' cyclopaedia of games.
11176 R
Young folks' cyclopaedia of persons.
and places. 4842 R
CHAMPLIN, Virginia
No 13 Rue Marlot. 11594 F
CHAMPNEY, Elizabeth W
Howling Wolf and his trick pony.
7212 J
Paddy O'Leary and his learned pig.
9377 J
Three Vassar girls abroad. 1314 J
— — — in England. 2197 J
— — — in France. 5466 J
— — — at home. 3386 J
— — ·— in Italy. 5467 J
— — — on the Rhine. 5469 J
— — — in South America. 5468 J

·itch Winnie. 9616 J
Witch Winnie in Holland. 12621 J
Witch Winnie's mystery. 9618 J
Witch Winnie in Paris. 9719 J
Witch Winnie at Shinnecock. 9619 J
Witch Winnie in Spain. 12610 J
Witch Winnie at Versailles. 9345 J

CHANDLER, Bessie A
Woman who failed and others. 7849F

CHANEY, George
Every day life and every day morals. 487 EE
F Grant & Co. 1119 J

CHANNING, William E
Lectures on elevation of laborers. 662 E
Prose works of. 6 vols. 666 E

CHAPIN, Anna Alice
Wonder tales from Wagner, told for young folks. 11066 J

CHAPIN, E H
Humanity in the city. 751 RE

CHAPMAN, John Jay
Emerson and other essays. 11387 E

CHARCOT, J M
Diseases of old age. 8721 S

CHARDENAL, C A
French exercises for advanced pupils. 11499 EE

CHARLES, Cecil
Honduras. 6342 V

CHARLES, Mrs Elizabeth
Against the stream. 6298 F
Early dawn. 414 F
Kitty Trevlyan, Diary of. 11738 F
Martin Luther. 325 B
Schonberg-Cotta family, Chronicles of. 4956 F
Victory of the vanquished. 1957 F
Winnifred Bertram. 4958 F

CHASE, Jessie Anderson
Three freshmen. 12555 J

CHASE, Warren
Life line of the lone one (an autobiography). 4736 B

CHATEAUBRIAND, M de
Martyr. 829 F

CHATFIELD-TAYLOR, H C (see Taylor, H C Chatfield)

CHAUCER Geoffrey
Canterbury tales. 47 P

CHAUVEAU, A
Comparative anatomy of domesticated animals. 7080 S

CHEEVER, H T
Island world of the Pacific; life in the Sandwich islands. 1622 V

"CHEIRO"
Language of the hand. 12206 S

CHENEY, Mrs Ednah D
Louise May Alcott, her life, letters and journals. 6051 B
Young folks' history of the civil war. 1134 J

CHENEY, John Vance
Out of the silence. 11967 P
Thistle drift. 89 P
Wood bloom. 98 P

CHERBULIEZ, Victor
Samuel Brohl and partner. 2991 F
With fortune made. 10289 F

CHESNEAU, Ernest
Education of the artist. 6434 A
English school of painting. 9169 A

CHESTER, E
Girls and women. 8137 EE

CHESTER, Norley
Stories from Dante. 12218 F

CHILD, G Chaplin
Benedicte. 8917 RE

CHILD, Theodore
Art and criticism. 8282 A
Praise of Paris. 7618 V
Spanish-American republics. 8842 H
Wimples and crisping pins. 8829 A

CHILDS, C W
New essentials of bookkeeping. 12490 EE

CHILDS, George W
Recollections. 7267 E

CHINIQUY, Father
Priest, woman and confessional. 5421 L

CHITTENDEN, L A
Elements of English composition.
8359 EE
CHOATE, Lowell
Romance of a letter. 3157 E
CHOATE, Rufus
Addresses and orations. 9314 E
CHOPIN, Kate
Bayou folk. 8344 F
CHRISTY, Robert
Proverbs, maxims and phrases, 2 vols. 6427 R
CHURCH, A H
Colour; and elementary manual for students. 6388 A
CHURCH, Alfred J
Burning of Rome. 6848 F
Count of the Saxon shore. 4256 F
Hammer, The. 6389 F
Henry V. 6782 B
Story of Carthage. 4355 H
Story of early Britain. 5369 H
Stories from English history. 10190 F
Stories from the Greek tragedians. 2206 F
Stories from Livy. 2204 H
Stories from Virgil. 2102 F
Roman life in the days of Cicero. 2203 H
Two thousand years ago. 2723 F
With the king at Oxford. 348 H
CHURCH, A W
Spenser, Life of. 1336 B
CHURCH, Ella Rodman
Home needle, The. 8935 A
How to furnish a house. 8933 A
CHURCH, Mary C
Dean Church. Life and letters of. 10382 B
CHURCH, R W
Bacon, Life of. 217 B
Beginning of the middle ages. 9375H
Spenser, Life of. 6686 B
CHURCH, Samuel C
John Marmaduke. 10727 F
CHURCHILL, Winston
The celebrity; an episode. 11067 F
CISNEROS, Evangelina
Story of herself told by herself. 11025 B
CLARK, Cecil
Little Alpine fox dog. 5040 J
CLARK, Eliza
Handel. 7255 B
Susianna Moore. 6347 B
CLARK, Frederick T
Valley of Havilah. 6965 F

CLARK, Francis E
Looking out on life. 7283 EE
Our journey around the world.10568V
Ways and means. 8099 EE
World wide endeavor, The story of. 12018 EE
CLARK, Mary Cowden
Girlhood of Shakespeare's heroines. 2 vols. 5669 F
CLARK, Edward H
Building of the brain. 6729 EE
Sex in education. 7030 EE
CLARKE, H Butler
Cid Campeador. 11883 B
CLARKE, James Freeman
Autobiography of. 7044 B
Ideas of the apostle Paul. 267 RE
Self-culture. 223 EE
Ten great religions., 2 vols. 7957 RE
CLARKE, John Bernard
Algebra. 11577 EE
CLARKE, Joseph T (trans)
Von Reber's history of mediaeval art. 4267 A
CLARK, Mrs Mary
Lost legends of nursery songs. 5058F
CLAY, Charlotte M
Baby Rue. 5119 F
CLAYDEN P W
Samuel Rodgers. Early life of. 7251 B
CLAYTON, Ellen C
Female warriors. 5018 B
CLEARY, Kate M
Like a gallant lady. 12238 F
CLEVELAND, Mary W and others
Villas and farm cottages. 1792 A
CLEMENS, Samuel L (see Mark Twain)
CLEMENTS, Clara E
Egypt, History of. 4226 H
Handbook of legendary and mythological art. 1773 A
Outline history of painting. 1764 A
Queen of the Adriatic. 8463 H
CLEMENT, J (ed)
Noble deeds of American women. 8940 F
CLEMENT, Clara Erskine and Laurence Hutton
Artists of the nineteenth century and their works. 10520 R
CLERKE, Agnes M
Astronomy, Popular history of. 1447S
CLEVELAND, H W S
Hints to riflemen. 8353 A
CLIFFORD, Edward
Father Damien de Venster; a journey from Cashmere to his home in Hawaii. 5736 B

CLIFFORD, Josephine (pseud Mrs Jackson McCrackin)
Another Juanita and other stories. 9478 F
Overland tales. 9479 F
CLIFFORD, Mrs W K
Aunt Anne. 7355 F
Flash of summer. 9963 F
Love letters of a worldly woman. 7236 F
Mrs Keith's crime. 10654 F
Wild proxy, A. 7826 F
CLODD, Edward
Pioneers of evolution from Thales to Huxley, with an intermediate chapter on the causes of the arrest of movement. 10384 S
Primer of evolution. 9759 S
Story of creation. 7307 S
CLOUGH, Arthur Hugh
Plutarch's lives, 5 vols. 10168 B
Poems of. 8262 P
COAN, Helen
Pen portraits of literary women. 1370 B
COATES, Henry T (ed)
Fireside encyclopaedia of poetry. 1550 R
COBB, James F
Off to California. 2154 J
COBB, Mary L
Poetical dramas. 17 P
COBB, Sophia Dickinson
Hillsboro farms. 11541 F
COBBE, Francis Power
Life of, 2 vols. 9301 B
Scientific spirit of the age
COBURN, F D
Swine husbandry. 9562 A
COCHIN, Augustin
Results of slavery. 499 H
COCKTON, Henry
Sylvester Sound, the somnambulist. 1095 F
CODY, Sherman
In the heart of the hills. 9832 F
COFFIN, C C
Boys of '76. 12109 J

Boys of '61. 4155 J
Building of the nation. 5547 H
Drumbeat of the nation. 4254 H
Following the flag. 2207 H
Freedom triumphant. 5842 H
Marching to victory. 5548 H
My days and nights on the battlefield. 2208 J
Old times in the colonies. 10185 J
Our new way around the world. 3268 V
Redeeming the republic. 5549 H
Seat of empire. 6981 H
Story of liberty. 5734 H
Winning his way. 2209 J
COFFIN, Charles Emmet
Gist of whist. 9511 A
COLEMAN, George
Broad grins. 5107 F
COLERIDGE, Edward P
Plays of Euripides, 2 vols. 9777 P
COLERIDGE, S T
Poetical works. 94 P
COLLAR, William C
Beginners' Latin book. 8352 EE
Practical Latin composition. 8357 EE
COLLIER, Jeremy
Meditations of Marcus Aurelius. 11781 E
COLLIER, William Francis
English literature. History of. 11689 H
COLLINGWOOD, Harry
Log of the Flying Fish. 12370 V
COLLINS, W Lucas
Butler. 9635 B
Thucydides. Lucian. Plantus. 615 H
Virgil. Illiad. Odyssey. 616 H
COLLINS, Mabel
Blossom and fruit. 4755 F
Star sapphire. 10367 F
COLLINS, Wilkie
Antonina, or The fall of Rome. 2335F
Armadale. 2332 F
Heart and science. 9012 F
Legacy of Cain. 6972 F
Man and wife. 11771 F
Moonstone. 8644 F
New Magdalen. 6971 F

Woman in white. 9169 F
COLLIS, Septima M
Woman's trip to Alaska. 7099 V
COLOMB, Capt. R
Slave catching in the Indian ocean.
5011 V
COLQUHOUN, Archiald
China in transformation. 12277 H
COLTMAN, Robert
Chinese, The. 8685 H
COLTON, Walter
Sea and sailor. 4705 V
COLVIN, Sidney
Landor, Life of. 6705 B
Woltman's history of painting.1760 A
COMBE, Andrew
Principles of physiology. 11500 S
COMBE, George
Constitution of man. 1518 S
COMINS, Lizzie
Marion Berkley. 7271 F
COMPARETTI, Domenico
Virgil in the middle ages. 11878 H
COMPAYRE, Gabriel
Pedagogy, History of. 8832 EE
COMPTON, Alfred G
Some common errors of speech.
11896 EE
COMPTON, Herbert (comp)
Particular account of the European
military adventures of Hindustan.
7651 H
COMPTON, Margaret
Snow bird and water tiger. 9368 J
CONDER, Claude
Judas Maccabaeus. 5737 B
Syrian Stone-lore. 7083 V
CONE, Helen (ed)
Pen portraits of literary women.
1999 B
CONGDON, Charles
Tribune essays. 448 E
CONKLING, Alfred R
City government in the United States.
9376 SS
CONRAD, Joseph
Children of the sea. 11809 F
CONSCIENCE, Blanche
Confessions of a society man. 9127 F
CONSCIENCE, Hendrik
Poor gentleman. 9038 F
CONVERSE, Frank H
Mystery of a diamond. 7345 F
Southern seas. 7021 F
Voyage to the gold coast. 7034 F
CONWAY, William Martin
Climbing and exploration in the
Karakoram-Himalayas. 9315 V

CONWELL, Russel H
James G Blaine, Life and public ser-
vices of. 5933 H
COOK, Clarence (ed)
Lubke's history of art, 2 vols. 4136 A
COOK, Eliza
New echoes and other poems. 23 P
Poetical works of. 13 P
COOK, James
Narrative of the voyages around the
world. 11738 V
Voyage to the Pacific ocean, 3 vols.
5275 V
COOK, Joseph
Occident, The. (being Boston Mon-
day lectures for 1883-4). 593 E
COOK, Lady
Essays on social topics. 11666 E
COOK, S E
Guiding lights; lives of the great and
good. 2164 B
COOKE, George Willis
George Eliot, Life of. 173 B
Ralph Waldo Emerson. Life of.
1266 B
COOKE, John E
Virginia, History of. 4288 H
COOKE, Josiah Parsons
New chemistry, The. 1388 S
Principles of chemical philosophy.
1524 S
COOKE, M C
Fungi; their nature and uses. 1397S
COOKE, Rose Terry
Happy Dodd. 8662 F
Huckleberries. 6748 F
Somebody's neighbors. 8663 F
Steadfast, the story of a saint and
sinner. 8661 F
COOLBRITH, Ina D
Perfect day and other poems. 7460 P
COOLIDGE, Susan
Barberry bush and eight other sto-
ries. 12113 J
Clover. 5550 J
Crosspatch. 112114 J
Eyebright. 12094 J
Just sixteen. 5551 J
Mischief's thanksgiving. 12112 J
What Katy did. 5551 J
What Katy did at school. 5558 J
What Katy did next. 513 J
COOLEY, Arnold
Cyclopedia of practical receipts.
4838 R
Instructions and cautions as to per-
fumes and cosmetics. 1760 R

COOLEY, Thomas M
Michigan, History of. 4287 H
COOPER, Eilwood
Forest culture and eucalyptus trees, 766 A
COOPER, J. Fennimore
Afloat and ashore. 2078 F
Borderers. 834 F
(Same as Wept of the Wish-Ton-wish)
Bravo. 2079 F
Chainbearer. 2069 F
Crater; or, Vulcan's peak. 2072 F
Deerslayer. 8293 F
Home as found; sequel to Home-ward bound. 2070 F
Homeward bound; a tale of the sea. 2070 F
Jack Frier. 2077 F
Last of the Mohicans. 8294 F
Lionel Lincoln. 2075 F
Mercedes of Castile. 2079 F
Miles Wallingford; sequel to Afloat and ashore. 2078 F
Monikins. 2065 F
Pathfinder. 8295 F
Pilot. 7028 F
Pioneers. 8296 F
Prairie. 8292 F
Precaution. 2071 F
Red rover. 9446 F
Redskins. 2073 F
Satantoe. 2069 F
Sea lions. 2077 F
Spy. 10784 F
Two admirals. 7030 F
Water witch. 7029 F
Ways of the hour. 2071 F
Wept of the Wish-Ton-Wish. 2067F
Wing-and-wing. 2074 F
Wyandotte. 2074 F
COOPER, Harriet C
Short studies in botany. 8133 S
COOPER, Samuel Williams
Three days. 7158 F
COOTE, Walter
Wanderings south and east. 5015 V

COPPEE, Henry
Conquest of Spain, History of. 11268 H
CORBIN, Mrs. Caroline Fairfield
His marriage vow. 8964 F
CORRELLI, Marie
Ardath; the story of a dead self. 12437 F
Barabbas; a dream of the world's tragedy. 8020 F
Cameos. 9589 F
Mighty atom. 11486 F
Romance of two worlds. 10782 F
Sorrows of Satan. 9998 F
Soul of Lilith. 8787 F
Thelma. 8030 F
Vendetta. 7985 F
Wormwood. 7916 F
Ziska; the problem of a wicked soul. 10473 F
CORNWALL, William C
Sound money monographs. 13637 SS
CORNWALLIS, Kinahan
Adrift with a vengeance. 2974 V
CORRAN, Frank
Curious facts in history of insects. 1547 S
COSSA, Luigi
Guide to the study of political econ-omy. 11631 SS
COSTELLO, F H
Master Ardick Buccaneer. 10290 F
COTES, Mrs Everard (see Duncan.Sara Jeanette)
COTES, V Cecil
Two girls on a barge. 7163 F
COTTERILL, James H
Applied mechanics. 7436 S
COTTON, Louise
Palmistry. 6531 S
COUBERTIN, Baron Pierre de
Evolution of France under the third empire. 11326 H
COUCH, T Quiller (see "Q")
COUES, Elliott
Key to North American birds. 1506 S
COULSON, Walter J
Diseases of the bladder. 8709 S

COULTAN, Harland
What may be learned from a tree.
50005 S
COUTTS, F B Money
Revelation of St. Love, the divine.
12352 P
COWAN, J T
Ice-boat boys. 7396 J
COWAN, John   "
Science of a new life. 8089 S
COWPER, William
Poetical works of, 3 vols. 6578 P
COWPERTHWAITE, J H
Money, silver and finance. 7065 SS
COX, George W
An introduction to the science of
comparative mythology and folk-
lore. 12498 F
Athenian empire. The. 5470 H
Crusades. The. 5480 H
Greeks and Persians. 5474 H
Lives of Greek statesmen, 2 vols.
9575 B
Mythology of the Aryan nations.
12195 F ·
COX, Jacob D
Battle of Franklin, Tennessee. Nov.
30, 1884. 10794 H
COX, Palmer
Brownies around the world. 9122 J
COX, Ross
Adventures on the Columbia river.
12533 V   .
COX, S S
Arctic sunbeams. 5730 V
Isles of the Princesses. 1621 V
Oriental sunbeams. 5403 V
CRABB, George
Mythology of all nations. 5087 F
CRADDOCK, Charles Egbert (pseud
Mary N Murfree)
Despot of Broomsedge Cove. 2107 F
Down the ravine. 3110 F
His vanished star. 8771 F
In the clouds. 311 F
In the Tennessee mountains
Juggler, The. 10846 F
Prophet of the Great Smoky moun-
tains
Story of the Keedon Bluffs. 5553 F
Young mountaineers and other sto-
ries. 10851 F
Where the battle was fought. 3109 F
CRADDOCK, Ida C
Heaven of the Bible. 10583 RE
CRAFT, Mabel Clare
Hawaii Nei. 12573 V

CRAIG, Mary A
House by the Medlar-tree. 5821 F
CRAIGIE, Mrs (see John Oliver
Hobbes)
CRAIK, Mrs D M (see Mrs Mulock)
CRAIK, Henry
State in its relation to education.
6811 EE
CRAIK, Henry (ed)
English prose. 10090 EE
CRAM, Ralph Adams
Black spirits and white. 10145 F
CRANE, Annie M
Opportunity. 2285 F
CRANE, Rev. Stephen
Jesus the Christ. 8513 RE
CRANE, Stephen
George's mother. 9833 F
Maggie, a girl of the streets. 10137F
Red badge of courage. 9830 F
CRANE, Walter
Claims of decorative art. 7367 A
CRANE, William
Politics. 6716 SS
CRAVEN, Mme A
Veil withdrawn. 11840 F
CRAWFORD, F Marion
Adam Johnstone's son. 9717 F
American politician. 2064 F
Casa Braccio, 2 vols. 9418 F
Children of the king. 7583 F
Cigarette maker's romance. 6066 F
Corleone, 2 vols. 10772 F
Doctor Claudius. 2062 F
Don Orsino. 7416 F
Greifenstein. 5554 F
Katherine Lauderdale, 2 vols.
Khaled, a tale of Arabia. 6138 F
Love in idleness. 6769 F
Marion Darche. 8022 F
Marzio's crucifix
Mr. Isaacs. 2061 F
Paul Patoff. 3148 F
Pietro Ghisleri. 7842 F
Ralstons, 2 vols. 9097 F
Roman singer. 1154 F
Rose of yesterday. 10442 F
Saint Ilario. 10562 F
Saracinesca. 10563 F   ·-
Tale of a lonely parish. 2145 F
Taquisara, 2 vols. 10091 F
Three fates. 9622 F
To leeward. 2063 F
With the Immortals. 4959 F
Zoroaster. 2553 F
CRAWFORD, T C
English life. 6963 H

CRAWFORD, Oswald
  Sylvia Arden. 6978 F
CREASY, Edward
  Ottoman Turks, History of. 12173 H
CREASY, E S
  Fifteen decisive battles of the world. 4183 H
  Rise and progress of English constitution. 9168 H
CREE, Nathan
  Direct legislation by the people.
CREIGHTON, Mandell
  Age of Elizabeth. 5486 H
  Cardinal Woolsey. 6774 B
CREMONY, John C
  Life among the Apaches. 155 H
CRESWELL, Frank O
  Handrailing and stair-casing. 11803A
CRIMM, Matt
  Adventures of a fair rebel. 7527 F
  In Beaver cove and elsewhere. 7528 F
CROCKETT. S R
  Bog-myrtle and peat. 10153 F
  Cleg Kelly, arab of the city. 10148 F
  Gray man. 10035 F
  Lad's love. 10370 F
  Lilac sunbonnet; a love story. 9335 F
  Men of moss-hags. 9334 F
  Sir Toady Lion. 10845 F
  Standard bearer. 11093 F
  Sticket minister and some common men. 8025 F
CROKER, B M
  Family Likeness. 7745 F
  Two masters. 6465 F
CROLY, George
  Salathiel, the immortal. 2716 F
CROLY, Mrs J C
  Thrown on her own resources.7447EE
CROMSE, Titus Fey
  Natural wealth of California. 1694 H
CROSS, Mrs (see Ada Cambridge)
CROSS, J G
  Electric shorthand dictionary.8354EE

CROSS, J W
  George Eliot, Life of, 2 vols. 1263 B
CROSS, M E (see George Eliot)
CROUCH, Archer P
  Senorita Montenar. 11068 F
CRUDEN, Alexander
  Complete concordance. 8458 R
CRUGER, Mrs van R (see Julien Gordon.)
CRUTTWELL, Charles Thomas.
  Roman literature, History of. 10641H
CUMMINGS, C F Gordon
  Two happy years in Ceylon, 2 vols. 7801 V
CUMMINS, Ella Sterling
  Story of the files. 10641 H
CUMMINS, Maria S
  El Fureidis. 10093 F
  Lamplighter. 5707 F
  Mabel Vaughan. 5706 F
CUNDALL, Frank
  Landscape and pastoral painters of Holland. 11153 B
CUNNINGHAM, Henry
  Coerulians, The. 3138 F
  Heriots,. The. 6063 F
  Wheat and tares. 6064 F
CUNNINGHAM, W
  Use and abuse of money. 7695 SS
CUNNINGHAM, William
  Growth of English industry and commerce. 12153 H
  Outlines of English industrial history. 12177 H
CURRIE, James
  Principles and practise of early and infant school education. 8807 EE
CURRIER, Mrs Sophronia
  By the sea. 11534 F
CURTEIS, A M
  Rise of the Macedonian empire. 5475 H
CURTIN, Jeremiah
  Myths and folklore of Ireland. 11270 F

Myths and folktales of the Russians, western slavs and Magyars. 11154 F
CURTIS, George Ticknor
James Buchanan, Life of, 2 vols. 12482 B
CURTIS, George William
Ars Recte Vivendi. 10735 E
From the easy chair. 7677 E
Goldendog. 2244 F
Howadji in Syria. 3445 V
Lotus eating. 7649 V
Nile notes of a howadji. 3318 V
Orations and addresses, 3 vols. 8241E
Potiphar papers. 804 F
Prue and I. 805 F
Trumps. 6300 F
CURTIS, William E
Venezuela, a land where it is always summer. 9588 H
CURZON, George N
Persia and the Persion question, 2 vols. 7555 H
Problems of the far east, Japan, Korea, China. 9305 H
CUSHING, Luther S
Rules of proceedure and debate. 322R
CUSTER, Elizabeth B
Boots and saddles.
Following the Guidon. 5750 H
Tenting on the plains. 11348 H
CUSTINE, Marquis de
Russia, History of. 4324 H
CYR, Cornelius W
Maroussia. 5962 F
CZEIKA
Operetta in profile. 3188 F

DABNEY, Virginia (ed)
Don Miff. 2905 F
DAGGETT, Mrs C S
Mariposilla. 10335 F
DAHN, Felix
Felicitas. 1174 F
DAINTREY, Laura
Eros. 8965 F
DALE, Darley
Lottie's wooing. 7986 F
DANA, James Dwight
Geological story briefly told. 7040 S
Manual of geology. 1474 S
System of minerology. 1509 S
DANA, Richard Henry
Two years before the mast. 2240 F
DANA, Mrs William Starr
How to know the wild flowers. 7856S
DANE, Daniel
Vengeance is mine. 6471 F

DANILEVSKI, G P
Princess Tarakanova. 6839 F
DANIELL, Alfred
Text book of the principles of physics. 9876 S
DANTE, Alighieri
The Vision; or, hell, purgatory and paradise. 49 P
D'ANVERS, Mrs Arthur Bell (pseud N R E Bell)
Elementary history of art. 11156 A
DARWIN, Charles
Descent of man, 2 vols. 1458 S
Evolution in man and animals. 1464S
Expression of the emotions.
Insectivorous plants. 11153 S
Journal of researches during the voyage of H M S Beagle. 4857 V
Origin of spieces. 9743 S
Variation of animals and plants under domestication. 1478 S
DASA, Philangi
Swedenborg, the Buddhist. 5287 B
D'AUBIGNE, J H Merle
Story of the reformation. 4042 H
DAUDET, Alphonse
Artists' wives. 7189 F
Belle Nivernaise and other stories. 7192 F
Head of the family. 11888 F
Nabob, The. 2971 F
Rose and Ninette. 7188 F
Port Tarascon, last adventures of Tartarin. 2982 F
Tartarin of Tarascon. 7192 F
(Humerous sketch of the volatile and bombastic type of southern Frenchman).
Tartarin on the Alps. 7190 F
Humerous extravaganza, burlesquing the pretensions of Alpine guides and travelers).
D'AUDIFFRET, Pasquier
Memoirs of Chancellor Pasquier, 3 vols. 8853 B
DAUNT, Achilles
Crag, glacier and avalanche. 11620 V
With pack and rifle in the far southwest. 2900 V
DAVENPORT, Benjamine R
Fifty best books of the greatest authors. 7136 L
DAVENPORT, R A
Bastile, The history of the. 11443 H
DAVENPORT, William E
Practical sermons. 11532 P

DAVIDS, C A Foley Rhys
Elements of general philosophy.
10102 S
DAVIDSON, E A
Drawing of carpenters and joiners.
11636 A
Drawing for stonemasons. 11635 F
Gothic stonework. 6386 F
Model drawing. 11703 F
DAVIDSON, Thomas
Education of the Greek people.
11179 EE
Virgil. Works of. 11692 EE
DAVIE, Oliver
Nests and eggs of North American
birds. 12154 S
DAVIES, Thomas
Preparation and mounting of micro-
scopic objects. 12172 S
DAVIS, Charles
Elements of analytical geometry.
8387 EE
DAVIS, George R
City of palaces. 12444 V
DAVIS, Harriet Riddle
Gilbert Edgar's son. 11751 F
DAVIS, J D
Joseph Hardy Neesima, Sketch of the
life of.
DAVIS, N S
Consumption; how to prevent it and
how to live with it.
DAVIS, Mrs R H
Doctor Warrick's daughters. 9513 F
Frances Waldeaux. 15094 F
DAVIS, Richard Harding
About Paris. 9346 V
Cuba in war time. 10444 V
Cinderella and other stories. 9730 F

Exiles and other stories. 8421 F
Gallegher. 7931 F
King's jackal. 11992 F
Our English cousins. 8407 F
Princess Aline. 9373 F
Rulers of the Mediterranean. 8145 V
Soldiers of fortune. 10642 F
Three gringos in Venezuela and Cen-
tral America. 9736 V
Van Bibber and others. 7656 F
West from a car window. 7366 V
DAVIS, Richard Harding, and others
Great streets of the world. 7805 V
DAVIS, S M H
Norway nights and Russian days.
3378 V
DAVIS, Varina Anne Jefferson
Romance of summer seas. 12208 F
Veiled doctor. 9365 V
DAVIS, William W
Nimrod of the sea. 2675 F
DAVIS, W W H
El Gringo; or, New Mexico and her
people. 745 V
DAWE, Carlton
Bride of Japan. 11412 F
DAWSON, Emma Frances
An itinerate house and other stories.
10095 F
DAWSON, J W
Fossil men and their modern repre-
sentatives. 12530 S
Modern science in Bible lands. 7278 S
Some salient points in the science
of the earth. 8671 S
DAY, Lewis F
Anatomy of pattern. 12181 A
Nature in ornament. 12184 A
Planning of ornament. 12182 A

DAY, Thomas
Sanford and Merton. 2714 F
DEANE, William J
Abraham, Life and times of. 297 B
DE BARY
Fungi, mycetozoa and bacteria. 7938S
DE CANDOLLE, Alphonse
Origin of cultivated plants. 5724 S
DE COSTA, B F
Lake George. 9091 V
DEFOE, Daniel
Robinson Crusoe. 10554 J
Works of. 8996 F
DE FOREST, J W
Playing the mischief. 2427 J
DE GARMO, Charles
Essentials of method. 5975 EE
DELACRETTELLE, Henri
Lamartine and his friends. 11607 B
DELAND, Ellen Douglas
Katrina. 12311 J
Malvern; a neighborhood story.
12295 J
Successful venture. 12296 J
DELAND, Margaret
John Ward ,preacher. 1359 F
Mr Tommy Dove, etc. 7837 F
Philip and his wife. 8774 F
Sidney. 5828 F
Story of a child. 7449 EE
Wisdom of fools. 10439 F
DELANO, Mrs Aline
Life on the plains and among the
diggings. 4330 V
Vagrant and other tales. 6470 F
DE LEON, T C and E Ledyard
John Holden, unionist. 8082 F
DENISON, John L
Pictorial history of navy of the United States. 4039 H
DENISON, Mary A
What not. 9391 F
DENNIE, John
Rome of today and yesterday. 8464H
DENTON, William and Elizabeth
Soul of things, or psychometric discoveries and researches. 11733 RE
DEPEW, Chauncey M
One hundred years of American commerce (1795-1895), 2 vols. 10922 H
Orations and after-dinner speeches.
6380 E
DEPONS, F
Voyage to the Spanish main in South
America in 1801-4, 3 vols. 3399 V

DEPPING, Guillaume
Wonders of bodily strength and skill.
1423 S
DE PUY, W H (ed)
University of literature, 20 vols.
10825 S
DE QUINCY, Thomas
Autobiographic sketches. 4177 E
Biographical and historical essays.
4173 E
Confessions of an opium eater. 4177E
Eighteenth century in scholarship
and literature. 4173 E
Essays in ancient history. 4172 E
Essays in philosophy. 4174 E
Essays on christianity, paganism
and superstition. 320 E
Literary criticism. 4176 E
Literary reminiscences. 4176 E
Narrative and miscellaneous papers.
4175 E
Politics and political economy. 4174E
Romances and extravaganzas.4275 E
DESCHANEL, A Privat
Elementary treatise of natural philosophy. 9856 S
DEWEY, John
Psychology. 7435 EE
DEWINDT, Harry
Gold fields of Alaska to Behring
straits. 11374 V
DEWITT, Julia
How he made his fortune. 5429 J
DEWITT, Madam
Private life of M. Guizot. 1281 B
DEXTER, Charles
In memoriam, versions and idle
measures. 12572 E
D'HOLBACH, Baron
System of nature. 1418 S
DIAZ, Mrs Abby Morton
Jimmy johns. 12102 J
John Spicer letters. 338 J
Lucy Maria. 12307 J
Polly Cologne. 12101 J
DICEY, A V
Introduction to the study of the law
of the constitution. 9586 SS
DICK, William B
Dick's recitations. 11001 P
(18 vols. bound in 6).
DICKENS, Charles
American notes. 8882 F
Battle of life and the haunted man.
8894 F
Barnaby Rudge. 2275 F
Bleak House. 2274 F
Child's history of England. 713 J

Christmas books. 2276 F
David Copperfield. 8879 F
Doctor Marigold's prescriptions. 8884 F
Dombey and son. 1006 F
Great expectations. 8885 F
Hard times. 1008 F
Little Dorritt. 8889 F
Martin Chuzzlewit. 2273 F
Mystery of Edwin Drood. 8887 F
Nicholas Nickleby. 2273 F
Old curiosity shop. 1008 F
Oliver Twist. 1012 F
Our mutual friend. 2272 F
Pickwick papers. 2275 F
Pictures from Italy. 1012 F
Tale of two cities. 2276 F
Uncommercial traveller. 1002 F
DICKINSON, Anna E
Ragged register of people, places and things. 2671 V
What answer? 11670 F
DICKINSON, Mrs Ellen
King's daughters. 7459 F
DICKINSON, Emily
Poems of. 6507 P
DICKINSON, H Howship
Albuminuria. 8713 S
DIEZ, Ambrose P
For our boys; a collection of original literary offerings. 11600 J
DILKE, Charles W
Greater Britain. 8675 H
Problems of Greater Britain. 6559 H
DILWORTH, James A B
Free banking a natural right.10973SS
DIMITRY, John (trans)
Three good giants. 3185 J
DISRAELI, B (see Lord Beaconsfield)
DISRAELI, Isaac
Amenities of literature. 576 E
Calamities and quarrels of authors. 291 E
Curiosities of literature, 3 vols. 577 E
DITSON, Lina B
Walewska. 12327 F
DIXIE, Lady Florence
In the land of misfortune. 5012 V

DIXON, Charles
Half hour recreations in natural history. 6404 S
DIXON, William Hepworth
Her majesty's tower, 2 vols. 4236 H
DIXSON, Zella Allen
Comprehensive subject index to universal prose fiction. 10755 R
DOBSON, Austin
Henry Fielding, Life of. 6694 B
DODDS, William
Beauties of Shakespeare. 502 P
DODGE, Mary A (see Gail Hamilton)
DODGE, Mary Mapes
Donald and Dorothy. 9646 J
Hans Brinker. 8654 J
When life is young. 8808 P
DODGE, Richard J
Our Wild Indians. 4100 H
Plains of the great west. 3393 H
DODGE, Theodore A
Bird's eye view of our civil war. 10493 H
DOGGETT, Kate Newell (trans)
Grammar of painting. 8088 R
DOLBEAR, A E
Matter, ether and motion. 7799 S
DOLE, Charles F
American citizen. 8679 SS
DOLE, Nathan Haskell
Score of famous composers. 8144 B
DOMESTICA, Acheta
Episodes of insect life. 6215 S
DOMETT, Alfred
It was a calm, still night. 11690 A
DONALD, R
Wonders of architecture. 12538 A
DONALDSON, Paschal
Odd-fellows text-book. 9131 E
DOUBLEDAY, C W
Reminiscences of Filibuster war in Nicaragua. 4357 V
DONNELLY, Ignatius
Atlantis, antediluvian world. 6437 S
Ragnarok, age of fire and gravel. 5606 S
DORCHESTER, David
Sign or problem in all ages. 3060RE

DORIS, Charles
  Secret memoirs of Napoleon. 12333B
D'ORSAY, Countess
  Clouded happiness. 2434 F
POTEN, Lizzie
  My affinity and other stories. 932 F
  Poems from the inner life of. 4 P
DOUGALL, L
  Beggars all. 9313 F
  Madonna of a day. 10449 F
DOUGLAS, Amanda M
  Bethia Wray's new name. 10221 F
  Claudia. 8164 F
  Floyd Grandson's honor. 7772 F
  Foes of her household. 10232 F
  Fortunes of the Faradays. 7775 F
  From hand to mouth. 7774 F
  Heirs of Bradley house. 7170 F
  Her place in the world. 10874 F
  Home nook. 6093 F
  Hope mills. 7773 F
  In the king's country. 8415 F
  In trust. 11845 F
  Larry. 10893 F
  Modern Adam and Eve in the garden. 7776 F
  Nellie Kinnard's kingdom. 6289 F
  Old man who lived in a shoe. 8163 F
  Osborne of Arrochar. 8165 F
  Out of the wreck. 10227 F
  Sherburne series
    Sherburne house. 7540 F
    Lyndell Sherburne. 10308 F
    Sherburne cousins. 10312 F
    Sherburne romance. 10309 F
    Mistress of Sherburne. 10310 F
    Stephen Dane. 6294 F
    Sydnie Adriance. 6290 F
    Whom Kathie married. 6291 F
    With fate against him. 11634 F
    Woman's inheritance. 6292 F
DOUGLAS, James
  Traveling anecdotes through Europe. 5211 F
DOUGLAS, Robert
  Adventures of a medical student, 3 vols. 5233 F
DOUGLAS, Robert K
  Li Hung Chang. 9449 B
DOUGLASS. Frederick
  Autobiography of. 4708 B
  China, History of. 4317 H
DOW, Lorenzo
  Life of. 1262 B
  Works of. 110 V
DOWDEN, Edward
  French literature, History of.11017EE
  Shakespeare, his mind and art. 399E
  Southey, Life of. 6679 B
  Studies in literature. 12199 EE
DOWIE, Menie Muriel (Mrs M M Norman)
  Crook of the bough. 12349 F
  Girl in the Karpathians. 7111 V
  Japanese girls and women. 7110 H
DOWNING, A J
  Cottage residences. 7706 A
DOWNING, Charles
  Selected fruits. 6727 A
DOWNING and Vaux
  Villas and cottages; a series of designs. 4731 A
DOYLE, A Conan
  Adventures of Sherlock Holmes. 7683 F
  Captain of the Polestar. 8318 F
  Desert drama. 11022 F
  Doings of Raffles Haw
  Exploits of Brigadier Gerard. 9514 F
  Firm of Girdlestone. 9598 F
  Great Shadow. 8065 F
  Memoirs of Sherlock Holmes. 9621 F
  Micah Clarke. 7783 F
  Refugees. 11047 F
  Round the red lamp. 9103 F
  Sign of the four. 8206 F
  Stark Munroe letters. 9366 F
  Uncle Bernac. 10504 F
  White company. 8178 F
DOYLE, J A
  English in America. 10586 H
DRAKE, Francis
  Indian history for young folks. 4141 J
DRAKE, Jeanie
  Metropolitans. 9919 F
DRAKE, Samuel Adams
  Book of New England legends. 882 F
  Making of the great west. 4253 H
  Making of New England. 4257 H
DRAPER, John W
  Conflict between religion and science. 1394 RE
  Human physiology. 11567 S
  Intellectual development of Europe. 2 vols. 4170 H
DREW, Thomas
  Digest of the history of ancient and modern nations. 4207 H
DROMGOOLE, William
  Valley path. 11905 F
DRUMMOND, Henry
  Addresses. RE
  Ascent of man. 8786 S

Greatest thing in the world. 5776 RE
Ideal life. 10975 RE
Monkey that would not kill. 11088 J
Natural law in the spiritual world.
  582 RE
DRUMMOND, Robert B
Erasmus, Life of, 2 vols. 1270 B
DRYDEN, John
Poetical works of. 54 P
Works of Virgil. 77 P
DU CHAILLU, Paul B
Country of the dwarfs. 3428 J
Equatorial Africa. 5751 V
Ivar, the Viking. 8003 J
Land of the midnight sun. 2 vols.
  3380 V
Lost in the jungle. 850 J
Stories of the gorilla country. 852 J
"DUCHESS" (pseud Mrs. M H Hun-
  gerford)
Beauty's daughters. 9094 F
Coming of Chloe. 10316 F
Duchess. 3416 F
Faith and unfaith. 9031 F
DUCOUDRAY, George
Ancient civilization. History of.
  5417 H
DUDEVANT, Mme A L A (see Sand,
  George)
DUDLEY, Marion
Poetry and philosophy of Goethe.
  EE
DUDLEY, Thos. Underwood
Church's need. The. 11626 RE
DUFFERIN, Earl of
Letters from high latitudes. 1614 V
DUFFY, Bella
Madam de Stael, Life of. 1261 B
Tuscan republics, etc. 7769 H
DUFFY, Charles G
Young Ireland (1840-1850). 8904 H
DUMAS, Alexandre
Count of Monte Cristo. 12421 F
Edmund Dantes, sequel to Count of
  Monte Cristo. 12422 F
D'artagnan series
Three musketeers. 9323 F
Twenty years after. 12423 F

Vicomte de Bragelonne. 12428 F
Queen's necklace series
Memoirs of a physician. 11454 F
Queen's necklace. 11455 F
Taking the Bastile. 11456 F
Countess of Charny. 11457 F
Chevalier of Maison Rouge. 11458F
Regency series
Conspirators. 2798 F
Regent's daughter. 8452 F
Valois series
Marguerite de Valois. 11459 F
Chicot, the jester. 2801 F
Forty-five guardsmen. 2794 F
DU MAURIER, George
Martian, The. 10503 F
Peter Ibbetson. 9996 F
Social pictorial satire. 11389 F
Trilby. 8732 F
DUNBAR, Charles F (compiler)
Laws relating to currency, finance
  and banking. 8839 SS
DUNBAR, Paul Laurence
Folks from Dixie. 11403 F
DUNCAN, P Martin (ed)
Cassell's natural history, 6 vols.
  1483 S
DUNCAN, Sarah Jeanette (pseud Mrs
  S J D Cotes)
Daughter of today. 9623 F
His honour and a lady. 9819 F
Simple adventures of a Memsahib.
  7787 F
Social departure. 6102 F
Story of Sonny Sahib. 11622 F
DUNN, J P
Indiana, History of. 4282 H
DUNPHY, T
Remarkable trials, 2 vols. 1377 F
DUPUY, Ernest
Great masters of Russian literature.
  6352 EE
DURUY, Victor
France, History of. 5571 H
Modern times, History of. 9568 H
DUVAL, Mathias
Artistic anatomy. 6433 A

DWIGHT, James
Practical lawn tennis. 7845 A
DYE, John Smith
Plots and crimes of the Great Conspiracy, History of. 4739 H
DYSON Mrs
Stories of the trees. 8131 J

EARLE, Alice Morse
Sabbath in puritan New England. 7675 H
Colonial days in old New York. 11284 H
Customs and fashions in old New England. 8012 H
Margaret Winthrop, Life of. 9380 B
EARLE John
Simple grammar of English now in use. 11911 EE
EARLE, Mary Tracy
Wonderful wheel, The. 9915 F
EASTLAKE, Charles L
Kugler s school of painting in Italy. 5280 A
EASTMAN, Charlotte Whitney
Evolution of Dodd's sister. 11930 F
EASTMAN, Julia
Striking for the right. 7329 J
EATON, Dorman B
Civil service in Great Britain. 8840 SS
EBERS, Georg
Bride of the Nile. 7182 F
Burgomaster's wife. 10820 F
Cleopatra, 2 vols. 8809 F
Egyptian princess, 2 vols. 1164 F
Elixir and other tales. 5989 F
Emperor, The. 7225 F
Homo Sum. 7174 F
Joshua, a biblical picture. 10781 F
Serapis. 2127 F
Story of my life. 7864 B
Uarda. 1041 F
Word, only a word. 1147 F
ECKSTEIN, E A
Chaldean magician. 1047 F
Hertha. 7155 F
Prusias, 2 vols. 1168 F
Quintus Claudius. 1166 F
EDDY, Mary B G
Science and health. 10532 RE
EDDY, Richard
Universalism in America, 2 vols. 8757 RE
EDGAR, J G
Footprints of famous men. 12280 B
War of the Roses. 4331 H

EDGEWORTH, Maria
Belinda. 2841 F
Castle Rackrent. 2842 F
Ennui. 2843 F
Fashionable life. 2844 F
Harrington. 2847 F
Irish bulls. 2842 F
Moral tales. 2820 F
Patronage. 2845 F
Popular tales. 2840 F
EDINGER, Ludwig
Structures of the central nervous system. 7120 S
EDMONDS, Cyrus R
Cicero s three books of offices. 9273 E
EDWARDS, Amelia B
Ballads. 675 P
Night on the borders of the Black forest. 6549 V
One thousand miles up the Nile. 5769 V
Pharoahs, fellahs and explorers. 12520 V
EDWARDS, M Betham
Dream Charlotte. 9831 F
EDWORDS, Clarence E
Campfires of a naturalist. 11377 F
EGBERT, Seneca
Manual of hygiene and sanitation. 11390 S
EGGLESTON, Edward
Beginners of a nation. 10044 H
Duffles. 7991 F
End of the world. 2682 F
Faith doctor. 8670 F
Mystery of Metropolisville. 2786 F
Stories of great Americans. 12636 J
EGGLESTON, Edward and Lillie E Seelye
Brant and Red Jacket. 9836 J
Montezuma. 9835 J
Pocahontas. 9834 J
Red Eagle. 9838 J
Tecumseh. 9837 J
EGGLESTON, George Cary (ed)
American war ballads, 2 vols. 9099 P
Strange stories from history. 2728 F
EGGLESTON, George Cary and Marbourg, D
Juggernauts. 5986 F
EGGLESTON, Nathaniel H
Home and its surroundings. 480 A
EGGLESTON, Thomas
John Peterson, Life of. 9307 B
EILOART, Mrs Elizabeth.
Boy with an idea. 8109 J
Curate's discipline. 2454 F

EISEN, Gustav
Raisin industry. 6896 A
ELBON, Barbara
Bethseda. 892 F
ELDER, Dr
Dr E K Kane, Life of. 111 B
ELIOT, Charles William
American contributions to civiliza-
tion, and other essays. 10795 E
ELIOT, George (pseud of Mrs. M E
Cross)
Adam Bede. 10472 F
Daniel Deronda, 2 vols. 2649 F
Felix Holt. 9024 F
Leaves from a note book. 476 E
Middlemarch. 698 F
Mill on the Floss. 2697 F
Poems of. 36 P
Romola. 2414 F
Scenes of clerical life and Silas
Marner. 3033 F
Silas Marner. 2655 F
ELLACOMBE, Henry N
Plant lore and garden craft of Shake-
speare. 10455 R
ELLET, Mrs E F
Court circles of the republic. 8924 L
Queens of American society. 8924 B
ELLIOTT, Henry W
Our Arctic province. 11032 V
ELLIS, Edward S
From the throttle to the president's
chair. 12494 J
ELLIS, Edward S
In the days of the pioneers. 10798 J
Lost in the Rockies. 12370 J
Shod with silence. 10450 J
ELY, Richard T
Introduction to political economy. SS
French and German socialism.9577SS

Outlines of economics. SS
Problems of today. SS
Socialism and social reform. 8656SS
EMERSON, Edward Waldo
Correspondence between John Ster-
ling and R W Emerson. 10901 E
EMERSON, Oliver Farrar
English language, History of. 8783EE
EMERSON, R W
Essays.
Letters and social aims.
Miscellanies. 674 E
Poems. 10167 P
Representative men. 1373 E
Society and solitude. 470 E
EMERTON, Ephriam
Introduction to the study of the mid-
dle ages. 9308 H
Mediavel Europe. 11045 H
ERMAN, Adolf
Life in ancient Egypt. 8841 H
EVANS, Augusta J (see Wilson, Mrs
A J E
EVANS, Henry Ridgely
Hours with the ghosts; or, XIX cen-
tury witchcraft. 11046 S
EVANS, W T
Esoteric Christianity, etc. 334 RE
EVERETT, C C
Poetry, comedy and duty. 11693 EE
EVERETT, Edward
George Washington, Life of. 144 B
EVETTS, Basil T A
New light on the Bible and Holy
land. 12192 RE
EWBANK, Thomas
Life in Brazil. 3297 V
EWING, Hugh
Castle in the air. 6885 F

EWING, Juliana H
Flat iron for a farthing. 5830 J
Great emergency. 6812 J
Jackanapes. 12098 J
Jan of the windmill. 4963 J
Lob-lie-by-the-fire.. 6816 J
Melchior's dream. 6799 J
Mrs. Overtheway's remembrance.
6813 J
Six and sixteen. 4964 J
We and the world. 6922 J

FABER, George Stanley
Origin of pagan idolatry. 3430 RE
FAGG, Michael
Life and adventures of a limb of the
law. 5236 B
FALCONER, Lanoe
Cecilia De Noel. 6843 F
FALCONER, William
Mushrooms; how to grow them.
6394 A
FALLOWS, Samuel
Dictionary of synonyms and anto-
nyms. 6550 R
FALLOUX, Count de
Writings of Madam Switchine. 950 E
FARADAY, Michael
Lectures on the various forces of
matter. 11735 S
FARMAN, Ella
Cooking club of Tu Whit hollow.
7398 J
FARMER, Lydia H
Boys' book of famous rulers. 5534 B
Girls' book of famous queens. 307 B
La Fayette, Life of. 12470 B
Story book of science. 9119 B
FARNHAM, Eliza
Woman and her era, 2 vols. 690 E
FARRAR, F W
Bible: its meaning and supremacy.
10751 RE
Christ, Life of. 4839 B
Early days of Christianity. 5413 RE
Julian Home, a tale of college life.
8102 F
Mercy and judgment. 7085 RE
Seekers after God. 11340 RE
Social and present day questions.
7694 SS
Solomon, Life and times of. 1350 B
FARROW, Edward S
Military encyclopedia, 3 vols. 8551 R
FARWELL, Eveline
Fingers and fortunes. 6530 S
FAWCETT, Edgar

Confessions of Claude. 3175 F
FAWCETT, Henry
Manual of political economy. 9175 SS
FAXON, C E
Beautiful ferns. 2715 S
FELLOW, A Rochester
Winnipeg country. 7718 V
FELTON, C C
Greece, ancient and modern. 2228 H
FENELON, F
Adventures of Telemachus. 2677 F
FENERBACH, A von
Caspar Hauser, Life of.
FENN, George Manville
Cormorant Crag. 9677 F
Haute noblesse. 6977 F
In honour's cause. 10076 F
Master of ceremonies. 11343 F
Mynn's mystery. 7020 F
FERGUSSON, James
Modern styles of architecture, 2 vols.
6501 A
FERN, Fanny
Fern leaves. 742 F
Ginger snaps. 954 F
FERRI, Enrico
Criminal sociology. 9532 SS
FERRIS, George T
Great Italian and French composers.
1374 B
FESSENDEN, T G
Complete farmer and rural economist
1803 A
FEUDGE, Fannie Roper
India. 4225 H
FEUILLET, Octave
Romance of a poor young man. 7184F
FICKES, David G
Oliver G Gray, Life of. 273 B
FIELD, Mrs C L
Highlights. 2703 F
FIELD, Eugene
House, The. 9540 F
Little book of profitable tales. 7055 F
Little book of western verse. 7424 P
Love affairs of a bibliomaniac. 9517F
Second book of verse. 7735 P
Songs and other verse. 12594 P
With trumpet and drum. 12647 P
FIELD, George
Rudiments of color and coloring.
6389 SS
FIELD, Henrietta
Muses up to date. 12004 P
FIELD, Henry M
Among the holy hills. 7325 V
Barbary coast, The. 8492 V

Greek islands and Turkey after the war. 7344 V
Our western archipelago. 9381 V
Story of the Atlantic telegraph. 7609H

FIELD, Kate
Ten days in Spain. 1176 V

FIELDE, Adele M
Corner of Cathay; studies from life among the Chinese. 9184 V

FIELDING, Henry
Amelia. 2868 F
Joseph Andrews. 2867 F
Tom Jones. 2 vols. 2865 F

FIELDS, Annie
Harriet Beecher Stowe. Life and letters of. 10872 B

FIELDS, James T
Yesterdays with authors. 10511 E

FIGUIER, Louis
Human race. 1456 S
Ocean world. 1540 S
Primeval man. 1469 S
Tomorrow of death. 11805 RE
Vegetable world. 1438 S
World before the deluge. 1481 S

FILIPPINI
One hundred ways of cooking eggs. 7524 A
One hundred desserts. 9716 A

FINCH, Marianne
An English woman's experience in America. 1625 V

FINCH, Henry T
Chopin and other musical essays. 11425 A
Wagner and his works. 11157 B

FINDLATER, Mary
Over the hills. 11818 F

FINLEY, John P
Tornadoes. 11680 S

FISH, Daniel W
Complete arithmetic. 8375 EE

FISHER, F C (see Christian Reid)

FISHER, George P
Benjamine Silliman, Life of. 2 vols. 139 B
Christian church, History of the. 4838 RE

FISHER, Sydney George
The true Benjamine Franklin. 12576 B

FISKE, Amos Kidder
Myths of Israel. 10747 F

FISKE, John
American political ideas. 8838 SS
American revolution, 2 vols. 6757 H
Beginnings of New England. 10501H
Civil government in the United States. 11169 H
Destiny of man. 331 RE
Discovery of America, 2 vols. 7428H
Excursions of an evolutionist. 1471 S
Idea of God. 8313 RE
Myths and myth-makers. 9796 F
Old Virginia and her neighbors, 2 vols. 10845 H
War of independence. 5440 H

FITCH, J G
Lectures on teaching. 8830 EE

FITCH, Thomas and Anna
Better days; or, A millionaire of tomorrow. 6883 F

FITCHETT, W H
Deeds that won the empire. 11912 F

FITZGERALD, Percy
Kings and queens of an hour, 2 vols. 5006 B

FLAGG, Wilson
A year among the trees. 514 E

FLAMMARION, Camille
Lumen. 11980 F

FLANDRAU, Charles M
Harvard episodes. 11980 F

FLEETWOOD, John
Christ, Life of. 663 B

FLEMING, George (pseud Julia Fletcher)
Andromeda. 2593 F
Kismet. 5675 F
Truth about Clement Ker. 6881 F
Vestigia. 2027 F

FLEMING, Mrs J M (Alice M Kipling)
Pinchback goddess. 10470 F

FLEMING, William H
How to study Shakespeare. 11410EE

FLETCHER, Banister
Architecture, History of. 11283 A
FLETCHER, C R L
Gustavus Adolphus and the struggle
of protestantism for existence. 11193 B
FLETCHER, Horace
Happiness. 10732 RE
FLETCHER, J C (see Fleming, George)
FLETCHER, J S
God's failures. 10409 F
FLINT, Annie
Sunbeam stories. 11917 J
FLINT, Robert
Vico. 7633 B
FLOWER, William Henry
The horse; a study in natural his-
tory. 7434 A
FLOWER, William Henry
Fashion in deformity. 6528 S
FLUGEL, Ewald
Thomas Carlyle, moral and religious
development. 7237 E
FOBES, Walter K (ed)
Five minute declamations. 10689 P
Five minute readings. 10690 P
FONTAINE, Edward
How the world was peopled. 9447 S
FONVEILLE, W de
Thunder and lightning. 277 S
FOOTE, Edward B
Medical common sense. 11716 S
FOOTE, Mary Hallock
Chosen valley. 7414 F
In exile and other stories. 8307 F
John Bodewin's testimony. 2475 F
Last assembly ball. 4942 F
Led horse claim. 4943 F
FORBES, Archibald
Barracks, bivouacs and battles. 6861 V
Camps, quarters and casual places.
9961 V
Chinese Gordon. 479 B
FORD, Isaac
Tropical America. 7748 V
FORD, Paul Leicester
Hon Peter Sterling. 9810 F
Prefaces, proverbs and poems of
Benj Franklin. 5968 L
Story of an untold love. 10733 F
True George Washington. 12631 B
FORD, Mrs Sallie Rochester
Grace Truman; or, Love and princi-
ple. 11504 F
FORD, Worthington
American citizen's manual. 8273 SS
FOREST, Julia B de
Short history of art. 7287 A

FORRESTER, Frank
Fish and fishing, 2 vols. 5783 A
FORRESTER, Mrs (pseud Mrs Bridges)
Diana Carew. 12160 F
Dolores. 12163 F
Fair women. 12157 F.
June. 12158 F
Once again. 12159 F F
Rhona. 12162 F
Viva. 12161 F
FORSTER, John
Charles Dickens, Life of, 2 vols. 133 B
FORTUNE, T Thomas
Black and white. 11610 F
FOSSETT, Frank
Colorado. 9048 H
FOSTER, J W
Pre-historic races of the United
States. 557 H
FOSTER, R S
Nature and blessedness of christ-
ianity. 10705 RE
FOTHERGILL, Jessie
First violin. 10423 F
From Moor Isles. 7478 F
Kith and kin. 10823 F
Oriole's daughter. 7817 F
Probation. 1180 F
Wellfields. 1181 F
FOTHERGILL, J Milner
Maintenance of health. 11544 S
FOUILLEE, Alfred
Education from a national stand-
point. 11574 EE
FOUQUE, De La Motte
Undine and other tales. 7480 F
FOWLER, Frank
Drawing in charcoal and crayon.
1768 A
Handbook of oil painting. 1778 A
FOWLER, O S
Hereditary descent. 1519 S
FOWLER, Thomas
Locke, Life of. 6696 B
FOWLER, W Warde
City state of the Greeks and Romans.
9578 H
Julius Caesar and foundation of
Roman imperial system. 11190 B
FOWLER, William W
Ten years in Wall street. 8926 L
FOX, John
Cumberland vendetta and other sto-
ries. 9505 F
Kentuckians, The. 11069 F
FOX, Norman
Christ in the daily meal. 12326 RE

FRACKELTON, S S
Tried by fire. 8014 A
FRANCILLON, R E
Gods and heroes. 7912 F
Real queen. 2977 F
FRANCIS, J G
Beach rambles in search of seaside
pebbles and crystals. 12528 S
FRANCIS, Laurence H
Schoolboys of Rookesbury. 11315 J
FRANCIS, M E
Duenna of a genius. 11938 F
FRANCO, Harry
Bankrupt stories. 5921 F
FRASER, Mrs Hugh
The Brown ambassador. 10456 F
FRASIER, Kirtland
Cyclopedia of anecdotes. 1204 R
FREDERIC, Harold
Copperhead. 8031 F
Damnation of Theron Ware. 10003F
Deserter and other stories. 12014 F
Gloria mundi. 12585 F
March hares. 10132 F
Seth's brother's wife. 5410 F
FREDUR, Thor
Sketches from shady places. 5121 E
FREEDLEY, E T
Opportunities for industry. 4734 L
FREEMAN, Mrs A M
Somebody's Ned. 11664 F
FREEMAN, E A
General sketch of history. 4241 H
Growth of the English constitution.
9119 H
Old English history. 10341 H
Race and language. 527 H
Sicily, History of, 2 vols. 9185 H
Some impressions of the United
States. 5117 V
FREMONT, Jessie Benton
Far west sketches. 2599 V
Souvenirs of my time. 2599 B
FREMONT, J C
Memoirs of his life. 276 B
FRENCH, A (see Thanet, Octave)
FRENCH, Harry W
Our boys in China. 11314 J
FRENCH, W Stewart
Realities of Irish life. 6968 F
FREYTAG, Gustav
Lost manuscript. 7364 F
Technique of the drama. 11266 EE
FRITH, Henry
King Arthur and his knights. 2184F
FRITH, Walter
In search of quiet. 9678 F

FRITH, W P
Autobiography, 2 vols. 5771 B
FRITSCH, Heinrich
Diseases of women. 8718 S
FROBISHER, John
Voyage to America, 1576-8. 3350 V
FROBEL, Friedrich
Education of man. 610 EE
FROISSART, Sir John
Chronicles of England, France and
Spain (1326-1400). 4244 H
FROST, John
Cyclopedia of eminent Christians.
7253 B
Pioneer mothers of the west. 6361 B
FROST, William Henry
Court of King Arthur. 10119 F
FROTHINGHAM, A B
George Ripley, Life of. 190 B
FROTHINGHAM, M L
Metrical pieces. 12 P
FROTHINGHAM, Richard
Rise of the republic of the United
States. 10618 H
FROUDE, James A
Bunyan, Life of. 6672 B
Caesar, a sketch. 1257 B
Carlyle, T; first 40 years of his life.
5844 B
Carlyle, T; life in London. 5845 B
Catharine Arragon, Divorce of.7850H
England, History of (1529-1603), 12
vols. 4072 H
English in the West Indies. 4258 V
Erasmus, Life and letters of. 9157 B
Oceana, or England and her colonies.
10394 H
Science of history. 527 H
Short studies on great subjects.584 E
FULLER, Anna
One of the pilgrims. 12578 F
FULLER, Andrew S
Grape culturist. 1809 A
Practical forestry. 9563 A
Small fruit culturist. 1810 A
FULLER, Henry R
Chatelaine of La Trinite. 7454 F
Chevalier of Pensiere-vani. 7113 F
Cliff dwellers. 7922 F
FULLER, Herbert
Vivian of Virginia. 11993 F
FULLER, Maurice
Thomas Fuller, Life and times of.
5220 B
FULLER, Richard F
Chaplain Fuller, Life of. 11721 B

FULLER, Thomas
  Abel Redevivus; or, The dead yet speaking. 1365 B
FURNEAUX, W
  Life in ponds and streams. 11273 S
  Out door word. 8256 S
FURNESS, Horace
  Variorum of Shakespeare, 10 vols. 1687 R

GABORIAU, E
  File No. 113. 10786 F
  Mystery of Orcival. 9021 F
  Other people's money. 7054 F
GAIRDNER, James
  Henry the Seventh. 6778 B
  Houses of Lancaster and York.5483 H
GALTON, Francis
  Hereditary genius. 6740 S
GARDINER, Samuel R
  English history for schools. 9279 H
  Puritan revolution. 5488 H
  Students' history of England. 11146 H
  Thirty years' war. 5487 H
GARDNER, Alice
  Julian, philosopher and emperor. 11184 B
GARDNER, E C
  Home interiors. 1813 A
  Illustrated homes. 6666 A
GARIBALDI, G
  Autobiography. 11578 B
GARLAND, Hamlin
  Rose of Dutcher's coolly. 9423 F
  Wayside courtships. 10719 F
GARLAND, Hugh
  John Randolph, Life of, 2 vols. 141B
GARNER, R L
  Speech of monkeys. 7861 S
GARNETT, James M
  Beowulf, and Anglo-Saxon poem. 6212 P
GARNETT, Richard
  Italian literature, History of. 11178 EE
GARRARD, Lewis H
  Wah-to-yah, the Taos trail. 1635 V
GARRETT, Edward (pseud Mrs I F

Mayo)
  At any cost. 2581 F
  Crooked places. 8059 F
  Equal to the occasion. 2375 F
  Gold and dross. 8061 F
  House by the works. 8966 F
  Occupations of a retired life. 8060 F
  White as snow. 5996 F
GASKELL, Mrs E C
  Cousin Phillis. 7625 F
  Cranford. 10096 F
GATTY, Horatia
  Juliana H Ewing and her books. 3104 B
GAUTIER, J
  Usurper, The. 2015 F
GAY, Mr
  Fables. 5128 R
GAY, Sidney H
  James Madison, Life of. 186 B
GAYE, Selina
  World's lumber room. 3246 J
GAYLEY, Charles Mills
  Classic myths, illustrated. 8870 R
GEIKIE, Cunningham
  Holy land and the Bible, 2 vols. 5991 V
  Hours with the Bible, 6 vols. 8408 RE
  New Testament hours. 8511 RE
  Short life of Christ. 7281 B
GEIKIE, James
  Great ice age in North America. 1496 S
GELLIE, Mary E
  Steven, the school-master. 5283 F
GENONE, Hudor
  Inquirendo island. 417 F
GEORGE, Henry
  Perplexed Philosopher, (H. Spencer.) 7738 SS
  Progress and poverty. 8797 SS
  Science of political economy. 11031 SS
  Social problems. 196 SS
GERALD, Caroline Fitz
  Venetia Victrix and other poems. 6872 P

GERARD, Dorothea
An arranged marriage. 9136 F
Spotless reputation. 10536 F
Wrong man. 9S91 F
GERHARD, William Paul
Guide to sanitary house inspection.
11672 A
GERUNDO, Friar
Life and history of, 2 vols. 5259 H
GIBBON, Charles
Blood money and other tales. 4760F
Golden shaft. 3093 F
GIBBON, Edward
Decline and fall of the Roman em-
pire. 3 vols. 3433 H
GIBBS, Alfred S
Goethe's mother. 6359 B
GIBSON, John
Great waterfalls, cataracts and gey-
sers. S129 V
GIBSON, William
Rambles in Europe in 1S39. 11S50 V
GIBSON, William Hamilton
Camp life in the woods. S53 V
Eye spy: afield with nature among
flowers and inanimate things.11239S
Sharp eyes: a rambler's calendar.
6754 S
GIDDINGS, Joshua R
The rebellion; its authors and causes.
4001 H
GIDE, Charles
Principles of political economy. 2273
SS
GILBERT, Grove
Lake Bonneville. 6140 V
GILBERT, Humphrey
Voyage to America. 3350 V
GILBERT, William (ed)
Memoirs of a cynic, 3 vols. 9274 B
GILBERT, W S
Bab ballads, with which are included
songs of a savoyard. 12223 P
GILDER, Jeanette L
Taken by siege. 11070 F
GILDER, Richard Watson
Five books of song. S781 P
GILFILLAN, George
Bards of the Bible. 11837 B
GILL, Wilfred Austin
Edward Cracraft Lefroy: his life and
poems. 10749 P
GILLMAN, Henry
Ha-san, a Fellah: a romance of Pal-
estine. 11095 F
GILMAN, Arthur
Shakespeare's morals. 11395 E

GILMAN, Arthur
Boston, Story of. 5628 H
Rome, Story of. 4352 H
Saracens, Story of. 4351 H
GILMAN, Daniel C
James-Monroe, Life of. 185 B
GILMAN, Nicholas Paine
Socialism and the American spirit.
7739 SS
GILMAN, Parker (ed)
Biart's adventures of a young nat-
uralist. 1249 V
GILMORE, Minnie
Woman who stood between. 11727 F
GILMORE, Parker
Travel, war and shipwreck. 2178 V
GIRONIERE, Paul de la
Twenty years in the Philippines.
5932 V
GISSING, George
Charles Dickens, a critical study.
11375 B
Eve's ransom. 11580 F
Sleeping fires. 10135 F
GLADDEN, Washington
Christian way. 10899 RE
Cosmopolis city club. 12183 E
Santa Claus on a lark. 9841 J
Seven puzzling Bible books. 10858
RE
Tools and the man. 7736 RE
GLADSTONE, J H
Michael Farraday, Life of. 270 B
GLADSTONE, William E
Criticism of Robert Elsmere. 4665 E
Juventus' Mundi. 235 H
Kin beyond the sea. 527 E
GLASGOW, Ellen
Phrases of an inferior planet. 12586F
GLAZELBROOK, R T
Laws and properties of matter.11421S
GLAZELBROOK, R T and W N Shaw
Practical physics. 9872 S
GLAZIER, Willard
Down the great river. 7702 V
Three years in Federal cavalry.
4699 V
GLEIG, G R
The subaltern. 5050 F
GLOUVET, Jules de
Woodman, The. 7681 F
GNEIST, Dr Rudolfson
English parliament, History of. 11257
H
GODKIN, Edwin L
Unforeseen tendencies of democracy.
11445 SS

GODOLPHIN, Mary
  Aesop's fables. 9803 J
  Robinson Crusoe. 9522 J
GOEBEL, K
  Outlines of classification and mor-
    phology of plants. 5224 S
GOETHE, John W von
  Autobiography. 6890 B
  Dramatic works: Iphigenia in Tauris,
    Torquato Tasso, Goethe v. Berlich-
    ingen. 6892 P
  Elective affinities. 6891 E
  Faust; Anna Swanwick, trans. 5189 P
  Faust; A Hayward trans. 2909 P
  Travels in Italy, France and Switz-
    erland. 6891 E
  Werther, Sorrows of. 6891 E
  Wilhelm Meister's apprenticeship and
    travels. 6894 E
GOFF, George Paul
  Autobiography of a sailor boy.1174913
GOLDOS, B Perez
  Marianella. 1171 F
GOLDSMITH, Oliver
  Poems and plays of. 581 P
  Vicar of Wakefield. 2545 F
  Rasselas. 2545 F
GOMME, George Laurence
  Ethnology in folklore. 11423 F
  Village community. 9564 H
GOODALE, George Lincoln
  Physiological botany. 7700 S
GOODE, Francis
  The better covenant. 586 RE
GOODE, John M
  Memoirs of. 5111 B
GOODLOE, Abbe Carter
  College girls. 9414 F
GOODWIN, Christina
  How they learned housework. 8125 J
GOODWIN, William
  Adventures of Caleb Williams. 227 F
GOODYEAR, William Henry
  History of art. 12194 A
GORDON, H L
  Feast of the virgins and other poems.
    7056 P

GORDON, H R
  Pontiac, chief of the Ottawas. 10657J
  Tecumseh, chief of the Shawonoes.
    11375 J
GORDON, John
  Three children of Galilee; a life of
    Christ for young people. 11071 J
GORDON, Julien
  Diplomatic diary. 6664 F
  Marionettes. 7176 F
  Puritan pagan. 11719 F
  Successful man. 6410 F
GORDON, Mrs
  Memoir of John Wilson. 263 B
GORDY, Wilbur F
  United States history for schools.
    11894 J
GOSS, Warren Lee
  Tom Clifton. 7405 J
GOSSE, Edmund
  Critical kit-kats. 9816 E
  Gossips in a library. 8155 E
  Gray, Life of. 6703 B
  History of 18th century literature.
    6868 EE
  Modern English literature. 12003 EE
  On viol and flute. 9561 P
  Shakespeare to Pope. 9383 EE
GOSSE, Philip Henry
  Assyria, her manners and customs.
    12529 H
  Evenings at the microscope. 1499 S
GOUBAUX, Armand
  Exterior of the horse. 7058 A
GOUGH, John B
  Autobiography. 114 B
  Platform echoes. 585 E
GOULD, Florence
  Lute Falconer. 7208 F
GOULD, S Baring
  Arminell. 7004 F
  Bladys Stewponey. 11015 F
  Court royal. 12473 F
  Curious myths of the middle ages.
    6983 F
  Domita. 12552 F
  Germany, past and present. 9571 H
  John Herring. 7003 F

Kitty alone; a story of three fires.
11994 F
Legends of patriarchs and prophets.
6982 F
Mehalah. 7002 F
Penny-come-quicks. 4748 F
Germany, Story of. 4348 H
GOULDING, F R
Marooner's island. 7201 J
Sapelo. 7204 J
Young marooners on the Florida
coast. 856 J
GOW, Alexander M
Good morals and gentle manners.
8231 A
GOWING, L F
Five thousand miles in a sledge.
5418 V
GOWER, Ronald
My reminiscences. 1649 H
GRAHAM, Ennis (see Molesworth, Mrs
G
GRAHAM, P Anderson
Red Scaur. 10351 F
GRAHAM, Douglas
Treatise on massage. 7942 S
GRAHAM, James M
Son of the czar; an historical ro-
mance. 11023 F
GRAHAM, Mrs F
Reasonable elocution. 8382 EE
GRAHAME, Kenneth
Golden age, The. 10541 F
GRAND, Sarah
Heavenly twins. 7951 F
GRANT, Alexander H
Christian year; thoughts in verse for
Sundays. 11756 RE
GRANT, James
Secret dispatch. 893 F
GRANT, Robert
Art of living. 9490 A
Bachelor's Christmas and other sto-
ries. 9491 F
Face to face. 2293 F
Opinions of a philosopher. 11862 F
GRANT, Ulysses S
Personal memoirs of, 2 vols. 8953 B
GRANVILLE A B
Autobiography, 2 vols. 5019 B
GRAS, Felix
Reds of the Midi; an episode of the
French revolution. 10068 F
GRAY, Asa
Botany of California. 11144 S
Elements of botany. 12179 S
Lessons in botany and vegetable
physiology. 8380 S

Synoptical flora of North America.
6258 S
GRAY, David
Gallops. 12588 F
GRAY, George L
Children's crusade. 9298 J
GRAY, Maria G
Thoughts on self-culture addressed
to women. 5102 EE
GRAY, Maxwell (pseud M G Tuttiet)
A costly freak. 8320 F
An innocent impostor. 7928 F
Reproach of Annesley. 4020 F
Ribstone pippins; a country tale.
11072 F
Silence of Dean Maitland. 5959 F
Sweethearts and friends. 11018 F
GREELY, A W
Explorers and travelers. 8018 B
Three years of Arctic service, 2 vols.
3340 V
GREELEY, Horace
American conflict, 2 vols. 12190 H
Glances at Europe. 3398 V
Recollections of a busy life.
GREEN, Anna Katharine (pseud Mrs.
A K G Rohlfe)
Behind closed doors. 2290 F
Leavenworth case. 6438 F
Marked personal. 8172 F
GREEN, F W Eldridge
Memory and its cultivation. 11027 S
GREEN, Homer
Burnham Breaker. 7179 J
Coal and coal mines. 5436 J
GREEN, John Richard
Conquest of England. 11254 H
History of the English people, 5 vols.
4178 H
Making of England. 11255 H
Short history of the English people.
7990 H
GREEN, Mrs J R
Henry the Second. 6979 B
GREEN, William Spotswood
Among the Selkirk glaciers. 5983 V
GREENWAY, Kate
Book of games. 5431 J
GREENE, Sarah P McLean
Cape Cod folks. 2238 F
Stuart and bamboo. 10805 F
Vesty of the basins. 7539 F
GREENWOOD, Grace (pseud Lippin-
cott, Sara J)
Forest tragedy. 6184 F
Haps and mishaps of a tour in Eu-
rope. 6185 V
History of my pets. 7185 J

New life in new lands. 11848 V
Poems of. 6186 P
Queen Victoria. 1132 B
GREENWOOD, James
Adventures of Reuben Davidger.
5733 J
Hatchet throwers. 5188 J
GREEY, Edward
Wonderful city of Tokio. 3305 J
Young Americans in Japan. 11317 J
GREG, Percy
Across the Zodiac, 2 vols. 5263 F
GREGORY, Olinthus
Memoirs of the late John M Goode.
5111 B
GREVILLE, Charles C T
Greville memoirs; a journal of the
reign of George IV and William IV,
1818-1837. 1280 B
GREVILLE, Henry (pseud Alice Du-
rand)
Cleopatra. 2735 F
Zitka. 3121 F
GRIBBLE, Theodore Graham
Preliminary survey and estimates.
7564 S
GRIFFIN, H Hewitt
Athletics. 7542 A
Cycles and cycling. 7541 A
GRIFFIS, William Elliot
Brave little Holland and what she
has taught us. 8309 J
Japan in history, folklore and art.
8113 H
Japanese fairy world. 5976 J
Mikado's empire. 3446 H
Pilgrims in their three homes, En-
gland, Holland and America.11328H
GRIFFITH, Arthur
Chronicles of Newgate. 2884 H
Wellington; his comrades. 11987 B
GRIFFITH, Cecil
Victory Deane. 7161 F
GRIGGS, William
Fac-simile of text of Hamlet. 388 R
GRIMM, Herman
Goethe, Life and times of. 6706 B
Literature. 578 EE

Michael Angelo, 2 vols. 6357 B
GRIMM, James L and W K
Fairy tales. 2215 J
German popular tales, first series.
10117 J
German popular tales, second series.
10118 J
GRIMSHAW, Robert
Locomotive catechism. 11732 S
Steam engine catechism. 11732 S
GRINDON, Leo H
Phenomena of plant life. 1442 S
GRISWOLD, Hattie T
Home life of great authors. 10159 B
GROHMAN, W A Baille
Camps in the Rockies. 4710 V
GROOME, Francis H
In Gypsy tents. 2894 F
GROOS, Karl
Play of animals. 12561 S
GROSSE, Ernst
Beginnings of art. 10380 A
GROTE, George
Greece, History of, 4 vols. 4109 H
GROVE, George
Dictionary of music and musicians,
4 vols., with index. 8333 R
GRUISEN, A von
Holiday in Iceland. 3346 V
GUERBER, H A
Legends of the Virgin and Christ,
with special reference to literature
and art. 9989 F
Myths of northern lands. 11044 F
Romans, Story of. 11713 H
GUERNSEY, Alfred H
Health at home. 8938 S
Thomas Carlyle. 3238 B
GUERNSEY, Lucy Ellen
Lady Betty's governess. 9003 F
GUHL and Koner
Greeks and the Romans. Life of.
8276 H
GUILD, Curtis
Chat with celebrities. 10752 E
GUIMPS, Roger de
Pestalozzi; his life and work. 5967 B

GUINEY, Louise Imogen
Lover's Saint Ruth's and three other tales. 11988 F
GUIZOT, M
Civilization, History of, 2 vols. 42171I
England, History of, 4 vols. 7216 H
France, History of, 8 vols. 4101 H
Meditations on christianity. 372 RE
Private life of. 1281 B
GULSTON, A Stepney
Aphrodite and other poems. 8898 P
GUMMERE, Francis B
Germanic origins; study in primitive culture. 10163 H
GUNN, Thomas B
Physiology of New York boarding houses. 4738 L
GUNNING, William
Life history of our planet. 1472 S
GUNNISON, J W
Mormons of Salt Lake, History of. 4360 H
GUNSAULUS, Frank W
Monk and knight, 2 vols. 6456 F
GUNTER, Archibald C
Baron Montez. 8007 F
Florida enchantment. 12121 F
Miss Dividends. 8011 F
Miss Nobody of Nowhere. 10303 F
Mr Barnes of New York. 10125 F
Mr Potter of Texas. 7535 F
Small boys in big boots. 12467 F
That Frenchman. 7533 F
GUTHRIE, F A (see Anstey, T)
GUTTMAN, Paul
Handbook of physical diagnosis. 8711 S
GUY, William A
Factors of an unsound mind. 1502 S
GUYOT, Arnold
Earth and man. 1473 S

HABBERTON, John
Chautauquans. 7536 F
Helen's babies. 764 J
Lucky lover. 7690 F
Mrs. Mayburn's twins. 10626 F
Some folks. 8962 F
Trif and Trixy. 10730 F
HAECKEL, Ernst
Evolution of man, 2 vols. 1462 S
History of creation, 2 vols. 1477 S
HAGGARD, H Rider
Allan Quartermain. 10802 F
Cleopatra. 4745 F
Doctor Therne. 12642 F
Eric Bright-eyes. 7842 F
Heart of the world. 9625 F

Jess. 2816 F
Joan Haste. 9607 F
King Solomon's mines. 2818 F
Maiwa's revenge. 6303 F
Mr Meeson's will. 2820 F
Montezuma's daughter. 8174 F
Nada, the lily. 7273 F
People of the mist. 8792 F
She. 11995 F
Wizard. 10097 F
HAHNEMANN, Samuel
Organon of homeopathic medicine. 3254 S
HAINES, T L
Royal path of life. 8915 RE
HALE, Edward Everett
Bulfinch's age of fable. 5565 F
Christmas eve and Christmas day. 5573 F
Exercise, physical, mental and spiritual. 333 S
Fall of the Stuarts. 5494 H
Four and five. 7173 F
Franklin and France. 4362 H
George Washington, Life of. 1360 B
Gone to Texas. 4983 F
His level best and other stories. 4984 F
How to do it. 4985 F
In His name. 2190 F
Man without a country. 4986 F
Mrs Marriam's scholars. 4987 F
(Sequel to Ten times one is ten.)
My friend, the boss. 3409 F
New England boyhood. 7860 B
Ninety days of Europe. 6214 V
Our new crusade. 5574 F
Seven Spanish cities. 4992 V
Six of one by one half a dozen of the other. 4988 F
Spain, Story of. 4344 H
Stories of adventure. 8136 F
Stories of discovery. 8116 F
Stories of the sea. 8104 F
Stories of the war. 8103 F
Susan's escort and other stories. 10490 F
Sybaris and other homes. 4989 F
Sybil Knox. 7177 F
Ten times one is ten. 4990 F
Ups and downs. 5575 F
What career. 5576 EE
HALE, Gertrude Elizabeth
Little flower people. 7231 J
HALE, Lucretia P
Peterkin papers. 707 J
Peterkins, Last of the.

HALE, Susan
Mexico, Story of. 5372 H
HALES, John W
Notes and essays on Shakespeare.
6874 E
HALEVY, Ludovic
Abbe Constantine. 9903 F
(This charming tale of French love
is a perpetual answer to those who
hastily affirm that no pure fiction
comes out of Paris.)
HALIBURTON, John
Rule and misrule of the English in
America. 553 H
HALIBURTON, Thomas C (Sam Slick)
The attache, or Sam Slick in En-
gland. 888 F
HALL, A Wilford
Problem of human life. 7997 L
HALL, Bolton (ed)
Who pays your taxes. 7064 SS
HALL, Florence Howe
Social customs. 6057 EE
HALL, James
The west, its commerce and naviga-
tion. 11860 V
Wilderness and warpath. 6205 V
HALL, John
Familiar talks to boys. 2166 EE
HALL, Ruth
In the brave days of old. 12312 J
HALL, William
Irrigation development. 1822 A
HALLAM, Henry
Constitutional history of England, 2
vols. 4161 H
Introduction to literature of Europe.
4157 EE
Middle ages. History of, 2 vols. 4159H
View of the state of Europe during
the middle ages. 12545 H
HALLIWELL, J O
Voyage and travels of Sir John
Mainderville. 3303 V
HALLOCK, C
Sportsman's gazetteer. 1816 A
HALSTEAD, Murat
Cuba, Story of. 10917 H

HAMBLEN, Herbert E
Story of a Yankee boy. 12305 J
HAMERLING, Robert
Aspasia, 2 vols. 7352 F
HAMERTON, E
Golden mediocrity. 2886 F
HAMERTON, P G
Intellectual life. 229 E
Present state of the fine arts in
France. 6876 A
Thoughts about art. 11402 E
HAMILTON, Gail (pseud Mary A
Dodge)
A new atmosphere. 6196 E
Country living and country thinking.
6194 E
Summer rest. 6195 E
Woman's wrongs. 418 E
Wool gathering. 2880 E
HAMILTON, Kate M
The parson's proxy. 9516 F
HAMILTON, M
McLeod of the Camerons. 10373 F
HAMLIN, Augustus C
Leisure hours among the gems.
11223 S
HAMLIN, Cyrus
My life and times. 9358 B
HAMMOND, H L
New stories from an old book. 11313J
HAMMOND, Mrs J H
A woman's part in a revolution.
10863 F
HAMMOND, W A
Doctor Grattan. 1150 F
Lal. 2157 F
Mr Oldmixon. 2574 F
Sleep and its derangements.7697 S
HAMOUN, Leila
Tragedy at Constantinople. 1172 F
HANAFORD, Phoebe A
Daughters of America, or women of
the century. 8989 B
George Peabody, Life of. 8959 B
HANNA, Sarah R
Bible history. 361 RE
HANNAY, George B
Don Emilio Castelar. 9754 B

Rodney, George B. 6783 B
HANSON, Charles Henry
Stories of the days of King Arthur.
  8108 F
HANSON, John Wesley (compiler)
Children's speaker. 11333 P
HANSON, J W
  A pocket cyclopaedia; brief explana-
  tions of religious terms as under-
  stood by Universalists. 8765 RE
  Bible threatenings explained.8505 RE
  Manna; a book of daily worship.
  8761 RE
  New covenant, 2 vols. 8516 RE
  W H Ryder, Biography of. 8762 RE
HAPGOOD, Isabel F (trans)
  Recollections and letters of Ernest
  Renan. 7104 E
HARDY, A S
  But yet a woman. 2904 F
  Passe Rose. 5720 F
  Wind of destiny. 2895 F
HARDY, Mrs A S
  Hall of shells. 10971 J
HARDY, Lady Duffus
  Through cities and prairie lands.
  11547 V
  Love affairs of some famous men.
  10850 E
HARDY, E J
  How to be happy tho married. 6393E
  Manners maketh a man. 346 E
HARDY, Thomas
  Far from the madding crowd. 10001F
  Group of noble dames. 6473 F
  Jude, the obscure. 9415 F
  Life's little ironies. 8319 F
  Pair of blue eyes. 10427 F
  Return of the native. 7963 F
  Tess of the D'Urbervilles. 7882 F
  Trumpet major. 7964 F
  Two on a tower. 2981 F
  Under the greenwood tree. 10034 F
  Well-beloved, The. 10359 F
  Woodlanders, The. 2823 F
HARE, Augustus J C
  Cities of northern and central Italy.
  3 vols. 12459 V
  Days near Paris. 8844 V
  Florence. 4195 V
  Sketches in Holland and Scandinavia
  1617 V
  Studies in Russia. 4194 V
  Venice. 4197 V
  Walks in London. 4198 V
  Walks in Paris. 8796 V
  Walks in Rome. 8843 V
  Wanderings in Spain. 4196 V

HARKNESS, Albert
  Practical introduction to latin com-
  position. 8361 EE
HARLAND, H C (see Luska, Sidney)
HARLAND, Marion (pseud Mrs Mary
V. Terhune)
  Alone. 10933 F
  An old field school girl. 10756 F
  Empty heart. 10941 F
  Eve's daughters. 1155 A
  From my youth up. 9614 F
  Gallant fight. 7148 F
  Helen Gardner's wedding day. 9613 F
  Hidden path. 10930 F
  Husbands and homes. 9729 F
  Jessamine. 10938 F
  Judith; chronicle of old Virginia.
  5428 F
  Miriam. 10935 F
  Mr Wayt's wife's sister. 8167 F
  Moss-side. 10936 F
  My little love. 10940 F
  Nemesis. 10934 F
  Phemie's temptation. 9615 F
  Ruby's husband. 10937 F
  Sunny bank. 10932 F
  True as steel. 10939 F
HARRADEN, Beatrice
  In varying moods. 8645 F
  Ships that pass in the night. 8303 F
HARRIS, Amanda B
  Pleasant authors for young folks.
  2033 J
HARRIS, George
  Moral evolution. 9525 EE
HARRIS, Joel Chandler
  Balaam and his master. 6284 F
  Daddy Jake, the runaway. 7039 J
  Nights with Uncle Remus. 1129 J
  On the plantation. 11482 F
  Sister Jane. 10043 F
  Uncle Remus and his friends. 9725 F
HARRIS, John (compiler)
  Complete collection of voyages to all
  parts of the world, 2 vols., 1748.
  367 V
HARRIS, Mrs M C
  An utter failure. 7164 F
  Frank Warrington. 5819 F
  Missy. 5577 F
  Perfect Adonis. 5818 F
  Phoebe. 889 F
  Richard Vandermarck. 5705 F
  Rutledge. 5578 F
  St Philips. 5703 F
  Sutherlands. 5704 F
HARRIS, William
  Hegel's logic. 6553 EE

HARRISON, Benjamine
This country of ours. 10696 H
HARRISON, Mrs Burton
Anglomaniacs. 5963 F
Bachelor maid. 8801 F
Bric-a-brac stories. 2717 F
Daughter of the south, etc. 7154 F
Edelwiess of the Sierras. 7418 F
Errant wooing. 9344 F
Good Americans. 12587 F
Son of the Old Dominion. 11996 F
Sweet bells out of tune. 8023 F
HARRISON, E S
Santa Cruz county, History of. 738911
HARRISON, Frederic
Meaning of history, and other historical pieces. 8813 H
Studies in early Victorian literature. 11404 EE
William the Silent. 12204 B
HARRISON, James A
Greece, History of. 4345 H
HARRISON, John Thornhill
Creation and physical structure of the earth. 6419 S
HARRISON, Joseph La Ray (compiler)
Cap and gown; some college verse. 12618 P
HARRISON, W Jerome
Chemistry of photography. 9863 S
HARRISON, William H
The humorist. 5059 L
"HARRY GRINGO"
Tales for the mariners. 4700 F
HART, Albert Bushnell
Epochs of American history—formation of the union. 9855 H
Practical essays on American government. 12013 H
HART, James Morgan
German universities. 11224 EE
HARTE, Bret
Argonauts of North Liberty. 5579 F
Barker's buck and other stories. 10523 F
Bell-ringer of Angels, and other stories. 8814 F
By shore and sedge. 718 F
Clarence. 9425 F
Colonel Starbottle's client and some other people. 7062 F
Cressy. 5580 F
Crusade of the Excelsior. 2347 F
Frontier stories. 2337 F
Heritage of Dedlow marsh, and other stories. 5581 F
In the hollow of the hills. 9426 F
Luck of the Roaring camp, and other stories. 6639 F
Maruja. 717 F
Millionaire of Rough and Ready. 720 F
Mrs Skagg's husbands, and other sketches. 712 F
On the frontier. 716 F
Poetical works of. 80 P
Protegee of Jack Hamlin's, and other stories. 8182 F
Sally Dows and other stories. 7820 F
Tales of the Argonauts and other sketches. 4702 F
Tales of trail and town. 11347 F

Thankful Blossom; a romance of the Jerseys. 719 F
Wail of the plains. 6466 F
Ward of the Golden Gate. 5825 F
HARTE, Walter B
Meditations in motley. 10098 E
HARTLEY, May
Christie Carew. 894 F
HARTMAN, Franz
Magic, white and black. 11440 F
HARTMAN, Robert
Anthropoid apes. 1383 S
HARTWIG, Dr G
Aerial world. 1449 S
Dwellers in Arctic regions. 8130 V
Heroes of the Arctic regions. 8107 B
Polar and tropical worlds, 2 vols. 3330 V
HARTZLER, H B
Moody in Chicago. 11778 RE
HARVEY, Thomas W
Elementary grammar of English language. 8372 EE
HARVEY, W H
Coin's financial school. 9733 SS
HARWOOD, J B
One false, both fair. 2975 F
HASSALL, Arthur
Viscount Bolingbroke, Life of.12176B
HASSAUREK, F A
Four years among Spanish America. 3395 V
HASTINGS, H L
Guiding hand, The. 11575 RE
HAVARD, Henry
Dutch school of painting. 9112 A
HAVEN, E O
Rhetoric. 9067 EE
HAVERGAL, Frances Ridley
Poetical works of. 10508 P
Swiss letters and Alpine poems. 11535 P
HAVERGAL, M V G
Autobiography of. 1283 B
HAWEIS, H R
Christ and christianity. 329 RE
HAWKINS, Sir John
Voyages of, to America. 3350 V
HAWTHORNE, Julian
An American penman. 3190 F
Beatrix Randolph. 11726 F
Confessions and criticisms. 11398 F
Fool of nature. 9709 F
John Parmelee's curse. 11700 F
Love is a spirit. 9866 F
Six-cent Sams. 8083 F
HAWTHORNE, Nathaniel
Blithedale romance. 2896 F

Dr Grimshawe's secret. 2096 F
English note-books. 3364 V
Ethan Brand, and other stories. 4784 F
Grandfather's chair. 4965 F
House of the seven gables. 12431 F
Marble faun, 2 vols. 6882 F
Mosses from an old manse. 6882 F
Our old home. 961 F
Passages from American note-books. 1627 V
Passages from French and Italian note-books. 3338 V
Scarlet letter. 12433 F
Tanglewood tales. 4965 F
True stories from history. 4966 F
Twice-told tales. 734 F
Wonderbook. 10566 F
HAY, John
Bread-winners; a social study, Cleveland, Ohio. 7481 F
HAY, John
Castilian days. 1087 V
Poems of. 5777 P
HAY, John, and John G Nicolay
Abraham Lincoln, 10 vols. 6010 H
HAY, Mary Cecil
Old Middleton's money. 7018 F
Victor and vanquished. 6942 F
HAY, Mrs W Y
Adventures of Prince Lazy-bones. 879 J
HAYDN
Universal index of biography relating to all ages and nations. 1672 R
HAYES, Henry (see Kirk, Ellen Olney)
HAYES, I I
Land of desolation. 3327 V
Open polar sea. 3322 V
HAYS, John
Poems of. 5777 P
HAYWARD, Jane Mary
Bird notes. 11438 S
HAZARD, Rowland G
Essays on language. 6377 EE
Freedom of the mind in willing. 3453 EE
HAZLITT, William
Mary and Charles Lamb. 157 B
Miscellaneous works of, 5 vols.12447E
Napoleon. Life of, 3 vols. 1321 B
HEADLAM, Walter
Fifty poems of Meleager. 6068 P
HEADLEY, J T
Achievements of Stanley. 3354 V
Career of P H Sheridan. 1339 B

Farragut and our naval commanders.
4390 B
Napoleon and his marshalls, 2 vols.
6903 B
Oliver Cromwell, Life of. 6222 B
HEADLEY, P C
Campaigns and life of U S Grant.
5372 H
Empress Josephine, Life of. 10630 B
HEARN, Lafcadio
Chita; a memory of Last Island.
7072 F
Exotics and retrospectives. 12553 E
Gleanings from Buddha fields.11492V
Glimpses of unfamiliar Japan, 2 vols.
8794 V
Kokoro. 9592 V
Out of the east. 10133 V
Stray leaves from stray literature.
11220 EE
Two years in the French West Indes.
7086 V
HEARN, William Edward
Aryan household. 9760 H
HEAVEN, Louise P
Chata and Chinita. 5546 F
HEBER, Reginald
Jeremy Taylor, Life of the Right
Reverend, 2 vols. 5109 B
HECTOR, Mrs F A (see Alexander,
Mrs)
HEDGE, Frederic Henry
Hours with German classics.12472 EE
HEILPRIN, Angelo
Animal life of our seashore. 7699 S
Arctic problem. 8533 V
Distribution of animals. 5723 S
HEIMBURG, U
Her only brother. 7150 F
Penniless girl
Two daughters of one race. 9025 F
HEINE, Heinrich
Poems and ballads. 97 P
Travel pictures. 9183 E
HELMHOLTZ, Herman
Sensations of tone. 7731 A
HELPER, Hinton R
Impending crisis. 429 H

HELPS, Arthur
Friends in council, 2 vols. 749 E
Leaves from journal of our life in
Highlands. 8508 V
HEMANS, Mrs
Poetical works of, 2 vols. 50 P
HENDERSON, Howard
Practical hints on camping. 6395 A
HENDERSON, Marc
Song of Milkanwatha. 7314 P
HENDERSON, Peter
Gardening for profit. 6387 A
Handbook of plants. 7078 R
HENDERSON, W J
Afloat with the flag. 9382 J
Sea yarns for boys. 9340 J
HENDERSON, W J
How music developed. 12591 A
Preludes and studies. 7290 A
What is good music. 11016 A
HENNEQUIN, Alfred
Art of play writing. 12471 EE
HENNIKER, Florence
In scarlet and grey. 9991 F
HENRY, George
'89. 9008 F
HENSLOW, George
Origin of floral structures. 11363 S
HENTY, G A
Beric, the Britain. 7807 F
Boy knight. 11324 F
By England's aid. 6908 F
By pike and dyke. 6909 F
By right of conquest. 7808 F
By sheer pluck. 11323 F
Captain Bayley's heir. 10421 F
Condemned as a nihilist. 7393 F
Cornet of horse. 11318 F
Dash for Khartoum.
Final reckoning. 10414 F
For name and fame. 7809 F
Held fast for England. 7391 F
In freedom's cause. 7394 F
In Greek waters. 7810 F
In the reign of terror. 6912 F
In times of peril. 11321 F
Jack Archer. 2219 F
Jacobite exile. 8002 F

Lion of St Mark. 6911 F
Maori and settler. 10420 F
March on London. 10769 F
On the Irrawaddy. 10128 F
Orange and green. 11322 F
Redskin and cowboy. F
Reign of terror. 6912 F
St. Bartholomew's eve. 8006 F
Tale of Waterloo. 6910 F
Through the Sikh war. 8028 F
With Clive in India. 7395 F
With Cochrane, the Dauntless.10127F
With Frederick the Great. 10728 F
With Moore at Corunna. 10682 F
Young buglers. 11319 F
Young Carthaginian. 7895 F
Young colonists. 11320 F
Young franc-tireurs. 2181 F
HEPWORTH, George H
Hiram Golf's religion. 8158 F
HERBERT, William Henry
Memoirs of Henry the Eighth.11640B
Supplement to fish and fishing.5784A
HERFORD, C H
Age of Wordsworth. 12652 EE
HERING, C
Guiding symptoms, 7 vols. 9083 S
HERNDON, W H
Abraham Lincoln, Life of, 3 vols.
5348 B
HERODOTUS
Ancient world, History of the, 4
vols. 4211 H
(Edited by Rawlinson.)
HERRICK, Mrs S B
Chapters on plant life. 1439 S
Wonders of plant life. 1436 S
HERRON, George D
Christian state, The. 9317 RE
HERSCHEL, Sir J F W
Outline of astronomy. 1446 S
HERVEY, Mrs
Adventures of a lady in Tartary,
Thibet, 3 vols. 7934 V
HERVEY, A B
Sea mosses. 10979 S
HEYSE, Paul
Romance of the Canoness. 3135 F
H H (see Helen Hunt Jackson.)
HIATT, James M
Ribbon workers. 8392 SS
HIBBARD, S
Town garden, The. 3248 A
HICHENS, Robert S
An imaginative man. 10151 F
HICKIE, William James (trans)
Comedies of Aristophanes, 2 vols.
9775 P

HIGGINSON, Ella
From the land of the snow pearls.
11476 F
HIGGINSON, S J
Java, the pearl of the east. 8111 H
HIGGINSON, T W
Army life in a black regiment. 5965H
Book and heart; essays on literature
and life. 10318 E
Cheerful yesterdays. 11293 E
Common sense about women. 2874 E
Enchanted islands of the Atlantic,
Tales of the. 12643 F
Larger history of the United States.
4064 H
Malbone, an old port romance.6478F
Margaret Fuller Ossoli, Lite of.192 B
Monarch of dreams. 1220 F
Record of a human soul. 3224 F
Travellers and outlaws. 7270 F
HILDRETH, Richard
United States, History of. 4064 H
HILL, Alice Polk
Colorado pioneers, Tales of. 875 F
HILL, A S
Foundations of rhetoric. 7453 EE
Our english. 5419 EE
Principles of rhetoric. 8358 EE
HILL, Benjamin H
Addresses on life and services of.
1286 E
HILL, Chas T
Fighting a fire. 10793 L
HILL, David J
Principles and fallacies of socialism.
198 SS
HILL, George Birkbeck
Lord Chesterfield's worldly wisdom.
6864 E
HILL, George J
Story of the war in La Vendee.
10429 F
HILL, Nathaniel P
Speeches and papers on the silver
and postal telegraph. 7873 SS
HILL, Randolph
Tom, the ready; or up from the
lowest. 11325 J
HILL, Robert T
Cuba and Porto Rico. 12644 H
HILLIARD, G S
G B McLellan, Life and campaigns
of. 160 B
HINDE, Mary L
We two alone in Europe. 10162 V
HINDE, Sidney
Fall of the Congo arabs. 11285 V

HINDMARSH, Robert
Precious stones mentioned in sacred scripture. 10966 RE
HINES, Gustavus
Wild life in Oregon. 854 V
HINTON, James
Man and his dwelling place. 8942 RE
Physiology for practical use. 11546S
HITCHCOCK, Edward
Mary Lyon, Life and labors of. 143B
HITCHCOCK, Thomas
Unhappy loves of men of genius. 7438 F
HITTELL, Theo H
California. History of. 4 vols. 4165 H
HITTELL, John S
California, Resources of. 234 H
Culture, History of. 431 E
HOBBS, John Oliver (pseud Miss Craigie)
A bundle of life, etc. 8482 F
School for saints. 11073 F
The gods, some mortals and Lord Wickenham. 9518 F
The Herb-moon; a fantasia. 11623 F
HOCKING, Joseph
Mistress Nancy Molesworth. 12575 F
HODDER, Edwin
All the world over. 2 vols. 5092 V
Shaftesbury, Life and works of. 3 vols. 1332 B
HODGE, Archibald
Commentaries on the confession of faith. 11627 RE
HODGKIN, Thomas
Theodoric, the Goth, the barbarian champion of civilization. 11195 B
HODGKINS, Louise Manning
Guide to study of XIX century authors. 8655 EE
HODGSON, Fred T
Practical carpentry. 8254 A
Stair-building made easy. 8280 A
Steel square and its uses. 8281 A
HOEY, Mrs C
Blossoming of an aloe. 2496 F
The clients of Dr Bemagin. 5118 F

Thorvaldsen, Plons' life and works of. 1758 A
Startling exploits of Dr J B Quies. 2287 F
HOFBERG, Herman
Swedish fairy tales. 11308 J
Swedish folklore. 10983 F
HOFFMANN, E T W
Conjuring and magic. Secrets of. 11802 S
Magic at home. 8114 A
Modern magic. 488 A
Weird tales. 2558 F
HOFFMAN, Walter James
Beginnings of writing. 9372 S
HOFLAND, Mrs
Blind farmer and the children. 4777 J
HOGG, Jabez
The microscope. 7969 S
HOGG, James
Poems of. 6634 P
Tales of love and adventure. 8967 F
HOLBEACH, Henry
Shoemakers' village. 5095 J
HOLBROOK, Kennedy
'How? or, spare hours made profitable. 6919 J
HOLCOMBE, William H
Letters on spiritual subjects. 5785 RE
HOLDEN, Edward S
Our country's flag and flags of foreign countries. 12592 H
Primer of heraldry for Americans. 12593 R
Publications of Lick observatory. 7974 S
HOLDEN, Florence P
Audiences; a few suggestions to those who look and listen. 10317 E
HOLDER, Charles F
Along the Florida reef. 7402 V
Living lights. 1533 S
Marvels of animal life. 1532 S
The ivory king. 1534 S
HOLDEN, George H
Canaries and cage birds. 12205 S
HOLE, S Reynolds
Book about roses. 483 A

CENTRAL LODGING HOUSE.

HOLLAND, Frederic May
Douglas, Frederick, colored orator.
6537 B
HOLLAND, J G
Arthur Bonnicastle. 1067 F
Bay-path. 1068 F
Bitter-sweet. 5582 P
Every-day topics, series 1. 5584 E
Every-day topics, series 2. 5585 E
Gold foil. 5586 E
Jones family. 5588 E
Kathrina. 5583 P
Lessons in life. 5587 E
Miss Gilbert's career. 1070 F
Mistress of the manse. 5592 P
Nicholas Minturn. 1069 F
Plain talks. 5589 E
Puritans' guest,etc. 5591 P
Seven oaks. 3412 F
Titcomb's letters to young people.
5590 E
HOLLEY, Marietta (Josiah Allen's
wife)
Josiah Allen as a P A and P I.
9628 F
Miss Richard's boy and other sto-
ries. 2192 F
My opinion and Betsy Bobbett's.
2864 F
My wayward partner. 2863 F
Samantha among the brethren.
6736 F
Samantha in Europe. 10557 F
Samantha on the race problem.
8544 F
Samantha at the world's fair. 8798 F
Sweet Cicely. 511 F
HOLLOWAY, Laura
Ladies of the White House. 9125 H
HOLM, Adolph
Greece. History of. 4 vols. 10320 H
HOLMES, Alice
Very little dialogues. 10688 P
HOLMES, Edward
Mozart. Life of. 138 B
HOLMES, Mary J
Doctor Hathern's daughters.10948 F
Dora Deane. 10952 F
Forrest House. 10954 F
Gretchen. 10951 F
Madeline. 10955 F
Marguerite. 10953 F
Mildred. 10949 F
Queenie Hetherton. 10950 F
HOLMES, Oliver Wendell ·
Autocrat of the breakfast table.364E
Elsie Venner. 8321 F
Emerson, R W. Life of. 1240 B

Guardian angel. 8322 F
Our hundred days in Europe. 3385 V
Over the teacups. 6756 E
Poet at the breakfast table. 366 E
Poetical works. 6330 P
Professor at the breakfast table.
365 E
HOLTON, Isaac
New Grenada; twenty months in the
Andes. 4694 V
HOLUB, Emil
Seven years in South Africa, 2 vols.
4876 V
HOLME, David D
Incidents in my life. 5251 B
HONDIN, Robert
Tricks of the Greeks unveiled.1046 S
HOOD, Thomas
Poetical works of. 7784 P
Prose works of, 11 vols. 6640 L
Up the Rhine. 58 V
HOOK, Theodore
John Brag, 2 vols. 6178 F
HOOKER, Isabella B
Womanhood. 420 E
HOOPER, George
Wellington, Life of. 6539 B
HOOPER, Lucy Hamilton
Under the tri-color; American col-
ony in Paris. 11658 A
HOOPES, Josiah
Book of evergreens. 8875 A
HOPE, Anthony (pseud of Anthony
Hope Hawkins)
Change of air. 9149 F
Chronicles of Count Antonio. 9326 F
Comedies of courtship. 9515 F
Dolly dialogues. 9163 F
Father Stafford. 9707 F
Frivolous cupid. 9416 F
Indiscretion of the duchess. 9325 F
Man of mark. 9150 F
Mr Witt's widow. 9793 F
Phroso. 10186 F
Prisoner of Zenda. 10195 F
Rupert of Hentzau. 11997 F
Simon Dale. 11034 F
Sport Royal. 9319 F
HOPKINS, Albert A (ed)
Scientific American cyclopedia of
receipts. 8229 R
HOPKINS, Caspar T
Manual of American ideas. 11714 SS
HOPKINS, George M
Experimental science. 7562 S
HOPKINS, Livingston
Comic history of the United States.
1048 H

HOPKINS, Mark, Jr
World's verdict, The. 7181 F
HOPKINS, Nevil Monroe
Model engines and small boats.
11981 S
HOPPIN, James M
Early renaissance. 7268 H
Greek art on Greek soil.. 11277 H
Old England; its scenery, art and
people. 9306 V
HOPPUS, Mary
Great treason. 890 F
MOREY, William A
Mind reading and beyond. 1219 L
HORNADAY, William T
Two years in the jungle. 3440 V
HORNER, Susan and Florence
Walks in Florence, 2 vols. 7949 V
HORNUNG, E W
Rogue's march, The. 9987 F
HORTON, Mrs D H
Wife's messengers. 136 F
HOSMER, James K
As we went marching on. 2719 H
Samuel Adams, Life of. 1245 B
Jews, Story of the. 4350 H
HOTCHKISS, Chauncey
Colonial free-lance. 10639 F
HOUGHTON, Walter R
Kings of fortune. 8923 B
HOUSE, Edward H
Midnight warning and other stories.
7585 F
HOUSMAN, A E
A Shropshire lad. 10581 F
HOUSTON, Edwin J
Dictionary of electrical words, terms
and phrases. 11235 L
HOVELACQUE, Abel
Science of language. 1492 EE
HOWARD, Blanche W
Aulnay tower. 2578 F
Aunt Serena. 1195 F
Battle and a boy. 7844 J
Guenn. 2140 F
One summer. 9624 F
Open door. 5465 F
Tony, the maid. 3143 F

HOWARD, Blanche W and William
Sharp
Fellowe and his wife. 7159 F
HOWARD, Oliver Otis
General Taylor. 7644 B
HOWE, E W
Man story, A. 7180 F
Story of a country town. 7180 F
HOWE, Henry
Over the world. 10990 V
HOWE, Maud
San Rosario ranch. 1184 F
HOWELLS, George
Conflicts of labor and capital. 6070
SS
HOWELLS William Dean
An open-eyed conspiracy. 10803 F
April hopes. 3174 F
Boys' town, A. 6258 J
Chance acquaintance. 1056 F
Christmas every day, and other sto-
ries. 7578 J
Fearful responsibility, etc. 4021 F
Foregone conclusion. 1052 F
Hazard of new fortunes, 2 vols.5595F
Imperative duty. 6744 F
Indian summer. 1159 F
Italian journeys. 1053 V
Lady of the Aroostook. 4971 F
Landlord at Lion's Head. 10100 F
Minister's charge. 5636 F
Modern instance. 1059 F
Mouse-trap and other farces. 9164 F
Shadow of a dream. 5824 F
Rise of Silas Lapham. 2573 F
Sleeping car and other farces. 9172P
Story of a play. 12207 F
Suburban sketches. 1054 V
Their wedding journey. 1055 F
Traveller from Altruria. 8770 F
Undiscovered country. 1051 F
Venetian life. 1057 V
Woman's reason. 11485 V
World of chance. 7823 F
HOWERTON, G T
Short talks on character building.
7803 EE

HOYLE
American Hoyle; or Gentleman's handbook of games. 9823 A
HOYT, H M
Protection versus free trade. 204 SS
HOYT and Ward
Cyclopaedia of practical quotations. 6726 R
HOYT, John W
Studies in civil service. 197 SS
HUC, E R
Travels in Tartary, Thibet and China. 1639 V
HUBERT, Philip G
Inventors (Men of achievement se ries). 8016 B
HUDSON, Thomas J
Laws of psychic phenomena. 8149 S
HUDSON, W H
Birds in a village. 11674 S
Idle hours in a library. 10806 EE
Naturalist in La Plata. 7650 V
Studies in interpretation. 11396 E
HUG, Lina and R Stead
Switzerland, Story of. 9116 H
HUGHES, Thomas
David Livingston, Life of. 6841 H
Gone to Texas. 6543 V
Rugby Tennessee. 6871 H
Tom Brown at Oxford. 9652 J
Tom Brown's school days. 9730 J
HUGHES, Mrs T
Among the sons of Ham. 5112 V
HUGO, Madam
Victor Hugo, Life of.
HUGO, Victor
Dramatic works, 2 vols. 8599 P
Hans of Iceland. 8598 F
History of a crime. 8601 F
Hunchback of Notre Dame. 8603 F
Les Miserables. 3 vols. 8596 F
Man who laughs. 8604 F
Ninety-three. 8602 V
Things seen. 343 V
Toilers of the sea. 8605 F
Up the Rhine. 4382 V
William Shakespeare, Life of. 1335 B
HULL, Moses
The question settled; careful comparison of Biblical and modern spiritualism. 9474 RE
HULLAH. Mary E
In hot haste. 7473 F
HULME, F Edward
History, principles and practise of heraldry. 6859 A
History, principles and practise of symbolism in christian art. 6857 A

HUMBOLDT, Alex von
Cosmos, 5 vols. 237 S
HUME, David
England, History of, 6 vols. 4067 H
HUME, Fergus
Aladdin in London. 7419 F
Carbuncle clue. 10353 F
When I lived in Bohemia. 7742 F
HUME, Martin A S
Year after the Armada. 11382 H
HUMPHREYS, Mary Gay
Catherine Schuyler, Life of. 10776 B
HUNGERFORD, Mrs (see "Duchess")
HUNT, Ezra M
Principles of hygiene. 7305 S
HUNT, Leigh
Imaginary conversations of Pope and Swift. 3233 E
Table-talk. 3233 E
HUNTER, Fanny
Western border life. 4733 V
HUNTER, P Hay
James Inwick, ploughman and elder. 10459 F
HUNTER, Robert
Encyclopaedia dictionary, 14 vols. 6573 R
HUNTER, Robert
Popular treatise on bronchitis. 500S
Popular treatise on colds. 659 S
HUNTINGTON, F D
Sermons for the people. 9473 RE
HURLL, Estelle
Child-life in art. 11432 A
HURST, Julius H
Stephen Lescombe, bachelor of arts. 10395 F
HUSMANN, George
Grape culture and wine making in California. 6915 A
HUTCHINGS, J M
California magazine, 1857, 2 vols. 6223 V
Scenes and wonders of curiosity in California. 6209 H
HUTCHINSON, Horace G
Record of a human soul. 3224 F
HUTCHINSON, H N
Autobiography of the earth. 12532 S
Story of the hills. 6862 S
HUTCHINSON, Joseph C
Physiology and hygiene. 8371 S
HUTTON, Barbara
Tales of the white cockade. 2177 F
HUTTON, Laurence
Boy I knew and four dogs. 11380 J

Literary landmarks of Florence. 10327 V
— — of Jerusalem. 9159 V
— — of London. 1309 V
— — of Rome. 10325 V
HUTTON, Richard Holt
Criticisms on contemporary thought and thinkers, 2 vols. 9494 E
Essays in literary criticism. 9196 E
Sir Walter Scott, Life of 6681 B
HUTTON, W H
King and baronage, 1135-1327. 9799H
HUXLEY, Thomas H
Biological and geological essays. 8688 S
Darwiniana. 8485 S
Evidence as to man's place in nature. 8483 S
Hume, Life of. 6691 S
Method and result. 8484 S
Physiography. 10160 S
Science and culture. 8487 S
Science and education. 8486 S
Science and Hebrew tradition essays. 8278 S

———

IBSEN, Henrik I
Prose dramas, 3 vols. 5836 P
IHNE, W
Early Rome, from foundation of the city to its destruction by the Gauls. 10585 H
INGE, William
Society in Rome under the Caesars. 9569 H
INGELOW, Jean
Don John. 5710 F
Fated to be free. 944 F
Mopsa, the fairy. 6274 J
Off the Skelligs. 4975 F
Poems of. 9655 P
Sarah De Berenger. 4976 F
INGERSOLL, Ernest
Ice Queen, The. 2189 J
INGERSOLL, Robert
Ghosts, etc. 5232 F
Some mistakes of Moses. 5253 F

INGLIS, Robert
Gleanings from the English poets. 11557 EE
INGRAM, John H
Claimants to royalty. 260 B
Edgar Allen Poe, Life of, 2 vols. 1327 B
Sunny south. 6204 F
IRELAND, Alexander
William Hazlitt, Life of. 7250 B
IRELAND, Joseph N
Mrs Duff (American actor series.) 11609 B
IRES, John
Electricity as a medicine. 1535 S
IRON, Ralph (see Schreiner, Olive)
IRONQUILL
Some rhymes of. 7858 P
IRVING, Fannie Belle
Six girls; a home story. 11932 J
IRVING, Pierre
Washington Irving. Life and letters of, 4 vols. 120 B
IRVING, Washington
Alhambra, The. 10821 H
Astoria. 9062 L
Bonneville. Captain. 2089 F
Bracebridge hall. 2091 F
Columbus, Life and voyages of. 105B
Conquest of Granada. 2087 F
Crayon miscellany. 9010 F
Goldsmith, Oliver. 2091 B
History of New York. 2094 H
Mahomet and his successors. 2093 B
Sketch book. 2280 F
Tales of a traveller. 2095 F
Washington, George, Life of, 3 vols. 5341 B
IRWIN, Eyles
Voyage up the Red sea in Arabia and Egypt and through the desert of Thibais, 1772. 4882 V

———

JACKSON, Frank C
Decorative design. 12197 A
JACKSON, George
First things first. 9843 RE

———

JACKSON, George Anson
  Son of a prophet. 7305 F
JACKSON, Helen Hunt (H H)
  Between whiles. 1029 F
  Bits of talk about home matters.
    5456 A
  Century of dishonor. 203 H
  Glimpses of three coasts. 8845 V
  Ramona. 8633 F
  Letters from a cat. 5455 J
  Mercy Philbrick's choice. 783 F
  Verses. 11164 P
  Zeph. 781 F
  Pansy Billings and Popsy. 11927 J
  Hetty's strange history. 782 F
JACKSON, Margaret
  A woman of today. 6939 F
JACKSON, Mary Anna
  General Thomas J Jackson, Life and
    letters of. 6753 B
JACOBUS, M W
  Notes on the gospels; John. 5148RE
JAEGER, Gustav
  Problems of nature. 12002 S
J A K
  Birchwood. 4977 J
  Fitch club. 4978 J
  Giant wharf. 7199 J
  Professor Johnny. 4979 J
  Riverside museum. 4980 J
  Rolf and his friends. 7331 J
  Who saved the ship. 4982 J
JAMES, G P R
  Arrah Neil. 2348 F
  Castle of Ehrenstein. 2356 F
  Commissioner. 2354 F
  Convict. 2486 F
  Fate, The. 2358 F
  Forest days. 2349 F
  Gowrie. 2487 F
  Memoirs of celebrated women, 2 vols.
    5246 B
  Old oak chest. 2353 F
  Pequinillo. 2352 F
  Russell. 2351 F
  Sir Theodore Broughton. 2350 F
  'Tis thirty years since. 2355 F
  Ticonderago. 2357 F
JAMES, Henry
  American, The. 1097 F
  Aspern papers. 6469 F
  Bostonians, The. 2156 F
  Confidence. 1061 F
  Daisy Miller. 1064 F
  Europeans, The. 1098 F
  Hawthorne, N. 6692 B
  In the cage. 12590 F
  Passionate pilgrim, etc. 1062 F
  Portraits of places. 1065 F
  Princess Casamassima. 2561 F
  Real thing. 7730 F
  Riverberator. 6449 F
  Roderick Hudson. 1096 F
  Tragic muse, 2 vols. 11572 F
  Transatlantic sketches. 1619 V
  Watch and ward. 1066 F
  What Maisie knew. 10723 F
JAMES, William
  The will to believe and other essays
    in popular philosophy. 10403 EE
JAMESON, Anna
  Memoirs of celebrated female sov-
    ereigns. 6709 B
  Sacred and legendary art, 2 vols.
    8232 A
JAMESON, Mrs C V
  Lady Jane. 11471 J
  Seraph, the little violinist. 12297 J
  Story of an enthusiast. 3177 F
  Toinette's Philip. 8775 J
JAMESON, James S
  Rear column. 7295 H
JANIN, Jules
  Asmodeus. 2147 F
JANVIER, Thomas A
  An embassy to Provence. 11800 F
  In the Sargasso sea. 12211 F
  Stories of old and new Spain. 6329F
JARRIN, G A
  Italian confectioner. 5929 A
JARVES, James Jackson
  Glimpse at the art of Japan. 12221 A
JAY, M W L
  Shiloh; or, Without and within.
    11730 F
JAEFFRESON, John Cordy
  Book about lawyers. 11856 L
JEBB, R C
  Bentley. Life of. 6675 B
JEFFERSON, Joseph
  Autobiography. 12236 B
JENKINS, John F
  Explorations and adventures. 2124 V
JENKINSON, Thomas B
  Amazula; or the Zulus. 4266 H
JENKS, Edward
  Australasian colonies, History of.
    12496 H
JENNESS, Mrs Theodora
  Two young homesteaders. 7272 J
JENNINGS, David
  Jewish antiquities. 5022 H
JENNINGS, Robert
  Cattle and their diseases. 1802 A
  Horses and their diseases. 1801 A

JEPHSON, Henry
Platform, its rise and progress.
7089 SS
JERNINGHAM, Mrs
Journal of. 18 P
JEROME, Jerome K
Idle thoughts of an idle fellow.
10600 F
Diary of a pilgrimage. 6742 F
Novel notes. 8041 F
On the stage and off. 6746 F
Sketches in lavender, blue and green.
10497 F
Three men in a boat. 6175 F
JERROLD, Blanchard
Douglass Jerrold, Life and remains
of. 11601 B
JESSOPP, Augustus
Coming of the friars. 12497 H
JEVONS, W Stanley
Money and the mechanism of ex-
change. 1408 SS
JEWETT, Sarah Orne
Betty Leicester. 5598 J
Country of the pointed firs. 10528 F
Country doctor. 2169 F
Deep haven. 6657 F
Friends ashore. 1189 F
King of Folly Island and other peo-
ple. 4973 F
Life of Nancy (short stories). 9408 F
Marsh island. 2580 F
Mate of the daylight. 1189 F
Native of Winby. 8084 F
Normans, The story of the. 4354 H
Old friends and new. 6656 F
White heron and other stories. 2652F
JEWETT, Lewellyn
Ceramic art of Great Britain. 1757 A
JEYS, S N
Joseph Chamberlain, Life of. 9751 B
JOHNSON, A H
Normans in Europe. 5179 H
JOHNSON, Charles F
Elements of literary criticism.
110333 EE
JOHNSON, Clifton (ed)
District school as it was. 10791 E

JOHNSON, Edward Gilpin
Sir Joshua Reynold's discourses on
art. 7573 A
JOHNSON, James F
Chemistry of common life, 2 vols.
1522 S
JOHNSON, Laurence
Medical formulary. 8717 S
JOHNSON, Oliver
William Lloyd Garrison and his
times. 4328 B
JOHNSON, Rossiter (ed)
Famous single and fugitive poems.
7223 P
Little classics, viz:
Comedy. 11526 F
Fortune. 11528 F
Heroism. 11527 F
Intellect. 11522 F
Laughter. 11523 F
Love. 11524 F
Poems narrative. 11529 F
War of secession, History of. 4367H
JOHNSON, Samuel
Lives of the poets. 7265 B
Rasselas, prince of Abyssinia.
JOHNSON, Virginia W
Genoa, the superb. 8481 H
Lily of the Arno. 7425 H
JOHNSON, William Henry
King's henchman. 11094 F
JOHNSTON, Alexander
American politics, History of. 12167
SS
Connecticut. 4006 H
United States; its history and con-
stitution. 8257 H
JOHNSTON, Annie Fellows
Little colonel, The. 11292 J
JOHNSTON, Henry
Doctor Congalton's legacy. 9538 F
JOHNSTON, Richard Malcolm
Mr Billy Downs and his likes. 7828F
Mr Fortner's martial claims. 7678 F
Old Mark Langston. 1033 F
Primes and their neighbors. 7129 F
JOHONNOT, James
Georaphical reader. 8110 EE

Little folks in feathers and furs J
JOKAI, M
Green book. 10314 F
Lion of Janina; or, The last days of
the Janissaries; a Turkish novel.
11074 F
JONES, Arthur T
Horse story. 5923 F
JONES, Charles C, Jr
Negro myths from the Georgia coast.
3219 F
JONES, Charles H
Famous explorers and adventurers
in Africa. 11723 V
JONES, Lynde E
Best reading. 11774 EE
JONES, M
Captain Cook's three voyages round
the world, 3 vols. 2158 V
JONES, Owen
Grammar of ornament. 12216 R
JONES, William Carey
Illustrated history of the University
of California. 9397 L
JONSON, Ben
Poems of. 37 P
JONSON, Kristofer
Spell-bound fiddler. 7258 F
JORDAN, David Starr
Care and culture of men. 9789 E
Foot-notes to evolution. 12634 E
Manual of vertebrate animals. 1531 S
Science sketches. 356 S
Story of the innumerable company.
9890 E
JORDAN, Elizabeth G
Tales of the city room. 11606 F
JORDAN, J Henry
Review of Alexander Hall against
Universalism. 8512 RE
JOSEPHUS, Flavius
Our young folks' Josephus; simpli-
fied by W S Shepard
JOYCE, P W
Short history of Ireland from earli-
est times to 1608. 8223 H
J S of Dale (see Stimson, F J)
JUNE, Jennie
Talks on woman's topics. 469 E
JUNIUS
Handwriting of. 3000 L
Letters of. 1035 E
JUNKIN, D
W S Hancock, Life of. 6353 B
JUNIOR, Charles
Dead men's tales. 12325 F

JUSSERAND, J J
English wayfaring life in the middle
ages. 12478 H
_____

KANE, Elisha Kent
Arctic explorations. 7878 V
KAPP, Frederich
Letters of Alexander von Humboldt.
11707 E
KAROLY, Karl
Guide to the paintings of Venice.
9520 A
Raphael's madonnas. 9118 A
KARR, W H
Shores and Alps of Alaska. 3382 V
KAUFFMANN, Rosalie
Queens of England. 522 J
Queens of Scotland. 518 J
KAYE, J W
Essays of an optimist. 471 E
KEANE, T F
Six months in Mecca. 3342 V
KEARY, Annie
Clemency Franklin. 6452 F
Doubting heart. 6464 F
Janet's home. 6461 F
Nations around. 6560 V
Oldbury. 6462 F
York and Lancaster rose. 6463 F
KEARY, Annie and E
Heroes of Asgard. 6526 F
KEARY, C F
Herbert Vanlennert. 10445 F
Norway and the Norwegians. 7885 H
KEARY, E
Magic valley. 6489 J
KEATS, John
Poetical works of. 9174 P
KEELER, Ralph
Vagabond adventures. 959 F
KEENE, J Harrington
Fly-fishing and fly-making. 6396 A
KEELING, Elsa d'Estere
Orchardcroft. 7838 F
KEENAN, H S
Trajan. 1191 F
KEEP, Josiah
West coast shells. 1515 S
KEIGHTLEY, S R
Last recruit of Clare's. 10362 F
KEIGHTLEY, Thomas
Ancient Greek mythology. 558 F
KELLER, Ferdinand
Lake dwellings of Switzerland. 2
vols. 1452 S
KELLY, William D
Old south and the new. 5966 H

KELLOGG, Edward
Labor and capital. 195 SS
KELLY, Thomas Fitzmaurice
Spanish literature, History of. 12315
EE
KELLY, William D
Lincoln and Stanton. 206 11
KELLER, M J
Elementary perspective. 7525 A
KELSEY, Charles B
Diseases of rectum and anus. 8723 S
KELSEY, D M
Deeds of daring of both blue and
gray. 11599 F
KEMBLE, Marion (ed)
Art recreations. 11770 E
KENDALL, May
Such is life. 6286 F
KENEALY, Arabella
Dr Janet of Harley street. 11624 F
KENNAN, George
Campaigning in Cuba. 12638 H
Siberia and the exile system, 2 vols.
7087 V
Tent life in Siberia. 4856 V
KENNEDY, James
Modern poets and poetry of Spain.
5222 EE
KENNEDY, J P
Horseshoe Robinson. 741 F
Rob of the bowl. 671 F
KENNEDY, Walker
Javan Ben Seir. 12343 F
KENNEDY, William S
Art and life; a Russian anthology.
1771 E
Prima donna, The. 5047 F
KENRICK, John
Ancient Egypt and its pharaohs.
4248 H
KENT, James
Commentaries on American law.
11972 SS
KENT, William
Memoirs and letters of James Kent.
12011 E

KENYON, Frederic G
Letters of Elizabeth Browning, 2
vols. 12227 E
KERNAHAN, Coulson
Captain Shannon. 12075 F
KERR, David
Boy explorers in Central Asia. 1175 J
Into unknown seas. 641 J
KESTER, Paul
Tales of the real gypsy. 11974 F
KIDD, Benjamin.
Control of the tropics. 12290 H
Social evolution. 8690 S
KIDD, John
Adaptation of external nature to
the physical condition of man.
11582 S
KIDD, Robert
Elocution and vocal culture. 8362
EE
KIMBALL, R B
Undercurrents. 5248 F
KINDERSLEY, Edward C
Good knight Bayard, History of.
523 F
KING, Charles
An army wife. 9792 F
Between the lines. 11468 F
Cadet days. 8406 F
Campaigning with Crook. 6043 F
Captain Close and sergeant Croesus.
9277 F
Colonel's daughter. 11998 F
Deserter; From the ranks. 11483 F
Foes in ambush. 7835 F
Garrison tangle. 10000 F
Laramie; or, The Queen of Bedlam.
6042 F
Marion's faith. 3205 F
Ray's recruit. 11040 F
Soldier's secret. 8070 F
Starlight ranch, etc. 6101 F
Story of Fort Frayne. 9348 F
Sunset pass. 6100 F
Trooper Ross and Signal Butte.9825F

Trumpeter Fred; a story of the plains. 9708 F
Under fire. 8821 F
Waring's peril. 8306 F
Warrior Gap. 11039 F
War-time wooing.

KING, Charles F
Methods and aims in geography. 8831 EE

KING, Clarence
Mountaineering in the Sierras.4851V

KING, Edward F (ed)
Golden spike. 2725 F
10,000 wonderful things. 2707 L

KING, Grace
Balcony stories. 8068 F

KING, James
Voyage to the Pacific ocean. 5277 V

KING, Katharine
Our detachment. 2493 F

KING, Pauline
Christine's career. 10028 J

KING, Rufus
Ohio, History of. 4280 H

KING, S P
Sylvia's world. 11618 F

KING, T Starr
Substance and show, or facts and farces and other lectures. 3425 E
White hills, The. 318 V

KING, Thorold
Haschisch. 1089 F

KINGLAKE, Charles
Eothen, or traces of Nowhere. 7531V
Invasion of the Crimea, 6 vols. 7549 H

KINGSLEY, Charles
Alton Locke. 2538 F
Claucus, or wonders of the shore. 8331 S
Health and education. 381 E
Hereward, the last of the English. 2540 F
Letters and memoirs of his life. 6073 E
Hermits, The. 7483 F
Heroes, The; or Greek fairy tales. 6441 F
Hypatia. 8008 F
Madam How and Lady Why. 5404 J
Poems of. 10771 P
Roman, The and the Teuton. 9176H
Town geology. 1480 S
Two years ago. 6236 F
Water babies. 2541 J
Westward ho! 2536 F
Yeast. 2537 F

KINGSLEY, Florence Morse
Paul, a herald of the cross. 10399 F
Stephen, a soldier of the cross. 11978 F
Titus, a comrade of the cross.10570 F

KINGSLEY, Henry
Austin Elliot. 11841 F
Ravenshoe. 2879 F

KINGSLEY, John Sterling
Riverside natural history, 6 vols. 8748 R

KINGSTON, W H G
Adventures among the Indians. 3087 J
At the south pole. 3377 J
Cruise of the Frolic. 9041 J
My first voyage to southern seas. 2710 V
New Grenada. 2142 F
Notable voyages. 2252 V
On the banks of the Amazon. 8121 J
Salt water. 9040 J

KINNEY, Abbott
Eucalyptus. 10009 A

KINSLEY, William W
Old faiths and new facts. 10405 RE

KIP, Leonard
Nestlenook. 9018 F

KIP, W Ingraham
Early days of my Episcopate.7647RE
Unnoticed things of Scripture.386RE

KIPLING, Rudyard
Captains courageous. 10715 F
Day's work. 12289 F
Jungle book. 9507 J
Departmental verses; barrack room ballads. 8260 P
Life's handicap; being stories of mine own people. 6841 F
Many inventions. 7840 F
Phantom 'Rickshaw, etc. 7053 F
Plain tales from the hills. 6450 F
Second jungle book. 9432 J
Soldiers three. 6988 F

KIPLING, Rudyard and W Balestier
The Naulahka. 9606 F

KIRBY, Mrs G B
Autobiography (Years of experience) 287 B

KIRBY, Mary and Elizabeth
Aunt Martha's corner cupboard. 537 J
The sea and its wonders. 8126 J
Things in the forest. 8132 J

KIRK, Eleanor
Selections from Henry Ward Beecher's works. 339 E

KIRK, Mrs E W O
Ciphers
Daughter of Eve. 6458 F
Lesson in love. 6454 F
Queen money. 3169 F
Revolt of a daughter. 11035 F
Sons and daughters. 3116 F
Story of Lawrence Garthe. 8819 F
Story of Margaret Kent. 2723 F
Walford. 5823 F
KIRK, Edmund
Among the pines, or the south in
secession times. 812 H
Rear-guard of the revolution. 2883 H
KIRKLAND, E S
Dora's housekeeping. 7372 J
France, Short history of. 6368 J
Six little cooks. 6054 J
Speech and manners for home and
school. 9282 J
KIRKLAND, Joseph
McVeys, The. 5601 F
Zury, the meanest man in Spring
county. 2294 F
KIRKPATRICK, E A
Inductive psychology. 9771 EE
KIRKWOOD, Daniel
Meteoric astronomy. 1445 S
KITCHEN, J M W
Consumption. 1507 S
KLINGLE, George
Getting to be women. 11849 EE
KNEELAND, S
Earthquakes and volcanoes. 4996 S
KNIGHT, Charles
Popular history of England, 1856 to
1867, 6 vols. 4113 H
KNIGHT, Charles (ed)
Half-hours with the best authors, 6
vols. 1209 L

Half-hours of English history, 4
vols. 4313 H
KNIGHT, Edward H
Mechanical dictionary, 4 vols. 1682 R
KNIGHT, Helen
Lady Huntington and her friends.
660 B
KNIGHT, William
Hume, Life of. 7630
KNOW, Robert
Races of men. 6197 S
KNOWER, Daniel
Adventures of a forty-niner. 9130 V
KNOWLES, Frederick Lawrence (ed)
Cap and gown. 12619 P
Golden treasury of American songs
and lyrics. 12511 P
KNOWLTON, I C
Thro' the shadows. 404 F
KNOX, Thomas W
Boy travellers in Australasia. 5453 J
— — on the Congo. 948 J
— — in the far east, 4 parts. 3308 J
— — in Russia. 5454 J
— — in South America. 3307 J
Decisive battles since Waterloo.
4255 H
John Boyd's adventures. 8004 J
Henry Ward Beecher, Life of. 1253 B
Robert Fulton, Life of. 1273 B
Underground world. 5791 V
KOHLRAUSCH, Frederick
Germany, History of. 4041 H
KOOPMAN, H Lyman
Mastery of books. 10358 EE
KOUNS, Nathan
Dorcas, daughter of Faustina. 11851 F
KREHBIEL, Henry
How to listen to music; hints and
suggestions to untaught lovers of
the art. 11150 A

KRUGER, Myra
Hyperaesthesia. 2724 F
KRUMMACHER, F W
The risen Redeemer. 3452 RE

LABOULAYE, E
Last fairy tales. 880 J
LACHAMBRE, Henri
Andre's balloon expedition in search of the north pole. 11025 V
LA FONTAINE, J de
Fables. 7224 J
LAGRANGE, F
Physiology of bodily exercise. 11360S
LALOR, John J (ed)
Cyclopaedia of political science, 3 vols. 12517 R
LAMARTINE, Alphonse de
Past, present and future of the republic. 6369 H
LAMB, Charles
Eliana. 11617 F
LAMB, Charles
Elia, Essays of. 566 E
Mrs Leicester's school and other writings. 11383 F
Works of. 1027 F
LAMB, Charles and Mary
Shakespeare, Tales from, 2 vols. 6048 J
LA MOTTE, Touque Friedrick de
Undine and other tales. 8995 F
LAMBERT, L A
Notes on Ingersoll. 1376 E
LANCIANI, Rodolfo
Ancient Rome in light of recent discoveries. 5746 H
Pagan and christian Rome. 8327 H
LANDOIS, L
Text book on human physiology. 7071 S
LANDON, Judson S
Constitutional history and government of the United States. 12150 H
LANDON, Melville D (Eli Perkins)
Kings of the platform and pulpit. 10921 B
Wit, humor and pathos. 5411 L
LANDOR, Walter Savage
Citation and examination of William Shakespeare. 1453 EE
Imaginary conversations. 11539 E
Prose dialogue in verse and epigram, 2 vols. 9559 P
LANDSBOROUGH, D
Popular history of British zoophytes. 11673 S

LANDSIER, John
Sabean researches. 4871 R
LANG, Andrew
Book of dreams and ghosts. 11914 E
Books and bookmen. 7593 EE
Cock-lane and common sense. 11358E
Custom and myth. 881 F
Essays in little. 7792 E
Letters on literature. 12180 EE
Letters to dead authors. 11222 E
Library, The. 7602 EE
Monk of fife. 9424 F
Old friends. 11165 E
LANG, Andrew (ed)
Blue fairy book.
Green fairy book. 10418 J
Red fairy book. 10417 J
True story book. 8251 J
Yellow fairy book. 8778 J
LANG, Andrew (Walter Metleaf, etc, trans)
Illiad of Homer in prose. 9192 EE
LANG, Andrew and S H Butcher trans
Odyssey of Homer. 9193 EE
LANG, Mrs A
Dissolving views. 2006 F
LANGHORNE, John and William
Plutarch's lives. 4208 B
LANIER, Sidney
Poems. 9549 P
Science of English verse. 9161 EE
LANMAN, Charles
Journal of A Ely, a prisoner of war in Richmond. 649 H
LANOYE, F de
Rameses the Great, or Egypt 3,300 years ago. 12537 H
LA RAME, Louise de (see "Ouida")
LARCOM, Lucy
New England girlhood. 5438 J
Poetical works of. 11247 P
LAFARGUE, Philip
New judgment of Paris. 6845 F
LARNARD, J N (ed)
History for ready reference, 5 vols. 9884 R
LARNED, Augusta
In woods and fields.10807 E
LATHROP, George Parsons
Spanish vistas. 8846 V
LATIMER, Elizabeth, Wormely
France in the 19th century. 7866 H
Russia and Turkey in the 19th century. 8092 H
LAUGHTON, John Knox
Nelson and his companions in arms. 10123 B

LAURIE, Andre
School boy days in France. 9993 J
LAURIE, S S
Historical survey of pre-christian education. 9757 EE
Institutes of education. 8001 EE
LAURIE, Thomas
The Ely volume, or The contributions of our foreign missions. 9290S
LAVATER, John C
Essays on physiognomy. 1510 S
LAWLESS, Hon Emily
Ireland, Story of. 534 H
Maelcho. 8826 F
LAWTON, William C
New England poets, a study of Emerson, Hawthorne. Whittier, Lowell and Holmes. 12549 EE
LAZARUS, Emma
Poems of, 2 vols. 3422 P
LAZARUS, Josephine.
Spirit of Judaism. 11394 RE
LEA. Henry C
The inquisition, History of, 3 vols. 4369 H
LEANDER. R
German fantasies. 3136 F
LEAR. Edward
Nonsense songs. 78 P
Nonsense book. 99 F
LEBON, Andre
Modern France. 1789-1895. 12186 H
LE BON, Gustave
The crowd; a study of the popular mind. 9990 SS
LECKY, W E H
Democracy and liberty, 2 vols. 9737H
England, 18th century, History of, 8 vols. 4395 H
European morals, History of. 2 vols. 4403 H
Political value of history. 12499 H
Rationalism in Europe, 2 vols. 4401H
LE CONTE, Joseph
Elements of geology. 1475 S
Evolution; its relation to religious thought. 5430 RE

LEE, Mary Catherine
In the cheering-up business. 8665 F
Quaker girl of Nantucket. 8664 F
Soulless singer. 9558 F
LEE, Sidney
Stratford-on-Avon. 6860 V
LEE, Yan Chow
When I was a boy in China. 12308 J
LEEDS, W H
Rudimentary architecture. 279 A
LE ESTRANGE, Roger
Seneca's morals. 362 E
LEFEVRE. Andre
Philosophy, historical and critical. 1420 EE
Race and language. 11365 EE
LEFFMANN, Henry
Examination of water. 7094 S
LE GALLIENNE, R
Prose fancies. 10510 E
Religion of a literary man. 8684 RE
Romance of Zion chapel. 11075 F
LEGGE, James
Chinese classics. 6986 EE
LEGH, M H Cornwall
How Dick and Molly saw England. 10343 J
How Dick and Molly went around the world. 10344 J
LEHMAN, Walter
Memoirs of an old actor. 289 B
LEIGHTON, Robert
Rome, History of. 8219 H
Wreck of the Golden Fleece. 8029 F
LEITH. Adams
Geoffrey Stirling. 4749 F
LELAND, Charles
The algonquin: legends of New England. 2242 F
LELAND. Lilian
Woman's journey around the world. 6665 V
LELAND, Thomas (trans)
All the orations of Demosthenes. 12544 E
LELONG, B M
Treatise in citrus culture. 1806 A

LEMMON, J G
Hand book of west American conc-
bearers. 9475 S
LENORMANT, Francois
Beginnings of history. 12523 11
LENT, William Bement
Across the country of the little king.
11961 V
Halcyon days in Norway, France and
the Dolomites. 11966 V
LEONHART, Rudolph
Either or. 8946 F
LEONOWENS, A 11
English governess at Siamese court.
6337 V
LE PILEUR, A
Wonders of the human body. 1490 S
LE QUEUX, William
Scribes and pharisees. 12556 F
Temptress, The. 9632 F
Whoso findeth a wife. 11913 F
Zoraida. 9439 F
LE SAGE, A R
Gil Blas, Adventures of. 2685 F
Vanillo Gonzales, or the merry bach-
elor. 1356 F
LESDERNIER, de
Hortense. 6176 B
LESTER, C Edwards
Charles Sumner, life and public ser-
vices of, 2 vols. 11590 B
LETOURNEAU, Charles
Biology. 1435 S
LEVER, C J (pseud of Cornelius
O'Dowd)
Charles O'Malley, the Irish dragoon.
10816 F
Harry Lorrequer. 3222 F
LEVETT-YEATS, S
Galahad of the Greek. 10537 F
Widow Lamport. 10538 F
LEVY, Arthur
Private life of Napoleon, 2 vols.
8499 B
LEWES, George Henry
Biographical history of philosophy.
1416 EE
Physiology of common life. 1517 S
LEWIS, Angelo J (see Hoffmann, E
T W)
LEWIS, C B
Sawed-off sketches. 2158 F
LEWIS, M G
The monk, 2 vols. 5261 F
Romantic tales. 5216 F
LEWIS, W M
People's practical poultry book.
1798 A

LEWIS, Meriwether, and Clark
History of the expedition to the
sources of the Missouri, and to the
Pacific ocean in 1804-1805-1806.
1638 V   b
LIDDELL, H G and Robert Scott
Greek-English lexicon. 12627 R
LIDDON, H P
Some elements of religion. 11667 RE
LIEFDE, J B de
Maid of Stralsund. 6299 F
LILJENCRANTZ, Ottilie A
The scrape that Jack built. 11076 J
LILLIE, Lucy C
Jo's opportunity. 643 J
Mildred's bargain and other stories.
6270 J
My mother's enemy. 7194 F
LIN, Frank (pseud of Gertrude Ather-
ton)
What dreams may come. 7033 F
LINDLEY, W, and J P Widney
California of the south; its physical
geography, climate, resources, routes
of travel and health resorts. 6338 V
LINDNER, Gustav
Manual of empirical psychology.
5974 EE
LINTON, E Lynn
Joshua Davidson, Life of. 11498 B
New woman. 9285 F
LINTON, W J
Wood engraving in America, History
of. 1782 A
LIPPINCOTT, Mrs S J (see Greenwood,
Grace)
LITTLE, John
The coming conflict; Sunday agita-
tion. 402 RE
LLOYD, J W
Drugs and medicines of North Am-
erica. 12654 S
LLOYD, John Uri (compiler)
Etidorhpa, or the end of the world.
10778 F
LOCHER, A
With star and crescent. 11782 V
LOCKE, David
The demagogue. 5988 F
LOCKE, D R
Morals of Abou Ben Adhem. 11752
LOCKE, John
Conduct of understanding. 315 E
LOCKER, Frederick
London lyrics. 11737 P
LOCKHART, J G
Memoirs of Sir Walter Scott, 10 vols.
149 B

Napoleon, Life of. 119 B
LOCKYER, J Norman
  Astronomy. 6636 S
  Dawn of astronomy. 8494 S
  Spectrum analysis. 1403 S
LODGE, Henry Cabot
  Alexander Hamilton. Life of. 182 B
  Daniel Webster. 183 B
  English colonies in America. 12151H
  Hero tales from American history.
    9498 F
  Historical and political essays.7597H
  Modern Europe, History of. 4290 H
  Studies in history. 4040 H
LODGE, Oliver J
  Modern views of electricity. 6548 S
LOFTIE, W J
  Windsor castle. 1616 H
LOGAN, A S
  Jesus in modern life. 11871 RE
LOGAN, John A
  Great conspiracy. 216 H
  Volunteer soldier of America.8918 H
LOGAN, Olive
  Get thee behind me, Satan. 2673 A
LOGAN, William
  Words of comfort for parents be-
    reaved of little children. 11811 RE
LONG, C
  Central Africa. 3295 V
LONG, George (trans)
  Discourses of Epictetus. 9773 E
  Thoughts of the emperor M. Aurelius
    Antoninus. 9802 E
LONG, John Luther
  Madame Butterfly and other stories.
    12589 F
LONG, Joseph W
  American wild fowl shooting.11698 A
LONG, Lily A
  Apprentices to destiny. 8175 F
LONGFELLOW, H W
  Christus. 10991 P
  Hyperion. 2998 F
  Outre Mer. 2997 V
  Poetical works. 60 P
  Song of Hiawatha. 14 P
LONGMAN, F W
  Frederick the Great and the seven
    years' war. 5491 B
LONGMORE, T
  Optical manual. 11669 A
LOOMIS, A W
  Confucius and the Chinese classics.
    4329 EE
LORD, John
  Beacon lights of history
  Antiquity. 4120 H

  Great women. 4124 H
  Jewish heroes and prophets. 6032 H
  Middle ages. 4122 H
  Old pagan civilizations. 6033 H
  Renaissance and reformation. 4121H
  Warriors and statesmen. 4123 H
LORD, John
  Two German giants, Frederick the
    Great and Bismarck. 8228 B
LORD, William
  Blue and gold. 10582 P
LOSSING, Benson J
  Civil war in America, 2 vols. 4014 H
  Eminent Americans. 164 B
  Mary and Martha Washington.5739B
  1776, or the War of Independence.
    4000 H
LOTHROP, Mrs H M S (see Sidney,
  Margaret)
LOTI, Pierre (pseud of L M J Viaud)
  An Iceland fisherman. 5401 F
  Child's romance. 9792 F
  From lands of exile. 5679 F
  Jeany Berny, sailor. 11847 F
  Ramuntcho. 11077 F
LOTZE, Hermann
  Microcosmus. 496 S
LOUDON, Mrs
  Encyclopaedia of plants. 1549 R
LOUGHEAD, Flora Haines
  The abandoned claim. 7215 F
LOUNSBURY, T R
  James Fenimore Cooper, Life of.189B
LOVELL, Kate R
  Nature's wonder workers. 6426 S
LOVER, Samuel
  Handy Andy. 1060 F
LOW, Hugh
  Savarvak; its inhabitants. 4696 V
LOWE, Charles
  German emperor, William II. 9752 B
  Prince Bismark. 9534 B
LOWELL, Edward J
  Hessians and other German auxiliar-
    ies of Great Britain in the revolu-
    tionary war. 4235 H
LOWELL, James Russell
  Among my books. 569 E

Biglow papers. 730 E
Last poems of. 9567 P
My study windows. 797 E
On a certain condescension in for-
eigners. 527 E
Poetical works of. 9668 P
LOWELL, Percival
Mars. 9742 S
Noto, an unexplored corner of
Japan. 6339 V
Occult Japan. 9300 V
LOWELL, Robert
Antony Brade. 5719 F
LOWER, M A
Essays on English surnames, 2 vols.
5038 EE
LUBBOCK, Sir John
Ants, bees and wasps. 5725 S
Beauties of nature, etc. 7444 E
Fifty years of science. 6402 E
Flowers, fruits and leaves. 11437 S
On the senses, instincts and intelli-
gence of animals. 5402 S
Pleasures of life. 337 E
Prehistoric times. 1455 S
Use of life. 8782 EE
LUKIN, J
Boy engineers. 7374 J
LUMMIS, Charles F
Awakening of a nation; Mexico of
today. 11029 H
Land of the Poco Tiempo. 11237 V
Man who married the moon. 8816 F
Some strange corners of our country.
7431 V
Spanish pioneers. 8416 H
Tramp across the continent. 7430 V
LUSH, Charles K
The federal judge. 10662 F
LUSKA, Sidney (pseud of Henry Har-
land)
As it was written: a Jewish musi-
cian's story. 2595 F
Grandison Mather. 5288 F
Latin quarter courtship. 5289 F
Mrs Peixada. 5290 F
Yoke of Thorah. 3167 F
LUTHER, Martin
Watchwords for the warfare of life.
325 RE
LUYS, J
The brain and its functions. 11362 S
LUYSTER, I M (trans)
Memoirs of Madam Recamier. 220 B
LYALL, Alfred
Warren Hastings. B
LYALL, Edna (pseud of A E Bayly)
Autobiography of a slander. 7987 F

Derrick Vaughan, novelist. 6975 F
Donovan; a modern Englishman.
6989 F
Doreen; the story of a singer. 8525 F
Hardy Norseman. 9637 F
In the golden days. 6990 F
Knight errant. 5291 F
To right the wrong. 8021 F
Wayfaring men. 10683 F
We two; sequel to Donovan. 5292 F
Won by waiting. 6476 F
LYELL, Charles
Students' elements of geology.11494S
LYMAN, Henry M
Anaesthetics. 8716 S
LYNCH, Lawrence L
Shadowed by three. 11861 F
LYON, Mary
Power of christian benevolence.
11780 RE
LYON, Sidney
For a mess of pottage. 11632 F

MAARTENS, Maarten (pseud of J M
Poorten-Schwartz)
God's fool. 8314
Greater glory, The. 8176 F
Her memory. 12581 F
My lady nobody. 9438 F
MABIE, Hamilton Wright
Books and culture. 10006 E
Essays in literary interpretation.
7445 E
My study fire. 6521 E
Norse stories retold. 5285 F
Under the trees and elsewhere.6383E
M'ALLISTER, Ward
Society as I have found it. 8417 F
McANALLY, D R, Jr
Irish wonders. 3218 L
MACAULAY, T B
Critical and historical essays, 2 vols.
10173 EE
England, History of, 4 vols. 4126 H
Frederick the Great, Life of. 1272 B
Miscellaneous writings of, 2 vols.
11852 E
Poetical works of. 7945 P
Reviews and essays. 473 E
McCABE, James D, Jr
Campaigns of Robert E Lee. 112 B
From farm to president's chair; life
of Garfield. 254 J
New York by sunlight and gaslight.
4321 L
McCARTHY, Justin
Dictator. 7824 F
Epoch of reform. 5493 H

History of our own times, 3 vols. 4169 H
History of the four Georges. 5392 11
Maid of Athens. 2928 F
Riddle ring. 10067 F
McCARTHY, Justin H
Ireland since the union. 1789-1886. 4065 H
McCARTY, L P
Annual statistician, 1886-1898, 10 vols. 1666 R
McCLURE, Robert
Diseases of American horse, cattle and sheep. 1799 A
McCOOK, Henry
Tenants of an old home. 3423 S
MACCORD, C W
Practical hints to draughtsmen. 7640 A
McCORMICH, Brooks
Nature's young nobleman. 6969
McCOSH, James
Psychology; the cognitive powers. 555 E
McCRACKEN, W D
Romance of Switzerland. 11167 H
Teutonic Switzerland. 11168 H
McCRAY, F T
Harriet Beecher Stowe, Life work of 7259 B
McCULLOCK, Hugh
Men and measures of half a century. 4384 H
MACDONALD, George
Adela Cathcart. 6315 F
Alec Forbes of Howglen. 2450 F
Annals of a quiet neighborhood.677F
At the back of the north wind.8038 J
David Elginbrod. 5374 F
Donal Grant. 5375 F
Flight of the shadow. 7157 F
Guild court. 5376 F
Heather and snow. 7832 F
Lilith. 9421 F
Malcolm. 2740 F
Marquis of Lossie. 5377 F
Mary Marston. 9002 F
Phantastes: the portent. 11614 F
Ranald Bannerman's boyhood.6259 F
Robert Falconer. 2263 F
Rough shaking. 6888 J
St George and St Michael. 5378 F
Salted with fire. 10718 F
Seaboard parish: sequel to Annals of a quiet neighborhood. 818 F
Sir Gibbie. 5379 F
Steven Archer. 2013 F
There and back. 7121 F

Thomas Wingfold, curate. 2262 F
Weighed and wanting. 5380 F
What's mine's mine. 2738 F
Wilfred Cumbermede. 2739 F
MACDONALD, J R L
Soldiering and surveying in east Africa. 10864 V
MACE, Frances L
Under pine and palm. 5802 P
MACE, Jean
History of a mouthful of bread. 4288
MACFARLANE, Charles
Napoleon Bonaparte, Life of. 11665B
MAC GAHAN, J H
Campaigning on the Oxus, or the fall of Khira. 3324 V
McGlashan, C F
Donner party, History of the. 391 H
McGLASSON, Eva Wilder (pseud of Eva Wilder Brodhead)
An earthly paragon. 7582 F
Bound in shallows. 10304 F
Diana's livery. 7586 F
MAC GREGOR, J
1000 miles in the Rob Roy canoe. 3125 V
Rob Roy on the Jordan. 3285 V
McINTOSH, William
Philistine sermons. 12360 RE
McKAY and Windgate
Famous American actors of today. 11327 B
MACKAY, Charles
Memoirs of extraordinary and popular delusions. 6614 L
McKEEVER, Harriet B
Maude and Miriam. 8391 F
McKENDRICK, John Gray
Life in motion. 11865 S
MACKENZIE, Morell
Diseases of pharnyx, larynx and trachea. 8710 S
MACKENZIE, Robert
Nineteenth century. 4406 H
MACKEY, Albert G
Lexicon of freemasonry. 8873 R
MACKEY, H O
One thousand new illustrations.7313R

MACKIE, John
They that sit in darkness. 12335
MACKINNON, Capt
Atlantic and transatlantic sketches. 1624 V
MACKINTOSH, James
Electrical theory of the universe. 3095 S
Miscellaneous works of. 437 E
MACKINTOSH, John
Scotland, Story of. 8784 H
MACKLIN, Herbert
Monumental brasses. 6858 A
McKNIGHT, Charles
Old fort Duquesne. 9092 F
MACLAREN, Archibald
System of physical education. 6714S
MACLAREN, Ian (pseud of John Watson)
Beside the bonnie brier bush. 9712 F
Christianity and idealism. 10410 RE
Clerical life; a series of letters to ministers. 11376 RE
Companions of the sorrowful way. 11422 RE
Days of auld lang syne. 9410 F
Kate Carnegie. 9902 F
Mind of the master. 10530 RE
Schelling's transcendental idealism. 8087 EE
MACLEAN, J P
Mound builders. 12535 H
McLEAN, Sally P (pseud of Mrs S P M Greene)
Cape Cod folks. 2238 F
Moral imbeciles. 12224 F
Some other folks. 11940 F
McLELLAN, J A
Applied psychology. 9770 EE
McLENNAN, William
Spanish John. 11079 F
McLEOD, Donald
Mary. Queen of Scotts. Life of. 285B
MACLEOD, Fiona
Green fire. 9997 F
Sin-eater. 10141 F
MACLEOD, Norman
The startling. 7162 F
McMAHAN, Anna B
Best letters of Horace Walpole. 7244E
Best letters of William Cowper. 7852E
McMAHON, Bernard
American gardener's calendar. 8507A
McMANUS, L
Silk of the kine. 10448 F
McMASTER, John B
Benjamin Franklin. 2 vols. 1236 B

People of the United States, 3 vols. 7557 H
With the fathers; studies in the history of the United States. 9744 H
McMILLAN, Hugh
Roman mosaics. 1620 H
McMILLAN, Walter G
Treatise on electro-metallurgy. 7091 S
MACQUOID, Katharine
Cosette. 9035 F
Elizabeth Morey. 7007 F
Haunted fountain. 7009 F
Miss Eyon of Eyon court. 7006 F
Patty. 6851 F
MACY, Jesse
Our government. 7378 SS
MADOC, Fayr
Margaret Jermine. 6921 F
Story of Melicent. 891 F
MAEL, Pierre
Land of the tawny beasts. 12334 J
MAGILL, Mary Tucker
Pantomimes, or wordless poems. 11538 P
MAGRUDER, Allan
John Marshall. Life of. 1243 B
MAGRUDER, Julia
Across the chasm. 2586 F
Princess Sonia. 9411 F
Realized ideal. 11078 F
Violet. 9913 F
MAHAFFY, J P
Alexander's empire. 535 H
Descartes. 7636 B
Greek world under Roman sway. 10350 H
Old Greek education. 11166 H
Rambles and studies in Greece. 10177 H
Social life in Greece from Homer to Menander. 10737 H
MAHAFFY, J P and J E Rogers
Sketches from a tour through Holland and Germany. 6447 V
MAHAN, A T
Interest of America in sea power, present and future. 11272 H
Influence of sea power upon the French revolution, 2 vols. 8225 H
Influence of sea power upon history. 5740 H
Nelson, the embodiment of the sea power of Great Britain, 2 vols 10587B
MAHAN, A
Modern mysteries explained and exposed. 8253 L
MAIN, Robert
Rudimentary astronomy. 1491 S

MAINE, H S
Ancient law. 11206 H
Dissertations on early law and custom. 10584 H
Lectures on the early history of institutions. 11205 H

MALDEN, Mrs Catherine
Jane Austen. 6346 B

MALET, Lucas (pseud of Mrs. M K Harrison)
Little Peter. 8515 J
Mrs Lorimer, a sketch in black and white. 5718 F

MALLESON, G B
Indian mutiny of 1887. 12152 H

MALLOCK, William Hurrell
Aristocracy and evolution; Study of the right origin and social functions of the wealthier classes. 11391 SS
Heart of life. 9362 F
Is life worth living? 7421 F
New republic. 7761 F
Old order changes. 3130 F
Property and progress. 205 SS

MALTHUS, T R
An essay on principle of population. 3156 SS

MANACEINE, Marie de
Sleep, its physiology, pathology and hygiene. 11901 S

MANN, Horace
Lectures of. 300 EE

MANN, Mary E
Susannah. 9748 F

MANSFIELD, C V
Paraguay, Brazil and La Platte. 5243 V

MANTEGAZZA Paolo
Physiognomy and expression. 7854 S

MANTELL, G A
Wonders of geology. 2 vols. 12462 S

MANTON, Walter P
Handbook of field botany. 1441 S
Insects; how to catch and prepare them. 1543 S

MACHESI, Mathilde
Machesi and music: passages from the life of a famous singing teacher. 11383 B

MARCHMONT, Arthur W
By right of sword. 10737 F

MARDEN, Orbion S
Architects of fate. 9734 EE
Secret of achievement. 12340 L
Success: a book of ideals, helps and examples. 10796 EE

MAREY, E J
Animal mechanism. 1393 S

MARGUERITE, Julia de
Ins and outs of Paris. 4712 V

MARION, Charles
Russian campaign vs the Turconians. 3344 H

MARKHAM, Clements R
Peru, History of. 7859 H
Sea fathers; lives of great navigators. 1375 B
Travels in Peru and India. 3368 V

MARKHAM, R (ed)
Chronicles of the Cid. 524 F
Colonial days. 4261 J

MARLITT, E (pseud of Eugenie John)
At the councillors
Bailiff's maid. 1104 F
Countess Gisela. 2440 F
Gold Elsie. 10064 F
In the Shillings court. 10021 F
Lady of the rubies. 10065 F
Little moorland princess. 10012 F
Old mam'selle's secret. 11779 F
Owl's nest. 10019 F
Second wife. 10057 F

MARRIOTT, J A R
Makers of modern Italy. 6561 H

MARRYAT, Frank
Children of the New Forest. 2512 F
Dog fiend. 2517 F
Frank Mildway. 2503 F
Jacob Faithful. 2505 F
Japhet in search of a father. 2507 F
King's own. 2515 F
Little savage. 2268 F
Mr Midshipman Easy. 2509 F
Masterman Ready. 2526 F
Mission; or scenes in Africa. 2524 F
Monsieur Violet. 2511 F
Mountains and molehills. 1630 V
Newton Foster. 2520 F
Olla podrida. 2521 F
Pacha of many tales. 2506 F
Percival Keene. 2516 F
Peter Simple. 2519 F
Phantom ship. 2504 F
Pirate. 2522 F
Poacher. 2518 F
Poor Jack. 2514 F

Settlers in Canada. 2513 F
Valerie; an autobiography. 2510 F
MARRYAT, Florence
Parson Jones. 7834 F
MARSH, John B
Robin Hood, Life and adventures of. 7484 F
Story of the jubilee singers. 10801 F
MARSHALL, Alfred
Principles of economics. 7082 SS
MARSHALL, Emma
Alma. 7185 F
Dorothy's daughters. 7954 F
Lady Alice. 7956 F
MARSHALL, Henry R
Aesthetic principles. 11747 A
MARSHALL, Julian M
Tennis rachets, etc. 7543 A
MARSHALL, William
Men of mark in British church history. 8120 B
MARSHMAN, John Clark
Memoirs of Sir Henry Havelock. 6623 B
MARTIN, Annie
Home life on an ostrich farm. 7307V
MARTIN, Charles
Civil customs of England. 1770 SS
MARTIN, Edward S
A little brother of the rich. 7652 J
MARTIN, Edward W
Behind the scenes in Washington. 11773 L
MARTIN, Francis
Kilda Hall. 5082 F
MARTIN, George A
Fences, gates and bridges; a practical manual. 9579 A
MARTIN, George Madden
Angel of the tenement. 11929 J
MARTIN, Henri
Popular history of France, 3 vols. 4034 H
MARTIN, Mrs Herbert
Lindsay's girl. 10447 F
MARTIN, Theodore
Horace. 8230 P
MARTINEAU, Harriet
Biographical sketches. 129 B
Household education. 3252 A
MARTINGALE, Hawser
Mark Rowland. 11605 F
MARVEL, I K (pseud; see Mitchell, Donald G)
MASON, George
Pirates. History of the. 5187 L

MASON, Otis Tufton
Woman's share in primitive culture. 8780 S
MASPERO, G
Life in ancient Egypt and Assyria. 8848 H
Struggle of the nations, Egypt, Syria and Assyria. 11288 H
MASSON, David
T de Quincy, Life of. 6687 B
MASSON, Tom
The Yankee navy. 12344 J
MASSY, Dawson
Romans, History of the. 11718 H
MATHER, Increase
Troubles in New England, 6220 R
MATHER, Marshall
John Ruskin; his life and teaching. 12219 B
MATHERS, Helen
Hedri; or blind justice. 6970 F
MATHEW, J
Clio; or a discourse on taste. 4695 E
MATHEWS, Charles T
Story of architecture; outlines of styles in all countries. 11043 A
MATHEWS, Shaler
The social teaching of Jesus; an essay in Christian sociology. 10790 RE
MATHEWS, William
Getting on in the world. 739 E
Great conversers. 7588 E
Literary style, etc. 7587 E
Men, places and things. 321 E
Wit and humor; use and abuse. 7590 E
MATSON, Henry
References for literary workers. 8090 R
MATTHEWS, J Brander
Aspects of fiction and other ventures in criticism. 10116 EE
Family tree and other stories. 7172 F
Last meeting. 2732 F
Outlines in local color. 10894 F
Poems of American patriotism. 8291 P
Story of a story and other stories. 7830 F
Tales of fantasy and fact. 9794 F
Tom Paulding. 7448 J
Vignettes of Manhattan. 8772 F
MATTHEWS, J Brander and L Hutton
Actors and actresses of Great Britain and the United States, 5 vols. 280 B
MAUD, Constance
Wagner's heroes. 10348 F

Wagner's heroines. 10453 F

MAUDSLEY, Henry
Responsibility in mental disease. 1391 S

MAUNDEVILE, Sir John
Voiage and travaile. 3303 V

MAUPAS, C E de
Story of the coup d'etat. 8945 F

MAUPASSANT, Guy de
Odd number. 6302 F
Two brothers. 6953 F

MAURY, M F
Physical geography of the sea. 1443S

MAYHEW, Edward
Horse doctor, illustrated. 12668 A

MAYO, I F (see Edward Garrett)

MAXWELL, Herbert
Robert the Bruce and the struggle for Scottish independence. 10323 B

MAXWELL, Mrs M E (ee Mrs Braddon)

MAY, Sophie (pseud of Clarke, Rebecca S
Ashbury twins. 5293 J
Doctor's daughter. 5294 J
Drone's honey. 3141 J
Janet. 5295 J
Our Helen. 5296 J
Quinnebasset girls. 2291 J

MAY, Thomas E
Constitutional history of England, 1760-1860, 2 vols. 9153 H
Democracy in Europe, 2 vols. 9155 H

MAYER, Alfred Marshall
Sound. 9873 S

MAYEUX, Henri
Manual of decorative composition. 12493 A

MAYNARD, Charles J
Eggs of North American birds. 11207 S

MEACHAN, A B
Wigwam and warpath. 1637 V

MEADE, L T (pseud of E F Smith)
Deb and the duchess. 7168 J
Girl of the people. 6987 F
Heart of gold. 6959 J

Lady of the forest. 11329 J
Young mutineer. 12372 J

MEANS, James (ed)
Aeronautical manual for 1896.12188 S

MEDLEY, D J
Student's manual of English constitutional history. 9573 H

MEIGNAN, Victor
Over Siberian snows from Paris to Pekin. 5014 V

MELVILLE, G J Whyte
Cerise; a tale of the last century. 11562 F
In the Lena delta. 3300 V

MELVILLE, Herman
Redburn; his first voyage. 9471 F
Omoo; a narrative of adventures in the south seas. 8531 F

MENDENHALL, T C
Century of electricity. 5559 S

MENEFEE, C A
Sketch gook of Napa, Sonoma.9128 V

MENZIES, Louisa
Legendary tales of the ancient Britons. 2876 F

MERCIER, Charles
Sanity and insanity. 7696 S

MEREDITH, George
Diana of the crossways. 6477 F
Egotist. 5762 F
Harry Richmond. 6316 F
Lord Ormont and his Aminta. 8641 F
Ordeal of Richard Feverel. 5763 F
(Story of a motherless boy reared by his father strictly according to theory. The outcome is tragic.)
Rhoda Fleming. 2596 F
Shaving of Shagpat Farina. 7788 F

MEREDITH, Owen
Lucille. 10635 P
Poetical works of. 8901 P
Ring of Amasis. 2594 F

MERIVALE, Charles
Romans under the empire. 4 vols. 4219 H
Roman triumvirates. 5476 H

MERIWETHER, Lee
Afloat and ashore on the Mediterranean. 7450 V
Tramp at home. 7296 V
Tramp trip. How to see Europe on fifty cents a day. 1618 V
MERMAID SERIES
I—Best plays of Christopher Marlowe, edited by Havelock Ellis. 8186 P
II. — —Thomas Otway, edited by Roden Noel. 8187 P
III. — — John Ford, edited by Havelock Ellis. 8188 P
IV-V. — — Philip Massinger, edited by Arthur Symonds. 8189 P
VI. — — Thomas Heywood, edited by A W Verity. 8191 P
VII. — — William Wycherley, edited by W C Ward. 8192 P
VIII. — — Nero and other plays, edited by H P Horne, etc. 8193 P
IX and X. — — Beaumont and Fletcher ,by J St Loe Strachey. 8194 P
XI. — — William Congreve, edited by Alex C Ewald. 8196 P
XII. — — Webster and Tourneur, by J A Symond. 8187 P
XIII and XIV. — — Thomas Middleton, by A C Swinburne. 8198 P
XIV. — — James Shirley, by Edmund Gosse. 8200 P
XVI. — — Thomas Dekker. by Ernest Rhys. 8201 P
XVII. XVIII and XIX. — — Ben Jonson. by Brinsley. etc. 8202 P
MERRIAM. C Hart (ed)
Hawks and owls of the United States. 7795 S
MERRIAM. Florence
Birds through an opera glass. 5435 S
Birds of village and field. 11330 S
Birding on a bronco. 10100 S
MERRIAM, George S
Samuel Bowles. Life and times of. 1255 B
MERRIAM. Henry Seton
In Kedar's tents. 10717 F
Phantom future. 11418 F
The sowers. 10558 F
MERRIMAN, T M
Pilgrims, puritans and Roger Williams. 10055 H
Trail of history; or history of religion and empire in parallel from · creation to the present. 4383 RE

MERZ, J Theodore
Leibnitz. 7628 B
METUGARD, Eliza
Doctor's little daughters. 11697 F
MEUNIER, Victor
Great hunting grounds of the world. 1652 V
M E W S
Home amusements. 8936 A
MEYER, Franz Sales
Hand book of ornament. 8936 A
MEYER, G H
Lamara and other poems. 9470 P
MEYER, Lucy Rider
Real fairy folks. 8115 J
MEYER, W E
Wrecked on the Bermudas. 7995 J
MICHAUD, Joseph F
Crusades, History of the, 3 vols. 4318 H
MICHELET, Jules
The insect. 1546 S
MICHELET, M
France, History of. 2 vols. 4032 H
Martin Luther, Life of. 11825 B
MIDDLETON, H C
Cicero, Life of, 2 vols. 4880 B
MIFFLIN, Lloyd
At the gates of song. 10741 P
MILES, Alfred H
Poets and poetry of the century, 8 vols. 9784 P
MILL, John Stuart
On liberty; the subjecting of women. 8836 SS
System of logic. 9113 EE
MILLER, Annie Jenness
Physical beauty. 7324 A
MILLER, E Kalley
Romance of astronomy. 6869 S
MILLER, Fenwick
Harriet Martineau. 6349 B
MILLER, Hugh
Old red sandstone. 6618 S
Testimony of the rocks. 6619 S
MILLER, Joaquin (pseud of C H Miller)
Danites. 2674 F
Shadows of Shasta. 2687 F
Ship in the desert. 2897 P
Songs of the summer lands. 12178 P
MILLER, Olive Thorne
Bird lover in the west. 8312 S
Bird ways. 7038 S
In nesting time. 7036 S
Little brothers of the air. 7037 S
Little folks in feathers and fur. 7035 J

Our home pets. 8660 S
MILLS, Wesley
Dog in health and disease. 7525 A
MILMAN, H H
Jews, history of the. 4125 H
Latin Christianity, 3 vols. 10590 H
MILNE, Frances M
A cottage gray. 9386 P
For to-day poems. 8288 P
Heliotrope; a San Francisco idyl of twenty-five years ago. 11959 F
MILNE, John
Earthquakes and other earth movements. 7715 S
MILNER, Thomas
Isaac Watts, Life of. 259 B
MILTON, John
Poetical works of, 2 vols. 32 P
MINES, John F
Tour around New York. 7622 V
MINSHULL, J (trans)
Creator's wonders in living nature. 4834 S
God's glorious creation, or marvels of the earth, sea and sky. 4835 S
'MINTO, William
Daniel Defoe, Life of. 6689 BF
MITCHEL, O M
Planetary and stellar worlds. 6722 S
MITCHELL, Donald G (Ik Marvel)
Bound together. 1138 E
Dream life. 9633 E
English lands, letters and kings, 4 vols. 10724 EE
My farm at Edgewood. F
Out of town places. 1128 E
Reveries of a bachelor. 672 E
Seven stories with basement. and attic. 803 E
MITCHELL, Ellen M
Study of Greek philosophy. 7624 EE
MITCHELL, James
Scotsman's library. 5217 H
MITCHELL, J A
That first affair. 10045 F
Last American. 7623 F
MITCHELL, Lucy M
Ancient sculpture, History of, 2 vols. 11208 A
MITCHELL, S Augustus
System of modern geography. 8367 EE
MITCHELL, S Weir
Characteristics. 7581 F
Doctor and patient. 8081 S
Hugh Wynne, 2 vols. 10757 F
In war time. 2345 F
Wear and tear. 8080 S

When all the woods are green.8791 F
MITFORD, A B
Tales of old Japan, 2 vols. 5213 F
MOBERLY, C E
Early Tudors, Henry VII-Henry VIII. 5184 H
MOCLOY, Edgar S
Journal of William Mocloy. 7263 H
MOFFAT, William D
Not without honor. 12243 F
MOFFETT, Cleveland
True detective stories. 11973 F
MOFFETT, S E
Suggestions on government. 8911 SS
MOLESWORTH, Mrs L S (pseud of Ennis Graham)
Little Miss Peggy. 3137 J
Nurse Heather-Dale's story. 6790 F
Third Miss St Quentin. 4853 F
MOLL, Albert
Hypnotism. 7437 S
MOLLETT, J W
An illustrated dictionary of art and archaeology. 12500 R
MOLTKE, Count H von
Franco-German war, 1870-1871. 11238 H
MOMBERT, J J
Charles the Great, A history of.125SH
MOMMSEN, Theodor
Provinces of the Roman empire, 2 vols. 9151 H
Rome, History of, 5 vols. 9427 H
MONCREIFF, Frederick
The x jewel. 9631 F
MONNIER, Marc
Wonders of Pompeii. 11173 L
MONROE, Lewis R
Manual of physical and vocal training. 11785 S
MONROE, Lewis R (ed)
Public and parlor readings.
Dialogues and dramas. 9908 P
Humorous. 9909 P
Miscellaneous. 99096 P
Young folks' readings. 9907 P
MONTAIGNE, M E de
Essays of. 489 E

MONTBARD, G
  Among the Moors; sketches of oriental life. 12481 H
MONTEIRO, Joachim
  Angola and the river Congo. 3301 V
MONTGOMERY, Walter
  Boys of the Sierras. 5680 J
MONTRESOR, F F
  At the Cross-roads. 10900 F
  The one who looked on. 10134 F
MOODEY, Martha L
  Alan Thorne. 5522 F
MOODY, Helen Watterson
  The unquiet sex. 11921 E
MOOR, C R
  Memorial of Sumner Ellis. 8759 B
MOORE, Charles L
  Book of day dreams. 7642 P
MOORE, Francis C
  How to build a home. 10799 A
MOORE, Frank
  Civil war in song and story. 9392 L
  Rebellion record, 3 vols. 4017 H
  Women of the war. 115 B
MOORE, James
  Kilpatrick and our cavalry. 8949 B
MOORE, Joseph W
  Picturesque Washington. 6898 V
MOORE, R
  Universal assistant and complete mechanic. 11872 R
MOORE, Thomas
  Ireland, Histor of, 2 vols. 4163 H
  Poetical works of. 8422 P
  Travels of an Irish gentleman. 6231V
MOOREHEAD, Warren R
  Warneta, the Sioux. 5961 F
MORANT, G F
  Poultry for profit. 11399 A
MORE, George H
  Treason of Charles Lee. 101 H
MOREY, William C
  Outlines of Roman law. 9565 H
MORFILL, W R
  Russia. Story of. 9182 H
MORGAN, Appleton
  Digesta Shakespeareana. 7970 R
  Shakespeare in fact and in criticism. 661 E
MORGAN, C Lloyd
  Psychology for teachers. 10357 EE
MORGAN, Horace H
  Historical World's Columbian Exposition. 9063 H
MORGAN, Lady
  O'Briens and O'Flahertys, 2 vols. 3052 F

MORGAN, T J
  Educational mosaics; a collection of thoughts bearing on the educational questions of the day. 4858 EE
MORIER, James
  Abel Allnutt. 2763 F
  Ayesha. 2762 F
  Hajji Baba of Ispahan. 2764 F
  Mirza. 2765 F
  Zahrab, the hostage. 2761 F
MORISON, James Cotter
  Gibbon, Life of. 6695 B
  Macaulay, Life of. 6702 B
  Saint Bernard, Life and times of. 6865 B
MORLEY, Henry (ed)
  Early prose romances. 6326 F
  English prose writings of John Milton. 11411 F
MORLEY, John
  Critical miscellanies, 3 vols. 11225 E
  Edmund Burke, Life of. 6676 B
  Richard Cobden, 2 vols. 12144 B
  Voltaire, Life of. 1357 B
  Walpole, Life of. 6781 B
MORLEY, Margaret Warner
  Song of life. 7641
MORRIS, Charles
  Aryan race; its origin and achievements. 10569 H
  Civilization, 2 vols. 11392 H
MORRIS, Charles (ed)
  Half-hours of American history, 2 vols. 11392 H
MORRIS, E E
  Age of Anne. 5490 H
  Early Hanoverians. 4416 H
MOORE, George
  Impressions and opinions. 11373 E
MORRIS, George S
  Kant's critique of pure reason.8086EE
MORRIS, Harrison S
  Tales from ten poets, 3 vols. 7684 F
MORRIS, Lewis
  Epic of Hades. 9542 P
  Works of. 9547 P
MORRIS, Mowbray
  Montrose. 6784 B
MORRIS, William
  Earthly paradise, 3 vols. 8212 P
  Lovers of Gudrom. 7116 P
  News from nowhere. 8238 F
  Socialism; its growth and outcome. 9160 SS
  Story of glittering plain, etc.7174 F
MORRIS, William O'C
  French revolution and first empire. 5492 H

MORRISON, W Douglas
Female offender. 10036 SS
Jews under Roman rule. 9117 11
Juvenile offenders. 10112 SS
MORROW, John T
Arithmetic of magnetism and elec-
tricity. 9878 S
MORSE, Edward S
Japanese homes and their surround-
ings. 3039 H
MORSE, John T Jr
John Adams. 177 B
John Quincy Adams. 178 B
Oliver Wendell Holmes, Life and
letters of. 9740 B
Thomas Jefferson, 179 B
MORSE, Lucy G
Chuzzles. The. 5635 J
MORTON, Mary A
Abbie Saunders; story of pioneer
days in Minnesota. 8403 B
MORTON, Samuel
Types of mankind. 1450 S
MOSBY, John S
My reminiscences. 4409 H
MOSCHELES, Felix
Letters of Felix Mendelssohn. 6360E
MOSENTHAL, Julius
Ostriches and ostrich farming.5016 A
MOSES, Bernard
Democracy and social growth in
America. 12557 SS
Establishment of Spanish rule in
America. 12558 SS
MOTLEY, John L
John Barneveld, Life of. 2 vols. 103B
Rise of the Dutch republic, 3 vols.
4022 H
United Netherlands, History of.
5344 H
MOTT, E H
Pike county folks. 3086 F
MOTTELAY and Copeland (ed)
Soldier in our Civil war, 2 vols.
7469 H
MOULTON, Louise Chandler
Lazy tours in Spain and elsewhere.
10364 V
MOULTON, Richard G
Ancient classical drama. 6071 EE
Shakespeare as a dramatic artist.
10158 EE
MOZOOMDAR, P C
Oriental Christ, The. 6725 RE
MOXOM, Philip Stafford
Religion of hope. 10408 RE
MUGGE, Theodore
Afraza. 962 F

MUHLBACH, L (pseud of Mrs C M
Mundt)
Andreas Hofer. 2617 F
Berlin and Sans-souci. 2620 F
Daughter of an empress. 6961 F
Empress Josephine. 2613 F
Frederick the Great and his court.
2610 F
Frederick the Great and his family.
4818 F
Goethe and Schiller. 2616 F
Henry the Eighth and his court.
4774 F
Joseph the Second and his court.
2608 F
Louise of Prussia. 2614 F
Marie Antoinette and her son. 2607F
Merchant of Berlin. 2621 F
Mohammed Ali and his house. 2606F
Napoleon and Blucher. 2618 F
Old Fritz and the new era. 2619 F
Prince Eugene and his times. 2615F
Queen Hortense. 2612 F
MUIR, John
Mountains of California. • 9280 V
MULFORD, Prentice
Your forces and how to use them.
7124 E
MULLER, Donizetti
Links from broken chains. 8789 F
MULLER, F Max
Auld lang syne. 11902 E
Biographies of words. etc. 515 EE
Memories; a story of German love.
7804 F
Science of language. 2 vols. 1493 EE
Science of thought. 2 vols. 7233 E
MRS MULOCK (pseud of Mrs Dinal
M Craik)
Agatha's husband. 2464 F
Brave lady. 2310 F
Christian's mistake. 10703 F
Hannah. 2309 F
Head of the family. 2463 F
John Halifax, gentleman. 9108 F
Life for a life. 5297 F
Miss Tommy. 2213 F
Mistress and maid. 5300 F
My mother and I. 5301 F

Noble life. 5298 F
Sermons out of church. 6381 RE
Woman s thoughts about woman.
5925 E
Young Mrs Jardine. 6305 F
MUNDT, Mrs C M (see Muhlbach, L)
Mungen, Theodore T
On the threshold. 7240 EE
MUNROE, James P
Educational ideal. 9758 EE
MUNROE, Kirk
At war with Pontiac. 8509 J
Cab and caboose. 7767 J
Flamingo feather. 3416 J
Golden days of '49. 5426 J
Ready rangers. 11934 J
Under orders. 11731 J
Wakulla. 2727 J
White conquerors. 8005 J
With Crockett and Bowie. 10738 J
MUNSON, James E
Complete phonographer. 11163 EE
MURDOCK, Harold
Reconstruction of Europe. 9536 H
MURFREE, Fannie N D
Felicia. 8547 F
MURFREE, M N (see Craddock,
Charles Egbert)
MURRAY, Alexander
Manual of mythology. 6732 F
MURRAY, Amelia
Letters from United States and Canada. 3271 V
MURRAY, David
Japan, Story of. 8488 H
MURRAY, David Christie
Aunt Rachel. 8646 F
He fell among thieves. 6840 F
In direst peril. 8162 F
Martyred fool. 9374 F
Schwartz. 6770 F
Weaker vessel. 6769 F
MURRAY, George
Introduction to the study of seaweeds. 12222 S
MURRAY, Gilbert
Ancient Greek literature, History of.
10376 EE
MURRAY, Hugh
Encyclopedia of all nations, 2 vols.
9454 R
MURRAY, John
Autobiography. 8767 B
MURREY, Thomas J
Salads and sauces. 9769 A
MUSICK, John R
Columbia. 5717 F
Estevan. 7520 F

Pocohontas. 7521 F
St Augustine. 7518 F
MYERS, F W H
Essays—classical. 9581 E
Wordsworth, Life of. 6700 B
MYERS, P V N
Outlines of mediaeval and modern
history. 8217 H
MYERS, Sarah A (trans)
Martin's natural history. 1501 S
MYRICK, Herbert
Sugar; a new and profitable industry.
10332 A

NADAILLAC, Marquis de
Prehistoric America. 7725 H
NAEGELI, Carl and S Schwendener
Microscope in theory and practise.
7092 S
NANSEN, Fridtjof
Farthest north, 2 vols. 10345 V
First crossing of Greenland. 10311 V
NANSON, Charles Henry
Wanderings of Aeneas and the
founding of Rome. 8124 F
NAPHEGJI, G M D
Ghardaia; adventure in oasis of Sahara. 3267 V
NASH, H S
Genesis of the social conscience.
10750 RE
NEAL, John
An autobiography. 945 B
NEEDELL, Mrs John H
Julian Karslake's secret. 4752 F
Noel Chetwynd's fall. 7171 F
NEELE, Henry
Romance of history; England. 4411H
— — France. 4410 H
— — India. 4413 H
— — Italy. 4412 H
— — Spain. 4414 H
NEELY
Parliament of religions. 8073 RE
NERUIS, John L
China and the Chinese. 3333 H
NESBIT, M L
Grammarland, or grammar in fun.
8118 J
NEWCOME, S P
Pleasant pages for young people.
941 J
NEWELL, C M
Kamehameha. 2575 F
NEWELL, Mrs Harriet
Life and writings of. 9341 B
NEWELL, N H
Orpheus C Kerr papers, 3 vols.6210L

NEWMAN, J H (cardinal)
Apologia pro vita sua. 6622 RE
Callista; tale of the third century.
743 F
NEWTON, J R
Modern Bethesda. 11548 F
NICHOL, John
Byron, Life of. 6674 B
Francis Bacon; his life and philosophy, 2 vols. 7627 B
NICHOLS, Mrs C (see Bronte, Charlotte)
NICHOLS, James R
Whence, what, where. 8872 RE
NICOLAY, John G and John Hay
Abraham Lincoln; a history, 10 vols.
6010 H
NICOLAY, John G and John Hay (ed)
Letters, speeches and state papers of
Abraham Lincoln, 2 vols. 8682 E
NICOLL, Henry
Great movements and those who
achieved them. 1368 H
NIEBUHR, B G
Lectures on the history of Rome.
3 vols. 6199 H
NINDE, Mary L
We two alone in Europe. 10162 V
NITSCH, Mrs Helen (see Owen, Catherine)
NOKAED, Dixie
Hidden truth. 10742 RE
NORDAU, Max
Degeneration. 10428 S
NORDENSKIOLD, A E
Voyage of the Vega. 3259 V
NORDHOFF, Charles
California for health, pleasure and
residence. 3288 V
Whaling and fishing. 11638 V
NORMAN, C B
Armenia and the campaign of 1877.
8903 H
NORMAN, B M
Rambles in Yucatan. 3269 V
NORMAN, Henry
People and politics of the far east.
9574 H
Real Japan. 7621 H
NORRIS, Frank
Moran of the Lady Letty. 12339 F
NORRIS, W E
Bachelor's blunder. 10783 F
Dancer in yellow. 9977 F
Fight for the crown. 11080 F
Misadventure. 6960 F
No new thing. 7122 F

NORTH, Marianne
Recollections of a happy life, 2 vols.
8501 B
Some further recollections of a happy
life. 7953 B
NORTON, Charles Eliot
New life of Dante Anghicre. 11424 B
NORTON, Charles Eliot (ed)
Letters of James Russell Lowell, 2
vols. 8036 E
Orations and addresses of George W.
Curtis, 3 vols. 8241 E
NORTON, Charles L
Hand book of Florida. 6544 V
NORTON, S F
Ten men of money island. 7537 SS
NOYES, Henry D
Diseases of the eye. 8726 S
NYE, Bill (pseud of Edgar Wilson
Nye)
Baled hay. 4792 F
England, History of. 9905 H
United States, History of. 6878 H
NYNE, Atey
Wilmot's child. 9388 F

OKEY, Alexander F
Home grounds. 8937 A
OBER, F A
Crusoe's island; a bird hunter's
story. 11036 J
Travels in Mexico. 3316 V
O'BRIEN, D H
My adventures during the late war.
5240 V
O'BRIEN, R Barry
Charles Stuart Parnell, Life of.
12641 B
OCKLEY, Simon
Improvement of human reason.
5055 EE
Saracens, History of the, 2 vols.
4872 H
O'CONNOR, T P
Parnell movement. 8916 H
O'DONOGHUE, Mrs Power
Ladies on horseback. 8908 A
OHNET, Georges
Doctor Rameau. 9023 F

Ironmaster. 5030 F
OLCOTT, Henry S
Buddhist catechism. 2060 RE
OLIPHANT, Laurence
St Elgin's mission to China and
Japan, 1857-9. 3298 V
Scientific religion. 7284 RE
OLIPHANT, Margaret
Laurence Oliphant, Memoir of the
life of. 6533 B
OLIPHANT, Mrs M O W
Dante, Life of. 11603 B
House in Bloomsbury. 11999 F
Jeanne D'Arc. 11191 B
Jerusalem, the holy city. 11357 H
Makers of Florence. 5406 H
Makers of modern Rome. 9822 H
Makers of Venice. 5407 H
Royal Edinburgh. 6069 H
Sheridan, Life of. 6680 B
Victorian age of English literature.
OLIPHANT, T L K
Sources of standard English. 3049EE
OLIVER, Samuel P
Off and on duty. 3306 V
OLLIVANT, Alfred
Bob, son of battle. 12635 F
OLLIVANT, Joseph Earle
Hine Moa, the Maori maiden. 5060 F
OLMSTEAD, Dwight H
Protestant faith, 2 vols. 12346 RE
OLMSTEAD, Frederick L
Journey in the seaboard slave states.
748 V
Journey through Texas. 3277 V
OMAN, C W C
Byzantine empire, Story of. 7427 H
OMAN, C W
Warwick, the king-maker. 6785 B
O'MEARA, Kathleen
Narka, the nihilist. 3129 F
OPPERT, Ernest
A forbidden land: voyages to Corea.
3343 V
OPTIC, Oliver   etaoi aoi
OPTIC, Oliver (pseud of W T Adams)
Young America abroad series.
Outward bound. 12083 J
Shamrock and thistle. 12495 J
Red cross. 12084 J
Dikes and ditches. 12466 J
Palace and cottage. 12085 J
Down the Rhine. 12086 J
Up the Baltic. 12078 J
Northern lands. 12077 J
Cross and crescent. 12081 J
Sunny shores. 12080 J
Vine and olive. 12079 J

Isles of the sea. 12082 J
O'REGAN, William
John Curran, Memoirs of life of.6221B
O'RELL, Max (pseud of Paul Blouet)
English pharisses, French crocodiles,
7234
Frenchman in America. 7075
Jacque Bonhomme. 6378
John Bull and his daughters. 3036
John Bull and his island. 3037
John Bull and his womankind. 6635
ORMSBEE, Agnes Bailey
House comfortable. 7368 A
ORPEN, Mrs Goddard
Perfection city. 10471 F
Stories about famous precious stones
7118 F
ORR, Ellen
Portraits and silhouettes of musi-
cians. 10870 B
ORR, Mrs Sutherland
Handbook of the works of Robert
Browning. 11435 R
Robert Browning, Life and letters of.
7105 B
ORRED, Meta
Glamour. 10460 F
ORTON, James
Andes and the Amazon. 3292 V
Underground treasures. 6403 S
OSGOOD, Mrs M A
Black Cato. 11804 B
OSSOLI, Margaret Fuller
Art, literature and the drama.11447E
OSTROM, Kurre W
Massage and the original Swedish
movements. 7069 S
OSWALD, Philip L
Summerland sketches. 3293 V
OTIS, James (pseud of James Otis
Kaler)
Charming Sally; a tale of 1765.12304J
District messenger boy and a necktie
party. 11926 J
Jenny Wren's boarding house. 12108J
Josiah in New York. 12300 J
Left behind; or ten days a newsboy.
12107 J
Mr Stubb's brother; sequel to Toby
Tyler. 12097 J
Morgan, the Jersey spy. 12362 J
Toby Tyler; or ten weeks with a
circus. 12096 J
With Lafayette at Yorktown. 12361J
With Warren at Bunker Hill. 12363 J
With Washington at Monmouth.
12364 J

OUIDA (pseud of Louisa de la Rame)
Ariadne. 2133 F
Beatrice Boville. 2134 F
Bimbi; stories for children. 2137 J
Chandos. 12315 F
Dog of Flanders. 12291 F
Granville de Vigne. 12314 F
Massarenes. 10553 F
Pascarel. 12322 F
Puck. 12321 F
Signa. 12320 F
Tricotrin. 12318 F
Two offenders. 12323 F
Under two flags. 12313 F
Village commune. 12317 F
Wanda. 12319 F
OVERMAN, Federick
Practical mineralogy. 262 S
OVERTON, Frank
Applied physiology. 11742 S
OWEN, Catherine (pseud of Mrs Helen
Nitsch)
Choice cookery. 8301 A
Gentle bread-winners. 6275 F
Molly Bishop's family. 10509 F
Ten dollars enough. 1812 A
OWEN, Edith
Rose and Josephine. 5076 F
OWEN, Robert Dale
Footfalls on the boundary of another
world. 11505 RE

PACKARD, A S
Entomology for beginners. 11159 S
Guide to the study of insects. 11210 S
Labrador coast. 7081 V
Zoology. 1527 S
PADDOCK, Mrs
Fate of Madam la Tour. 2547 F
PAEZ, Don Ramon
Wild scenes in South America. 3394V
PAGE, David
Advanced textbook of geology.11725S
PAGE, H A
Thoreau, his life and aims. 11444 B
PAGE, Jesse
C H Spurgeon, his life and ministry.
7800 B
PAGE, Thomas Nelson
Elsket and other stories. 6743 F
On New Found river. 7143 F
Two prisoners. 11092 J
PAIGE, Lucius R
Commentary of the Acts. 8738 RE
— on Corinthians. 8740 RE
— — Galatians to Judges. 8741 RE
— — Luke. 8737 RE
— — John. 8738 RE

— — New Testament. 8736 RE
— — Revelations. 8742 RE
— — Romans. 8739 RE
PAIN, Barry
Stories and interludes. 7682 F
PAINE, Caroline
Tent and harem. 3276 V
PAINE, Robert Treat
Works of. 6216 B
PAINE, Thomas
Age of reason. 10880 EE
PALFREY, John G
New England, History of, 3 vols.
552 H
PALGRAVE, Francis T (ed)
Golden treasury. 7221 P
Selections from lyrical poems of
Robert Herrick. 6855 P
PALGRAVE, W G
Central and eastern Arabia. 3282 V
PALMER, Charles F
Inebriety, its source, prevention and
cure. 11920 S
PALMER, Julius A (ed)
Mushrooms of America, edible and
poisonous. 1699 A
PALMER, Linda
One day's weaving. 822 J
PALOU, Francis
Padre Junipero Serra, Life of. 6739B
PANSY (pseud of Mrs I M Alden)
Chautauqua girls at home. 5306 J
Chrissy's endeavor. 12299 J
Cunning workmen. 5307 J
Doctor Dean's way. 5308 J
Ester Ried. 12088 J
Ester Ried yet speaking. 12087 J
Grandfather's darling. 5309 J
Her associate members. 12089 J
Interrupted. 6261 J
Judge Burnham's daughter. 12298 J
Pansy scrap book. 5311 J
Spun from fact. 5312 J
Those boys. 6262 J
What she said. 5313 J
PARIS J A
On diet and the digestive organs.
1529 S
PARKER, Francis W
Uncle Robert's visit. 10974 J
PARKER, Gilbert
Battle of the strong. 12583 F
Chief factor. 8171 F
Mrs Falchion. 11924 F
Pierre and his people. 8170 F
Pomp of the Lavilettes. 10354 F
Seats of the mighty. 10149 F
Trail of the sword. 11491 F

Translation of a savage. 11461 F
Trespasser. 11481 F
PARKER, John
A B C of Gothic architecture. 9170 A
PARKER, Joseph
Ecce Deus. 4848
PARKER, J Marsh
Thomas Edison and Samuel Morse. 7256 S
PARKER, T Jeffrey
Course of instruction in zootomy. 10491 S
Textbook on zoology, 2 vols. 11011 S
PARKES, Edmund A
Manual of practical hygiene, 2 vols. 8703 S
PARKES, S H
Unfinished worlds. 1448 S
PARKHURST, Charles
Our fight with Tammany. 9138 SS
Talks to young men. 10374 EE
Talks to young women. 10375 EE
PARKMAN, Francis
Conspiracy of Pontiac, 2 vols. 4190 H
France and England in North America. 8220 H
Fontenac and New France. 4186 H
Half century of conflict, 2 vols. 8221 H
Jesuits in North America. 4189 H
La Salle and the discovery of the great west. 4184 H
Montcalm and Wolfe, 2 vols. 4151 H
Old regime in Canada. 4185 H
Oregon trail. 4181 H
Pioneers of France in the new world. 4187 H
PARR, Mrs Louise
Dorothy Fox.
Squire, The. 7359 F
PARRY, C Hubert
Art of music. 8672 A
PARSONS, Samuel
Landscape gardening. 11096 A
PARSONS, Theophilus
Essays of. 463 E
PARTON, James
Aaron Burr, Life of. 2 vols. 7797 B
Andrew Jackson, Life of. 3 vols. 8919 B
Benjamin Franklin, Life of. 130 B
Butler at New Orleans. 5255 H
Captains of industry. 2218 J
Thomas Jefferson. 154 B
Washington Irving. 1287 B
PASTON, George
Career of Canada. 10412 H
PATER, Walter
Greek studies. 9194 E

Marius, the epicurean. 12237 F
Plato and Platonism. 7719 E
Renaissance. 9181 E
PATON, James
John G Paton, Story of. 12491 J
PATTISON, Mark
Milton
PATTON, A A
Voice as an instrument. 11597 EE
PATTON, J Harris
Democratic party. 199 SS
PAVY, F W
Food and dietics. 8720 S
PAYN, James
At her mercy. 5163 F
Best of husbands. 5169 F
Canon's ward. 5138 F
Cecil's tryst. 5164 F
County family. 5158 F
Fallen fortunes. 5172 F
Found dead. 5170 F
Gwendolen's harvest. 5194 F
Humorous stories. 5192 F
Kit; a memory. 5139 F
Marine residence. 5197 F
Married beneath him. 5193 F
Not wooed but won. 5199 F
One of the family. 2458 F
Some private views. 5201 F
Two hundred pounds reward. 5204F
PAYNE, E J
Works of Burke, 3 vols. 8827 SS
PAYNE, J B (ed)
Haydn's dictionary of biography. 1672 R
PAYNE, Will
Jerry, the dreamer. 9824 F
PAYNE, William Morton
Little leaders. 12007 E
PAYSON, Edward
Doctor Tom. 11817 F
PEABODY, A P
Christianity, the religion of nature. 363 RE
PEACOCK, J Love
Headlong hall. 6838 F
Maid Marian. 6835 F
Melin court. 6836 F
Misfortunes of Elphin. 6834 F
Nightmare abbey. 6833 F
PEALE, R S (ed)
Home library of useful knowledge. 4714 R
PEARS, Edwin
Fall of Constantinople. 4279 H
PEARSON, Charles H
National life and character; a forecast. 12217 S

PEARY, Robert E
Northward over the great ice, 2 vols.
12341 V
PEATTIE, Ella W
America, Story of. 5916 H
PECK, Harry Thurston (ed)
Harper's dictionary of classical lit-
erature and antiquities. 11049 R
PECK, Jesse T
True woman, The. 1151 E
PECKE, Jesse
Central idea of christianity. 597 RE
PEEBLES, J M
Immortality and our employment
hereafter. 1218 RE
PELHAM, H F
Outlines of Roman history. 10500 H
PELLOW, George
John Jay, Life of. 9114 F
PEMBERTON, Max
Phantom army, The. 12582 F
PENDLETON, Edmund
Complication in hearts. 11579 F
Virginia inheritance. 9043 F
PENDLETON, Louis
Sons of Ham. 9134 F
Wedding garment. 9105 F
PEPPER, John Henry
Boys' book of metals. 12115 J
Scientific amusements. 8106 J
PERCY, Thomas
Relics of ancient English poetry.
7222 P
PERELAER, M T H
Ran away from the Dutch—Borneo.
3384 V
PERKINS, Eli (see Landon, Melville
D)
PERKINS, F B
Charles Dickens; a sketch of his life
and works. 10401 B
PERRY, Nora
Another flock of girls. 7369 J
Flock of girls. 793 J
Flock of girls and boys. 9506 J
Hope Denham. 8777 J
Rosebud garden of grils. 9651 J
Three little daughters of the revolu-
tion. 10032 J
Youngest Miss Lorton. 10120 J
PESCHEL, Oscar
Races of man, The. 1451 S
PETERMAN, Alexander L
Elements of civil government.9165SS
PETERSON, Alexander L
Girls' own indoor book. 5457 J
Girls' own outdoor book. 5458 J

PETERS, De Witt C
Pioneer life and frontier adventures.
3401 V
PETERSON, Henry
Modern Job, The. 11691 RE
PETO, S M
Resources and prospects of America.
4709 H
PETROFF, P
Ante-mortem depositions. 12016 S
PETTIGREW, T J
Superstition connected with the his-
tory and practise of medicine and
surgery. 5230 S
PHELPS, E S (now Mrs H D Ward)
A singular life. 9422 F
Avis, Story of. 5317 F
Beyond the gates. 1197 F
Burglars in paradise. 3142 F
Doctor Zay. 5709 F
Donald Marcy. 7785 F
Friends; a duet. 5708 F
Gates ajar. 815 F
Gates between. 3186 F
Gipsy books
Gipsy Breynton
Gipsy's cousin Jay. 12292 J
Gipsy's sewing and reaping. 12393 J
Gipsy's year at the Golden Crescent.
12294 J
Hedged in. 5605 F
Jack, the fisherman. 5137 F
Madonna of the tubs. 3105 F
Men, women and ghosts. 5314 F
Old maids' paradise. 3142 F
Sealed orders. 5315 F
Silent partner. 5316 F
Songs of the silent world. 34 P
Story of Jesus Christ. 10897 B
PHELPS, E S Ward and H D Ward
Come forth. 6051 F
Master of the magicians. F
PHELPS, Mrs Lincoln
Botany for beginners. 4828 S
PHILLIMORE, Catherine Mary
Tra Angelico, et als. 7711 B
PHILLIP, Robert
Devotional guide. 376 RE
PHILLIPS, L M
Miskel; a novel. 11750 F
PHILLIPS, Mary E
Reminiscences of William Wetmore
Story. 11426 B
PHILLIPS, Wendell
Speeches and lectures of. 491 E
PHILLPOTS, Eden
Folly and fresh air. 7463 E

PICARD, George H
A mission flower. 11516 F
O.d Boniface. 3150 F
PICK, Bernhard
The talmud; what it is. 5785 RE
PICKARD, Samuel T
John Greenleaf Whittier, Life and letters of, 2 vols. 8812 B
PICTON, J Allanson
Mystery of matter.1415 S
PIERCE, Edward L
Charles Sumner; memoirs and letters of, 2 vols. 8673 B
PIERCE, Gilbert
Dickens dictionary. 6436 L
PIERSON, Emma C
Gutenberg and the art of printing. 2016 A
PIFFARD, Henry G
Materia medica. 8722 S
PIKE, G Holden
Charles Haddon Spurgeon, Life of. 7529 B
PIKE, Nicholas
Sub-tropical rambles. 3266 V
PINKERTON, Allan
Spy of the rebellion. 4199 H
PITMAN, C B (trans)
Earthquakes. 7311 S
PITTENGER, William
Extempore speech; how to acquire and practise it. 11753 EE
PLANCHE, J R
Pursivant of arms. 5223 R
PLATT, James
Money. 7303 SS
PLON, Eugene
Thorvaldsen, his life and works. 11429 B
PLUMPTRE, E H
Tragedies of Aeschylos. 10876 P
Tragedies of Sophocles. 10877 P
PLUNKETT, Mrs H M
Josiah Gilbert Holland. 8347 B
PLYMPTON, A C
Betty, a butterfly. 8238 J
Dear daughter Dorothy. 8076 J
Little sister to Winifred. 8077 J
Robin's recruit. 8075 J
POE, Edgar Allen
Assignation and other tales. 3001 F
Narrative of A Gordon Pym. 1190 F
Poems and essays of. 10164 P
POLKS, Elise
Musical sketches. 11736 A
POLLARD, Alfred W
English miracle plays. 6505 EE

POLLARD, E A
Last year of the war. 4003 H
Second year of the war. 4002 H
The lost cause. 4005 H
POLLARD, Josephine
Bible and its story. 11301 J
Our hero general, U S Grant. 8968 B
POOL, Maria L
Dally. 8649 F
Mrs Gerald. 12122 F
Out of step. 9289 F
Redbridge neighborhood. 11021 F
Roweny in Boston. 7833 F
Two Salomes. 9288 F
POOLE, Stanley Lane
Barbary corsairs, Story of. 9115 H
Moors, Story of the. 4353 H
People of Turkey, 2 vols. 4336 H
Turkey. 4341 H
POOR, Agnes Blake
Boston neighbors in town and out. 11886 F
POORTEN, Schwartz J M W van der
see Maartens, Maarten,
POPE, Alexander
Poetical works of, 3 vols. 6629 P
PORRITT, Edward
Englishman at home. 8490 V
PORTER, Admiral
Adventures of Harry Marline. 5795 J
PORTER, H C (trans
Text book of botany. 11466 S
PORTER, James
Revised compedium of Methodism. 17701 RE
PORTER, Jane
Scottish chiefs. 2269 F
Thaddeus of Warsaw. 770 F
PORTER, Noah
Books and reading. 6719 EE
Elements of intellectual science. 456 EE
Fifteen years in the chapel of Yale college. 342 EE
Kant's ethics; a critical exposition. 8085 EE
PORTER, Robert F
Population and resources of Alaska. 8423 V
PORTER, Rose
The years that are told. 11507 F
POST, C W
I am well; The modern practise of natural suggestion. 12646 L
POTTER, Helen
Impersonations. 7658 EE
POTTER, Henry Codman
The scholar and the state. 10797 EE

POULET, Alfred
Foreign bodies in surgical practise. 8699 S

POULTON, Edward B
Charles Darwin and the theory of natural selection. 10189 B

POWELL, E P
Our heredity from God. 12276 S

POWER, Mrs S D
Children's etiquette. 462 J

POWERS, Laura Bride
Story of the missions of California. 8337 H

POYSER, Arthur W
Magnetism and electricity. 6529 S

PRAED, Mrs Campbell
Romance of a Chalet. 11797 F

PRAEGER, F
Wagner as I knew him. 7379 B

PRATT, Charlie and Ella (ed)
Little men and women. 11290 J

PRATT, Maria L
American history stories, 4 vols. 8803 J
Classic stories for language lessons. 9529 EE
Legends of Norseland. 9523 J
New calisthenics; a manual of health and beauty. 11204 S
Stories of colonial children. 9521 J

PRENTICE, Archibald
Tour in United States. 5924 V

PRENTICE, George D
Poems of. 74 P

PRENTISS, Elizabeth
Aunt Jane's hero. 5303 F
Flower of the family. 8478 F
Fred, Maria and me. 2034 F
Home at Greylock. 5304 F
Life and letters of. 11549 B
Stepping heavenward. 5305 F

PRENTISS, Henry M
Great polar current. 12336 S

PRESCOTT, E Livingston
Apotheosis of Mr Tyrawly. 9595 F

PRESCOTT, W H
Biographical and critical miscellanies. 4312 E
Ferdinand and Isabella, 3 vols. 4298H
Conquest of Mexico, 3 vols. 4301 H
Conquest of Peru, 2 vols. 4304 H
Philip the Second, 3 vols. 4306 H

PRESTON, Harriet Waters
Private life of the Romans. 9537 H

PRESTON, Howard W
Documents illustrative of American history, 1606-1863. 12166 H

PREYER, W
Mind of the child, 2 vols. 5424 EE

PRIME, E D G
Around the world. 3225 V
Forty years in the Turkish empire. 3321 V

PRIME, S I
Autobiography. 3424 B

PRIME, W C
Along the New England roads7599 E
Boat life in Egypt and Nubia. 3284V
I go a-fishing. 7452 E

PRINGLE, Andrew
Optical lantern for instruction and amusement. 9861 A

PROAL, Louis
Political crime. 12008 SS

PROCTOR, Richard A
Expanse of heaven. 10467 S
Light science for leisure hours. 8235 S
Moon, The. 7569 S
New star atlas. 6723 S
Pleasant ways in science. 8234 S
Stars in the seasons. 7570 S

PROTHERO, Rowland
Dean Stanley, Life and correspondence of, 2 vols. 8263 B

PRUDDEN, T Mitchell
Bacteria, Story of the. 7693 S

PRYDE, David
Highways of literature. 7245 EE

PUMPELLY, Raphael
Across America and Asia. 3270 V

PUSEY, E B
Confessions of St Augustine.. 317 E

PUTNAM, Eleanor
Woodland wooing. 6317 F

PUTNAM, George I
On the offensive. 8243 F

PUTNAM, M Louise
Abraham Lincoln, Children's life of. 7397 J

PYLE, Howard
Garden behind the moon. 9359 J
Rose of paradise. 3158 F
Story of Jack Ballister's fortunes. 9434 J

"Q" (pseud of A T Q Couch)
Astonishing history of Troy town. 11910 F
Blue pavilions. 11906 F
Dead man's rock. 11892 F
Delectable Duchy: stories, studies and sketches. 11530 F
Noughts and crosses. 11879 F

QUATREFAGES, A de
Human species. 1407 S
Pygmies. 9369 S
QUINBY, G W
Heaven our home. 405 RE
QUINCY, Josiah
Figures of the past. 11760 E

RAE, John
Contemporary socialism. 210 SS
RAGOZIN, L A
Assyria, Story of. 536 H
Chaldea, Story of. 4347 H
Media, Babylonia and Persia. 4343 H
Vedic India. 9191 H
RAIFE, Raymond
Sheik's white slave. 10454 F
RALEIGH, Walter
Robert Louis Stevenson. 11441 B
RALPH, Julian
Alone in China and other stories.
10385 F
On Canada's frontier. 7375 V
RAMABAI, Pundita
High cast Hindu woman. 4365 H
RAMBAUD, Alfred
Russia, History of. 3 vols. 4292 H
RAMEY, W Sanford
Kings of the battlefield. 11775 B
RAMSAY, C B
Reminiscences of Scottish life and
character. 7130 H
RAMSAY, James H
Lancaster and York. 2 vols. 12484 H
RAMSAY, Mrs
Summer in Spain. 5021 V
RAMSAY, W M
Impressions of Turkey during twelve
years' wanderings. 12476 V
RAND, Edward Sprague
Seventy-five popular flowers. 11675S
Rhododendron and American plants.
12534 S
RANDOLPH, John
H Adams. Life of. 187 B
H. Garland, Life of. 2 vols. 107 B
RANKE, L von
The popes; their church and state,
History of. 3 vols. 10533 H
Universal history.
RANNEY, Ambrose
Lectures on nervous diseases. 9090 S
RANSOME, Cyril
Rise of constitutional government in
England. 11415 H
RANSOME, Cyril (ed)
Battles of Frederick the Great.7608H

RATTAN, Volney
California flora. 10993 S
Exercises in botany. 10804 S
RAUM, George E
Tour around the world. 3306 V
RAWLINSON, George
Ancient Egypt, History of, 2 vols.
10113 H
Five great monarchies, 3 vols.4229 H
Manual of ancient history. 11542 H
Moses, his life and times. 1248 RE
Origin of nations. 7703 H
Partha, Story of. 9499 H
Phoenicia. 5373 H
Seventh great oriental monarchy.
4233 H
RAY, Anna Chapin
Cadets of Flemming hall. 7901 J
Half a dozen boys. 5831 J
Half a dozen girls. 7900 J
In Blue Creek canon. 7399 J
RAYMOND, Evelyn
Mixed pickles. 12309 J
RAYMOND, George Lansing
Genesis of art form. 9318 A
RAYMOND, Henry J
Abraham Lincoln, Life and public
services of. 9449 B
RAYMOND, Walter
Charity chance. 10372 F
RAYNER, E
Free to serve. 12076 F
READ, Opie P (Arkansaw Traveller)
An Arkansas planter. 10446 F
Emmet Bonlore. 8668 F
Jucklins, The. 10498 F
Kentucky colonel. 12117 F
Up Terrapin river. 8666 F
Waters of Caney Fork. 12568 F
READE, Charles
Cloister and health. 10426 F
Griffith Gaunt. 5167 F
Hard cash. 701 F
It is never to late to mend. 10415 F
New pastoral. 70 P
Peg Woffington. 2453 F
Put yourself in his place. 2382 F
Simpleton. 12438 F
REAL, Anthony (pseud of Fernand-
Michel)
Story of the stick. 246 F
REARDON, T H
Petriarch and other essays. 8101 E
RECLUS, Elisee
Africa, 4 vols. 5668 H
Asia, 4 vols. 5664 H
Europe, 4 vols. 4676 H
History of a mountain. 1498 S

North America, 3 vols. 6038 H
Oceanica. 5735 H
South America, 2 vols. 8686 H
REDDALL, Henry F
Fact, fancy and fable. 5638 R
REDDEN, Laura C
Sounds from secret chambers. 83 P
REED, Alonzo and B Kellogg
English composition and rhetoric.
11836 EE ·
REED, Elizabeth
Hindu literature; the ancient books
of India. 6558 EE
REED, S B
House plans for everybody. 1790 A
REEDER, A P
Around the golden deep. 6325 F
REES, James
Edwin Forrest, Life of. 148 B
REES, J Rogers
Diversions of a book worm. 7595EE
Pleasures of a book worm. 7594 EE
REEVE, Charles H
Prison question. 7516 SS
REEVES, John
Rothschilds, The. 7408 B
REID, Christian (pseud of Mrs F C F
Fiernan)
Miss Churchill. 3159 F
Roslyn's fortune. 9017 F
REID, Mayne
Desert home. 12104 J
Flag of distress. 12103 J
Lone ranch. 6263 J
Odd people. 12468 J
Ran away to sea. 12105 J
Scalp hunters. 10623 J
Stories about animals. 10996 J
REMSEN, Ira
Inorganic chemistry. 9879 S
REMUS, Uncle (pseud; see Harris,
Joel Chandler)
RENAN, Ernest
Future of science. 6527 S
Jesus, Life of. 472 B
Marcus Aurelius. 7660 B
Origins of Christianity. 7659 RE
People of Israel. 3 vols. 7567 H
Studies in religious history. 4270 RE
RENAUDOT, E
Ancient accounts of India and China.
5045 H
RENOUF, P Le Page
Religion of ancient Egypt. 12539 H
REVOIL, M B
In the bush and on the trail. 2899 V

REYNOLDS, George
Story of the book of Mormon. 8902
RE
REYNOLDS, G W M
Pickwick abroad. 2875 F
RHOADES, Henry E
Around the world with the blue
jackets. 11593 V
RHODES, W H
Caxton's book. 9029
RHOSCOMYL, Owen
Battlement and tower. 9710 F
Lady of Castell March. 12637 F
RIBOT, Th
Diseases of memory. 7433 S
Diseases of personality. 9295 S
Heredity. 1470 S
Psychology of attention. 9294 EE
Psychology of the emotions.11019EE
RICE, J M
Public school system of the United
States. 8247 EE
RICHARDS, Laura E
Captain January. 8650 J
Five minute stories. 8939 J
Hildegarde's holiday. 6889 J
Hildegarde's home.
Queen Hildegarde. 7370 J
Hildegarde's neighbors. 9714 J
Jim of Hellas. 9703 J
Joyous story of To To. 2698 J
Melody. 9702 J
Narcissa or the road to Rome.9701 J
Nautilus. 9654 J
Rosin the beau, sequel to Melody.
11938 J
Three Margarets. 11885 J
To To's merry winter. 3163 J
RICHARDSON, Benjamine W
Diseases of modern life. 1482 S
RICHARDSON, James (ed)
Wonders of the Yellowstone. 8414 V
RICHMOND, A P
Leaves from the diary of an old
lawyer. 11812 L
RICHTER, Jean St Paul
Life of. 2 vols. 11678 B
RICHTER, Victor von
Inorganic chemistry. 9853 S
RIDEING, William H
Boyhood of living authors. 1364 J
Saddle in the wild west. 3235 J
Young folks' history of London.
4150 H
RIDER, Annie
Hold up your heads, girls. 3180 J
RIDER, George T
Lyra Americana. 11827 P

RIDGWAY, Robert
Manual of North American birds. 7131 S
RIDPATH, John Clark
Great races of mankind. 4 vols. 11983 S
History of the world, 4 vols. 11983 S
United States, a history. 10576 H
William E Gladstone, Life of. 12623 B
RIGGS, Mrs K D (see Wiggin, Kate Douglas)
RIIS, Jacob A
Children of the poor. 7846 SS
How the other half lives. 7068 SS
Nisby's Christmas. 9715 J
Out of Mulberry street. 12640 F
RILEY, H H
Puddleford papers. 6206 L
RILEY, James Whitcomb
Afterwhiles. 7905 P
Armazindy. 8802 P
Child world. 10101 P
Flying islands of the night. 7920 P
Green fields and running brooks. 7921 P
Neghborly poems. 7917 P
Pipes O'Pan at Zekesbury. 7919 P
Poems here at home. 8098 P
Rhymes of childhood. 7992 P
Sketches in prose. 7918 F
RING, Max
John Milton and his times. 436 B
RIORDAN, Roger
Sunrise stories; a glance at the literature of Japan. 9591 F
RIORDAN, Anne
Records of Tennyson, Ruskin and Browning. 11231 E
RITCHIE, Leitch
France, Romance of history of. 1188H
RITTER, Frederic Louis
Music in America. 6392 A
ROBBINS, Mary Caroline
Rescue of an old place. 7282 A
ROBBINS, Mrs S S
Miss Ashton's new pupil. 7688 J
ROBERTS, Charles
Canada, History of. 10378 H
Forge in the forest. 10337 F
ROBERTS, Edwards
Shoshone. 7298 V
ROBERTS, Ellis H
Government revenue. 207 SS
New York, History of. 548 H
ROBERTS, Henry M
Rules of order. 323 R
ROBERTSON, Frederick
Lectures, addresses and other liter-

ary remains. 12164 E
ROBERTSON, George Croom
Hobbes. 7638 B
Making of the English nation. 9800H
ROBERTSON, William
Charles the fifth. 4309 H
Discovery and conquest of America. 955 H
ROBINSON, Edith
A loyal little maid. 11081 J
ROBINSON, Frederick S
The connoisseur. 10486 E
ROBINSON, H
Original letters about the Reformation. 442 RE
ROBINSON, H P
Pictorial effect in photography. 12477 A
ROBINSON, John
Ferns in their home and ours. 1440S
ROBINSON, J H
Expedition up the Orinoco. 5106 V
ROBINSON, Rowland E
Vermont. 7112 H
ROCHE, Charles
Memoirs of the Chancellor Pasquier, 3 vols. 8026 B
ROCHE, Regina Maria
Children of the abbey, 2 vols. 8062 F
ROCKHILL, William Woodville
Land of the Llamas. 7610 V
ROCKSTRO, W S
Mendelssohn. 9342 B
RODNEY, G B
In buff and blue. 10739 F
ROE, E P
Barriers burned away. 10239 F
Day of fate. 10240 F
Driven back to Eden. 10235 F
Earth trembled. 10242 F
Face illumined. 10214 F
From jest to earnest. 10217 F
He fell in love with his wife. 10215 F
His sombre rivals. 10236 F
Home acre, The. 5625 A
Knight of the 19th century. 10237 F
Miss Lou. 10238 F
Nature's serial story. 10233 F
Near to nature's heart. 10218 F
Opening a chestnut burr. 10313 F
Original belle. 9727 F
Taken alive, etc. 10234 F
What can she do? 10216 F
Without a home. 10300 F
Young girl's wooing. 10241 F
ROGERS, Clara Kathleen
Philosophy of singing. 7993 A

ROGERS, George A
Footprints of Jesus. 105 RE
ROGERS, James E
Holland, Story of. 5371 H
Six centuries of work and wages. 6554 SS
ROGERS, Samuel
Poetical works of. 65 P
ROGET, Peter Mark
Thesaurus of English words and phrases. 10519 R
ROHLFS, Mrs A K (see Green, Anna Katharine)
ROLFE, William J
Shakespeare, the boy. 9962 B
ROLLIN, Charles
Ancient history, 4 vols. 11518 II
ROLFE, William J and J A Gillet
Handbook of natural philosophy. 8364 S
ROMANES, George John
Animal intelligence. 6623 S
Darwin and after Darwin. 7667 S
Jelly-fish, star-fish and sea urchins. 5408 S
Mental evolution in man. 4847 S
ROOD, Ogden W
Modern chromatics. 1406 A
ROOK, E C and L J (ed)
Child's own speaker. 10685 P
ROOSEVELT, Theodore
New York. 7646 H
T H Benton, Life of. 1246 B
Winning of the west, 4 vols. 11211 H
ROPES, John C
First Napoleon, Life of the. 233 B
PORER, Mrs S T
Canning and preserving. 11229 A
Hot weather dishes. 11230 A
ROSCOE, Thomas
L de Tormes, Life and adventures of. 292 B
ROSE, Joshua
Practical machinist. 5646 S
ROSE, William Stewart (trans)
Orlando Furioso of Ludovico Aristo, 2 vols. 10919 P
ROSEBERRY, Lord
Pitt, Life of. 6777 B
ROSS, Denman W
Early history of land-holding among the Germans. 10619 H
ROSS, Peter
Scotland and the Scots. 6384 H
ROSSELL, Mrs H (trans)
Wanter's Flemish school of painting. 1772 A

ROSSETTI, Christina
Maud. 11474
ROSSETTI, Dante Gabriel
Dante and his circle. 11232 EE
Shadow of Dante. 12233 EE
ROSSITER, William
Illustrated dictionary of scientific terms. 4692 R
ROSTAND, Edmond
Cyrano De Bergerac. 12629 P
ROUSSELET, Louis
Ralph, the drummer boy. 2211 J
ROUTLEDGE, Robert (trans)
Marvels of the polar world. 2187 J
ROWBETHAM, Thomas
Art of sketching from nature. 1776A
ROWCROFT, Charles
Chronicles of the Fleet prison. 5067 H
ROWE, A D
Every day life in India. 2167 V
ROYCE, Josiah
California, History of. 4289 H
Conception of God. 10856 RE
Feud of Oakfield creek. 3153 F
Religious aspect of philosophy. 6519 RE
Studies of good and evil. 12006 RE
RUDOLPH, Prof
Wonders of nature. 3096 S
RUFFINI, G D
Doctor Antonio; a tale of Italy. 11621 F
Lavinia. 2870 F
RUGG, Henry W
The church. 8756 RE
RUSKIN, John
Art of England. 1767 A
Lectures on art. 1765 A
Modern painters, 2 vols. 3243 A
Mornings in Florence. 7538 V
Sesame and lilies.
Seven lamps of architecture. 3242 A
Stones of Venice. 3245 A
Venice, History of. 7989 H
RUSSELL, A P
In a club corner. 5677 E
RUSSELL, Henry B
International monetary conference. 11082 S
RUSSELL, Irwin
Poems of. 7220 P
RUSSELL, William
Normal training. 288 EE
Orthophony, or the cultivation of the voice. 8363 EE
RUSSELL, W Clark
Copsford mystery; or Is he the man?

9711 F
Emigrant ship, The. 8255 F
Ida Noble, Tragedy of. 7165 F
List, ye landsmen. 7741 F
Marooned. 11475 F
My shipmate Louise. 10422 F
Representative actors. 11705 B
Two captains, The. 10716 F
What cheer? 10122 F
Wreck of the Grosvenor. 2373 F
RUSSELL, William
  Modern Europe, History of, 3 vols.
    11694 H
RUSSELL, William H
  Eccentric personages. 219 B
  My diary, north and south. 1623 H
RYDER, Annie H
  Go right on, girls! 8141 EE

SABATIER, Paul
  St Francis of Assisi, Life of. 11172 B
SACHS, Julius von
  Lectures on the physiology of plants.
    7972 S
SAFFORD, Mary J M
  Health and strength for girls. 478 S
SAIGEY, M Emile
  Unity of natural phenomena. 11835S
SAINT-ARMAND, Imbert de
  Famous women of the French court.
    Marie Antoinette, 3 vols.
  Marie Antoinette and the end of the
    old regime. 5862 B
  Marie Antoinette and the Tuileries.
    7380 B
  Marie Antoinette and the downfall
    of royalty. 7381 B
  Empress Josephine, 3 vols
  Citizeness Bonaparte. 5863 B
  The wife of the first consul. 5860 B
  The court of the Empress Josephine.
    5865 B
  Empress Marie Louise, 4 vols.
  Happy days of Marie Louise. 5861 B
  Marie Louise and the decadence of
    the empire. 5864 B
  Marie Louise and the invasion of
    1814. 8323 B
  Marie Louise, the return from Elba
    and the hundred days. 6409 B
  Duchess of Angouleme, 2 vols.
  Youth of the duchess of Angouleme.
    8325 B
  Duchess of Angouleme and the two
    restorations. 8324 B
  Duchess of Berry, 3 vols.
  Duchess of Berry and the court of
    Louis XVIII. 7410 B
  Duchess of Berry and the court of
    Charles X. 7409 B
  Duchess of Berry and the revolution
    of July, 1830. 7657 B
  Women of the Velois and Versailles
    courts, 4 vols.
  Women of the Velois court. 7868 B
  The court of Louis XIV. 7924 B
  The court of Louis XV. 8091 B
  The last years of Louis XV. 8227 B
  The revolution of 1848. 9357 B
  Louis Napoleon and Mademoiselle de
    Montizo. 10326 B
  Napoleon III and his court. 11897 B
SAINT-BEUVE, C A
  Monday chats. E
SAINT-GERMAIN, Comte de
  Practical palmistry. 10330 S
SAINTSBURY, George
  Dryden, Life of. 6690 B
  Elizabethian literature, History of.
    6867 EE
  Flourishing of romance and rise of
    allegory. 10324 E   E
  Marlborough. 1366 B
SAINTSBURY, George (ed)
  Specimens of English prose style.
    7246 EE
SAJOUS, Charles E (ed)
  Annual of universal medical science
    for 1888-1889-1890, 15 vols. 9068 S
SALA, George A
  Things I have seen and people I have
    known, 2 vols. 11215 E
SALE, George (trans)
  Koran of Mahommed. 4417 RE
SALIS, Mrs de
  New-laid eggs. 7293 A
SALLUST
  Writings of. 475 H
SAM SLICK (see Haliburton, T C)
SAMUEL, S W
  From the forecastle to the cabin.
    1331 J
SANBORN, F B
  Goethe, Life and genius of. 6510 B
  Henry D Thoreau, Life of. 1238 B
  John Brown, Life of. 7107 B
SANBORN, F B (ed)
  Familiar letters of Henry D Thoreau.
    8817 E
SANBORN, Kate
  Truthful woman in southern Califor-
    nia. 7906 V
SAND, George (pseud of Mme A L A D
    Dudervant)
  Consuelo. 6053 F
  (Venice. Musical life).

Countess of Rudolstadt. 8647 F
(Sequel to Consuelo.)
Devil's pool. 11608 F
Impressions and reminiscences. 11806 EE
Monsieur Sylvestre. 6323 F
SANDERS, Lloyd C
Viscount Palmerston, Life of. 12174 B
SANGSTER, Margaret E
Easter bells. 10743 P
SAINT-PIERRE, J II B de
Paul and Virginia. 10978 F
SANKEY, Charles
Spartan and Theban supremacies. 4415 H
SANTAYANA, George
Sense of beauty. 10404 E
SANZAY, A
Wonders of glass making in all ages. 1774 A
SARGENT, John T (compiler)
Readings for the young. 7119 R
SARMIENTO, F L
Pauline Cushman. 4701 B
SAUNDERS, Frederick
Salad for the solitary and social. 6375 E
Story of some famous books. 341 E
SAUNDERS, Marshall
Beautiful Joe. 8549 J
King of the park. 10720 J
SAUNDERS, William
Insects injurious to fruit. 1545 A
SAVAGE, Richard Henry
Delilah of Harlem. 11581 F
Little lady of the Lagunitas. 8169 F
Passing shadow, The. 11531 F
SAVAGE, Thomas (ed)
Spanish-American manual, 1890-1891. 11834 R
SAXE, John Godfrey
Poems of. 10513 P
SAY, Leon
Turgot, Life of. 7249 B
SCARRETT, Helen
Letters to a daughter. 1050 J
SCHECHTER, S
Studies in Judaism. 11407 RE
SCHERER, W
German literature, Life of, 2 vols. 8497 EE
SCHILLER, J C F von
Poems of. 96 P
SCHINDLER, Rabbi
Dissolving views in the history of Judaism. 5415 RE

SCHLEGEL, August Wilhelm
Dramatic art and literature. 10340 EE
SCHMIDT, Oscar
Doctrine of descent and Darwinism. 1395 S
Mammalia in their relation to primitive times. 11367 S
SCHMUCHER, Samuel
Memorable scenes in French history. 6371 H
SCHNEIDER, Albert
Guide to the study of lichens. 12474 S
SCHOPENHAUER, Art
Art of literature. 6806 E
Counsels and maxims. 6808 E
Religion; a dialogue. 6810 E
Studies in pessimism. 6809 E
Wisdom of life. 6807 E
SCHOULER, James
Constitutional studies; state and federal. 10875 H
Historical briefs. 10103 H
United States, History of, 5 vols. 5978 H
SCHREINER, Olive (pseud of Ralph Iron)
Story of an African farm. 8069 F
SCHUBIN, Ossip
Erlach court. 4962 F
Our own set.
SCHUCHARDT, C
Schliemann's excavations. 7661 H
SCHURZ, Carl
Henry Clay, Life of. 175 B
SCHUTZENBERGER, P
Fermentation. 1400 S
SCHUYLER, Eugene
Fathers and sons. 2555 F
SCHUYLER, Montgomery
American architecture, Studies of.
SCHWATKA, Frederick
Along Alaska's great river. 3302 V
Children of the cold. 3279 J
Nimrod of the north. 5846 J
SCIDMORE, Eliza R
Alaska, its southern coast and the Sitka archipelago. 3315 V
Jinrikisha days in Japan. 6547 V
SCOLLARD, Clinton
Boy's book of rhyme. 10787 P
Man at arms. 11890 F
Under summer skies. 7441 V
SCOTT, Fred George
Elton Hazelwood. 11563 F
SCOTT, Robert H
Elementary meteorology. 7721 S
SCOTT, Sir Walter
Abbot, The. 2633 F

Anne of the Geierstein. 8987 F
Antiquary, The. 8989 F
Betrothed. 2641 F
Black dwarf. 2628 F
Bride of Lammermoor. 8980 F
Count Robert of Paris. 2646 F
Fair maid of Perth. 8973 F
Fortunes of Nigel. 8978 F
Guy Mannering. 8982 F
Heart of Mid-Lothian. 2629 F
Kenilworth. 8972 F
Lady of the lake. 10191 P
Lay of the last minstrel. 839 P
Marmion. 5003 P
Monastery. 8974 F
Old Mortality. 2627 F
Peveril of the peak. 2637 F
Pirate, The. 2635 F
Poems of. 4797 P
Quentin Durward. 8975 F
Red Gauntlet. 2640 F
Rob Roy. 2626 F
Tales of a grandfather. 2642 F
Talisman. 845 F
Waverly. 8982 F
Woodstock. 2643 F
SCRIPTURE, E W
  New psychology. 11889 EE
SCUDDER, Horace E
  Bodleys abroad. 6570 J
  Bodleys afoot. 6571 J
  Bodleys on wheels. 6569 J
  Bodleys' grandchildren in Holland. 6568 J
  Bodley family in town. 6565 J
  Book of fable. 7908 J
  Book of folk stories. 7907 J
  Childhood in literature and art. 8785 EE
  David Scudder, Life and letters of. 126 B
  Dwellers in five sisters' court. 6493 J
  English Bodley family. 6566 J
  Men and letters. 327 E
  Noah Webster, Life of. 191 B
  Viking bodleys. 6572 J
SCUDDER, Samuel H
  Butterflies. 1542 S
SEARS, Lorenzo
  Principles and methods of literary criticism. 12550 EE
SEAWELL, Molly Elliot
  History of Lady Betty Stair. 10681F
  Maid Marian, etc. 10518 F
  Rock of the lion. 11013 F
  Strange, sad comedy. 9818 F
  Virginia cavalier. 10104 F

SEDGWICK, Anne Douglas
  Dull Miss Archinard. 11884 F
SEEBOHM, Frederic
  English village community. 10697 H
  Era of protestant revolution. 5485 H
SEELY, John R
  Napoleon the First, Short history of. 1324 B
SEEMULLER, Annie M
  Reginald Archer. 11612 F
SEGUIN, L G
  Country of the Passion play. 4335 V
SEISS, Joseph A
  Miracle in stone. 6408 V
SELLAR, W Y
  Roman poets of the Augustan age. 11877 EE
SERGEANT, Adelina
  Idol-maker. 10196 F
  Life sentence. 4746 F
  Marjory Morse. 9809 F
SERGEANT, Lewis
  The Franks. 11968 H
SERGEANT, Lewis
  John Wyclif. 11189 B
  New Greece, History of. 4227 H
SERRANO, Mary J
  Journal of Marie Bashkirtseff. 5528 B
  Dona Perfecta. 9493 F
SESSIONS, Francis C
  In western levant. 6546 V
SEVERANCE, Mark Sibley
  Hammersmith; his Havard days. 10660 F
SEWARD, Olive Risley
  Around the world stories. 7214 J
SEWARD, William H
  John Quincy Adams, Life of. 125 B
SEWELL, Anna
  Black Beauty. 6884 J
SEYBERT, Henry
  Investigation of modern spiritualism. 1379 L
SHAFER, D R
  Foundation of success and laws of trade. 1203 EE
SHAIRP, J C
  Culture and religion in some of their relations. 6520 E
  Robert Bruce, Life of. 6673 B
SHAKESPEARE, William
  Complete works. Appleton edition, 11 vols. 12373 P
  — — Clarke and Wright edition, 12 vols. 1221 P
  — — Dr Johnson edition, 7 vols. 8626 P
  Varorium edition, 11 vols. 1687 R

SHALER, N S
American highways. 12226 S
Kentucky, History of. 4284 H
Outlines of the earth's history. 12215 S
SHARP, David
Walks abroad of two young naturalists. 8143 J
SHAW, Flora L
Sea change. 12306 F
SHEDD, Julia A
Famous painters and paintings. 11417 B
Famous sculptors and sculpture. 11416 B
SHEDD, W G T
Homilities and pastoral theology. 354 E
SHELDON, Charles M
In his steps—What would Jesus do? 12168 F
SHELDON, E A
Manual of instruction; object lessons. 261 EE
SHELDON, Louise V
Yankee girls in Zululand. 10995 V
SHELLEY, Mary W
Frankenstein. 2959 F
SHELLEY, Percy B
Poetical works of, 3 vols. 6590 P
SHELTON, William Henry
Last three soldiers. 10892 F
SHEPARD, Edward
Martin Van Buren, Life of. 1242 B
SHEPARD, Isabel S
.Cruise of the United States steamer Rush. 7297 V
SHEPARD, William (ed)
Pen pictures of modern authors. 6707 B
SHEPARD, William
Our young folks' Josephus. 8593 J
SHERER, J W
Conjuror's daughter. 5074 F
SHERIDAN, Richard B
Works of. 6624 P
SHERMAN, Francis
Matins. 10578 P
SHERMAN, Frank Dempster
Little folk lyrics. 11335 P
SHERMAN, John
Recollections of forty years in house, senate and cabinet, 2 vols. 10912 H
SHERMAN, W T
Memoirs, 2 vols. 117 H
SHERWOOD, M E W
Art of entertaining. 7289 EE

SHERWOOD, Mrs
Works of, 16 vols. 11641 F
SKIEL, Richard L
Sketches of the Irish bar. 2150 F
SHIELDS, G O
Crossings in the Cascades. 5639 V
Hunting in the great west, or Rustlings in the Rocky mountains.3090V
SHILLABER, B P
Ike Partington. 11560 F
Mrs Partington's knitting work. 11870 F
SCHUIKICHI, Shigemi
Japanese boy. 6538 B
SHINN, Charles H
Mining camps. 221 V
SHORTER, Clement K
Victorian literature. 10867 EE
SHORTHOUSE, J H
Blanche, Lady Falaise. 6817 F
Countess Eve, The. 6821 F
John Inglesant. 6818 F
Little schoolmate Mark. 6820 F
Sir Percival. 6819 F
SHUCK, Oscar T
California scrap-book. 439 H
Men of the Pacific. 11554 B
SHULDHAM, E B
Chronic sore throat. 11745 S
Stammering and its treatment.11745S
SIDNEY, Margaret (pseud of Mrs H M S Lothrop)
Five little peppers and how they grew. 9644 J
Five little peppers grown up. 9645 J
Five little peppers midway. 8595 J
Our town. 5302 J
Phronsie pepper. 10656 J
SIENKIEWICZ, H
Deluge, The, 2 vols. 8526 F
Pan Michael. 8250 F
Quo Vadis. 10369 F
With fire and sword. 8157 F
Yanko, the musician, and other stories. 8249 F
SIGOURNEY, Mrs L H
Daily counsellor. 11777 RE
Letters and life of. 646 B
Lucy Howard's journal. 11854 F
SILL, Edward
Hermitage, and other poems. 5597 P
SILVER, Abeel
The Holy word in its own defense. 5096 RE
SIMMONDS, T L
Commercial products of the sea. 1819 S

SIMMS, Joseph
Physiognomy illustrated. 7796 S
SIMMS, W Gilmore
Cassique of Kianah. 11710 F
Woodcraft. 6181 F
SIMON, A E Fritz
Historical epochs with system of mneumonics. 5728 EE
SIMON, Jules
Victor Cousin. 7390 B
SIMON, M Laird
Evenings with Moody and Sankey. 7300 RE
Holding the fort. 7285 RE
SIMS, J Marion
Story of my life. 1030 B
SINCLAIR, Catharine
Modern accomplishments. 5080 F
SINGER, Ignatious
Some unrecognized laws of nature. 114500 S
SINNETT, A P
Esotoric Buddhism. 1201 RE
Occult world. 6724 RE
Rationale mesmerism. 7304 RE
SITGRAEVES, L
Expedition down the Colorado and Zuri rivers. 3367 V
SKEAT, Walter
Concise etymological English dictionary. 1661 R
SKELTON, John
Poetical works of. 6188 P
SKENE, Alexander J C
True to themselves. 11725 F
SKINNER, Charles M
Myths and legends of our own land, 2 vols. 11041 F
SKINNER, Thomas
Excursion in India, 2 vols. 4974 V
SLADE, D D
Diphtheria. 9132 S
SLATER, John
Architecture, classic and early christian. 9166 A
SLAN, Samuel
Model architect, 2 vols. 7707 A
Homestead architecture. 1788 A
SLOSSON, Annie T
Seven dreamers. 6301 F
SMALLEY, George W
London letters and some others, 2 vols. 11419 E
Studies of men. 9370 E
SMEDES, Susan D
Southern planter. 7679 B
SMILES, Samuel
Art of living. 7235 EE

Brief biographies. 170 B
Character. 5366 EE
Duty. 5367 EE
George Stephenson, Life of. 8986 B
Huguenots in France. 11406 H
Industrial biography. 11844 B
Men of invention and industry. 226 B
Robert Dick, botanist. 6351 B
Self help. 5368 EE
Thrift. 452 EE
SMITH, Adam
Wealth of nations, 2 vols. 8528 SS
SMITH, A Donaldson
Through unknown African countries. 10865 V
SMITH, Albert H
Bayard Taylor. 9510 B
SMITH, Alexander
Dreamthorpe; a book of essays. 682E
Summer in Skye. 2951 V
Poems of. 11711 P
SMITH, Edward
Foods. 1382 S
Health. 11740 S
SMITH, Edward Fabian
Beecher's recitations and readings. 10687 P
SMITH, Emily James (trans)
Selections from Lucien. 7310 E
SMITH, Mrs E T (see Meade, T L)
SMITH, F Hopkinson
Caleb West, master diver. 11334 F
Colonel Carter of Cartersville. 7464 F
Day at Laguerre's and other days.
Gentleman vagabond and some some others. 9413 F
Gondola days. 11089 V
Tom Grogan. 9995 F
Well-worn roads of Spain, Holland and Italy. 11217 VV
White umbrella in Mexico. 4997 V
SMITH, G Barnett
Romance of colonization; the United States. 10871 H
SMITH, George
Ancient history from the monuments of Assyria. 12453 H
Assyrian discoveries. 5229 V
Chaldean accounts of Génesis. 5271 RE
SMITH, Gertrude
Rousing of Mrs Potter and other stories. 8159 F
SMITH, Goldwin
Guesses at the riddle of existence. 10411 RE
SMITH, Goldwin
Cowper, Life of. 6678 B

Lectures on the study of history. 3117 H

United States, The. 8248 H

SMITH, H (see Stretton, Hesba)

SMITH, Hannah
Music; how it came to be what it is. 11898 A

SMITH, Helen A
One hundred famous Americans. 5282 B

SMITH, Henry Preserved
The Bible and Islam, or the influence of the old and new testaments on the religion of Mohammed. 10789 RE

SMITH, J V C
Turkey and the Turks. 9266 H

SMITH, Laura A
Thro' Romany songland. 6852 P

SMITH, J Mayo (compiler)
Ancient Greek female costume.1779R

SMITH. Mary
The Browns. 12100 J
Their canoe trip. 12095 J

SMITH, Nora Archibald
Children of the future. 11037 EE

SMITH, R B
Rome and Carthage. 5477H

SMITH, Richard Mayo
Emigration and immigration.7613 SS

SMITH, Robert H
Cutting tools worked by hand and machine. 11720 A

SMITH, Robert Meade
Physiology of the domestic animals. 12330 S

SMITH, Roderick
Science of business. 606 EE

SMITH, S B
Teachings of the Holy Catholic church. 8519 RE

SMITH, S F (ed)
Knights and sea-kings of the middle ages. 8117 J

SMITH, Sydney
Essays, social and political. 3250 E
Works of. 457 E

SMITH, T Roger
Architecture, gothic and renaissance. 9167 A

SMITH, Uriah
Sanctuary, The. 408 RE
Thoughts on Daniel. 591 RE
Thoughts on Revelations. 5037 RE
United States in prophecy. 401 RE

SMITH, William
Dictionary of the Bible. 8459 R
Greece, History of. 11203 H

New classical dictionary. 11048 R

SMITH, William II
Evolution of Dodd. 11290 F

SMITH, W Robertson
Prophets of Israel. 11616 RE

SMITH, William Thayer
Human body and its health. 8366 S
Primer of physiology and hygiene. 8381 S

SMOLLETT, Tobias
Works of. 8897 F

SMYTH, J Peterson
How we got our Bible. 7279 RE

SMYTH, Lieut
Journey from Lima to Para. 5182 V

SNIDER, Denton
Freeburgers. 7175 F
Walk in Hellas. 7269 V

SOLEY, James Russell
Boys of 1812. 4947 J
Sailor boys of '61. 5286 J

SOLON, L M
Art of the old English potter. 1769 A

SOMERS, Jane R
Two bequests. 3118 F

SOMMERVILLE, Maxwell
Siam. 10861 V

SONNENSCHEIN, W S
Best books. 7079 R
Reade's guide to contemporary literature. 10360 R

SONREL, L
Bottom of the sea. 12536 S

SOREL, Albert
Montesquieu, Life of. 7247 B

SOULE, John B L
Polychords

SOULE, Richard
Dictionary of English synonyms. 7059 R

SOUTHALL, James C
Epoch of the mammoth. 12525 S

SOUTHWICK, Albert P
Wisps of wit and wisdom. 7446 L

SOUVESTRE, Emile
An attic philosopher in Paris. 3237E

SOWERBY, George B
The acquarium. 11686 S

SPRAGUE, William B
Visits to European celebrities.11513V

SPALDING. J L
Means and ends of education.9504 EE

SPARKS, W E
How to shade from models. 11431 A

SPAYTH, Henry
Game of draughts. 7996 A

SPEAR, Charles
Names and titles of the Lord Jesus

Christ. 5094 RE
SPEDDING, James
Francis Bacon; an account of life
and times of, 2 vols. 11355 B
SPENCER, Herbert
Education. 11807 EE
Essays, scientific, political and spec-
ulative. 6523 E
Principles of ethics. 7929 EE
Recent discussions in science, phi-
losophy and morals. 11699 E
Study of sociology. 1387 SS
Various fragments. 11024 E
SPENSER, Edmund
Fairy Queen. 52 P
Poetical works of. 3 P
SPOFFORD, Harriet Prescott
Priscilla's love story. 11090 F
SPRAGUE, William R
Excellent woman, The. 9133 A
SPRING, L W
Kansas, History of. 4285 H
SPRINGSTEED, Annie Frances
Expert waitress. 8495 A
SQUIRE, E G
Nicaragua, 2 vols. 3262 V
STABLES, Gordon
Every inch a sailor. 12365 V
Greenland and the pole. 12366 V
Hints about home and farm favorites
6940 A
On special service. 4744 V
STAEL, Madam de
Corrinne. 1038 F
Germany, History of. 11219 H
STAINER and Barrett (ed)
Dictionary of musical terms. 8534 R
STALKER, James
Jesus Christ, Life of. 9680 B
STALLO, J B
Concepts and theories of modern
physics. 11433 S
STANLEY, A P
Lectures on history of Jewish church.
4246 RE
STANLEY, Henry M
Congo, The, 2 vols. 3437 V
In darkest Africa, 2 vols. 5917 V
Livingstone, lost and found. 3439 V
My Kalulu. 4287 V
Thro' the dark continent, 2 vols.
9813 V
Thro' south Africa. 11909 V
STANLEY, Wallace P
Our week afloat, or how we explored
the Pequonset river. 11312 V
STANLEY, W M
Mile of gold. 11585 V

STANNARD, Mrs H E V P (see Winter
John Strange)
STANTON, Anthony
Woman suffrage, History of, 3 vols.
4325 SS
STANTON, Mary O
Physiognomy, 2 vols. 7675 S
STANWOOD, Edward
Presidential elections, History of.
8835 H
STAPFER, Edmond
Jesus Christ before his ministry.
10407 RE
STATHAM, H Heathcote
Modern architecture. 11384 A
STEARNE, E J
Notes on Uncle Tom's Cabin. 629 E
STEARNS, Albert
Sindbad, Smith & Co. 9916 J
STEARNS, Winifred
Wrecked on Labrador. 7200 J
STEBBINS, Genevieve.
Delsarte system of expression .6391
EE
STEBBINS, Giles
American protectionist manual. 6715
SS
Progress from poverty. 628 SS
STEBBING, Thomas R R
Crustacea, History of. 11401 S
STEDMAN, Edmund C
Blameless prince. 73 P
Library of American literature.
3448 P
Nature and elements of poetry.
7601 EE
Poetical works. 10866 P
Poets of America. 11218 P
Victorian poets.
Victorian anthology, 1837-1895.10571P
STEEL, Mrs F A
From the five rivers. 11584 F
In the permanent way. 10722 F
Miss Stuart's legacy. 8024 F
On the face of the waters. 10398 F
Red Rowans. 10853 F
STEEL, J Dorman
Fourteen weeks in geology. 1476 S
— — n physics. 1414 S
— — in physiology. 1538 S
— — in zoology. 1539 S
Introduction to botany. 1437 S
New descriptive astronomy. 1444 S
STEELE, Willis
Isidra. 3211 F
STEERE, M J
Footprints heavenward. 8514 RE

STEEVENS, G W
  Land of the dollar. 10599 F
  With the conquering Turk. 11372 F
STEPHEN, James F
  Liberty, equality and fraternity. 11493 SS
STEPHEN, Leslie
  Alexander Pope, Life of. 6704 B
  Hours in a library. 11200 EE
  Samuel Johnson, Life of. 6701 B
  Swift, Life of. 6684 B
STEPHENS, Alexander H
  War between the states, 2 vols. 4153 H
STEPHENS, H Morse
  Portugal, Story of. 9123 H
STEPHENS, Henry
  Book of the farm. 8878 A
STEPHENS, John L
  Gustavus Adolphus, History of.228B
  Travels in Yucatan, 2 vols. 3257 V
STEPHENS, Robert N
  An enemy to the king. 11971 F
  Continental dragoon. 12595 F
  Road to Paris. 12622 F
STEPNIAK, S
  Russian peasantry. 6446 H
STERLING, John
  Onyx ring. 11637 F
STERN, Herman J
  Gods of our fathers. 11448 F
STERNDALE, Robert
  Afghan knife. 5053 F
STERNE, Lawrence
  Tristam Shandy, 2 vols. 3230 F
STERNE, Simon
  Constitutional history and political development. 12165 H
STEVENS, C A
  Knockabout club. 644 J
  Knockabout club along shore. 1250J
  Young moose hunters. 2856 J
STEVENS, C Ellis
  Sources of constitution of the United States. 8491 H
STEVENS, John Austin
  Albert Gallatin, Life of. 181 B
STEVENS, Lydia W
  Heart problems. 69 P
STEVENS, Thomas
  Around the world on a bicycle, 2 vols. 5969 V
STEVENSON, Robert L
  Across the plains. 12415 E
  Ballads. 12123 P
  Black arrow and other tales. 12408F
  David Balfour. 12406 F
  Dr Jeckyll and Mr Hyde, Strange case of. 12407 F
  Fables. 9918 F
  Familiar studies of men and books. 12414 E
  Inland voyage, travels and essays of. 12412 E
  In the south seas. 12419 V
  Island night's entertainments.8722 F
  Kidnapped. 12405 F
  Letters and miscellanies. 12417 F
  Master of Ballantrae. 12409 F
  Memories and portraits. 12413 E
  Merry men, The. 12407 F
  New Arabian nights. 12401 F
  St Ives; being adventures of a French prisoner in England. 10770F
  Travels with a donkey in the Cevennes. 5210 V
  Treasure island. 12402 F
  Underwood. 86 P
  Virginibus purisque. 12413 E
  Weir of Hermiston plays. 12420 F
STEVENSON, Robert L and Fanny Van de G
  Dynamiter, The
STEVENSON, Robert L and Lloyd Osborne
  Ebb tide. 9291 F
  Wrecker. 8209 F
  Wrong box. 5325 F
STEVENSON, Sarah H
  Boys and girls in biology. 2721 J
STEWART, Aubrey
  Tale of Troy. 3181 F
STEWART, Baljour
  Conservation of energy. 1389 S
STEWART, John A
  Letters to living authors. 7598 E
STICKNEY, Albert
  A true republic. 8524 SS
  Democratic government. 202 SS
STILLE, Charles J
  Studies in mediaeval history.10869 H
STILLMAN, W J
  Old Italian masters. 9171 A
STIMSON, F J (J S of Dale)
  Crime of Henry Vane. 2155 F
  First harvests. 5566 F
  In the three zones. 7747 F
  Kink's own. 2185 F
  King Noanett. 10027 F
STINSON, John
  Organon of science. 1101 S
STOCKTON, F R
  Adventures of Captain Horn. 9321 F
  Amos Kilbright; his adscititious experience. 6324 F
  Ardis Claverden. 5960 F

Captain Chap. 9911 J
Casting away of Mre Leeks and Mre. Aleshine. 5318 F
Clocks of Rondaiue. 7455 J
Dusantes. 5319 F
(Sequel to Mrs Leeks and Mrs Ale-shine)
Girl of Cobhurst. 11085 F
House of Martha. 7043 F
Hundredth man. 3228 F
Lady or the tiger? and other stories. 784 F
Late Mrs Null. 786 F
Mrs Cliff's yacht. 10105 F
Personally conducted. 5320 V
Pomona's travels. 9629 V
Round about rambles. 5321 J
Rudder Grange. 785 F
Squirrel Inn. 6747 F
Story-teller's pack. 10365 F
Watch-maker's wife and other stories. 7988 F
What might have been expected. 5522 J
STODDARD, A R (compiler)
Library of choice literature, 10 vols. R
STODDARD, Charles A
Beyond the Rockies. 8349 V
STODDARD, Charles W
Poems of. 1
Summer cruising in the south seas. 5041 V
South sea idyls. 7457 F
STODDARD, Richard H (ed)
Bric-a-brac series, 10 vols. 11555 E
STODDARD, Richard Henry
Prosper Merimee. 6918 B
Under the evening lamp. 7605 E
STODDARD, W O
Chuck Purdy. 6469 J
Chumley's post. 9840 J
Crowded out of Cro'field. 7691 J
Inside the White House in war time. 7276 J
Little smoke. 7401 J
Lives of the presidents, viz.
George Washington. 5382 J
John Adams and Thomas Jefferson. 5383 J
James Madison, James Monroe and John Quincy Adams. 1363 J
Andrew Jackson and Martin Van Buren. 299 J
William H Harrison, J Tyler and James K Polk. 5386 J
Z. Taylor, M Fillmore, F. Pierce and James Buchanan. 5387 J

Abraham Lincoln and A Johnson. 5388 J
Ulysses S Grant. 5389 J
R B Hayes, J A Garfield and C A Arthur. 5390 J
Grover Cleveland. 5391 J
Men of business (Men of achieve-ment series). 8015 B
On the old frontier. 8074 J
Partners. 9535 J
Red Beauty. 3212 J
Swordmaker's son; a story of the year 30 A D. 9914 J
Taking leaves. 5281 J
Two arrows. 2011 J
STOKES, Anson P
Joint metallism. 10054 SS
STOKES, Alfred C
Microscopy for beginners. 12499 S
STONE, James Kent
Invitation heeded. 11514 RE
STONE, Mary E
Riddle of luck. 7786 F
STORIES by American Authors, 10 vols. 5357 F
STORY, Alfred Thomas
Building of the British empire, 2 vols. 11899 H
STORY, Joseph
History of the constitution. 9570 H
STORY, William Wetmore
Conversations in a studio. 6497 A
Roba de Roma, 2 vols. 467 V
STOWE, Harriet Beecher
Agnes of Sorrento. 3414 F
Chimney corner; house and home papers. 607 A
Men of our times. 6198 B
Minister's wooing. 2753 F
My wife and I. 673 F
Oldtown folks. 2822 F
Pearl of Orr's island. 800 F
Poganuc people. 8058 F
Stories, sketches. 11346 J
Uncle Tom's cabin. 12441 F
We and our neighbors. 3415 F
(Sequel to My wife and I).
STOWE, J W
Probate confiscation. 11867 SS
STRAIN, E H
A man's foes. 11630 F
STRANGE, Edward F
Alphabets; a manual. 11446 A
STRAUB, Jacob
Consolations of science. 8768 RE
Prophecy and the prophets. 8760 RE
STRAUS, Oscar S
Roger Williams, Life of. 8852 B

STRECKFUS, Adolph
Quicksands. 2165 F
STREET, Alfred B
Poetical works of, 2 vols. 19 P
STRETTON, Hesba (pseud of Sarah
Stretton)
Bede's charity. 2546 F
Carola. 2237 F
Cassy. 6277 F
Cobwebs and cables. 5327 F
David Lloyd's last will. 5829 F
Doctor's dilemma. 5956 F
Hester Morley's promise. 5955 F
Her only son. 640 J
In prison and out. 5328 F
King's servants. 6280 F
Lost Gip. 6278 J
STRICKLAND, Agnes
Tales from English history. 10627 J
True stories from ancient history.
9022 J
STROHM, Gertrude
Universal cookery art. 7288 A
STRONG, Grace
Worst foe, The. 6741 F
STRONG, Josiah
Twentieth century city. 11969 SS
STROTHER
Virginia illustrated. 2688 V
STUART, Esme
Arrested. 10413 F
Cast ashore. 11793 F
STUART, George
Caesar. 8355 B
STUART, Ruth McEnery
Golden wedding, etc. 7819 F
In Simpkinsville. 10647 F
Moriah's mourning. 12209 F
Solomon Crow's Christmas pockets.
10106 F
Story of Babette. 11508 F
STUBBS, William
Constitutional history of England, 3
vols. 9178 H
Early Plantaganets. 5481 H
STURGIS, Julian
An accomplished gentleman. 2119 F
Folly of Pen Harrington. 10640 F
STURGIS, Russell
European architecture. 10107 A
SUE, Eugene
Mysteries of Paris. 11294 F
Paula Monti. 5244 F
Wandering Jew. 11305 F
SULLIVAN, T R
Tom Sylvester. 8032 F
SULLY, James
Outlines of psychology. 5987 EE

SUMNER, Charles
Notes of travel in northern Europe.
3332 V
Recent speeches and addresses.647 E
SUMNER, William G
American currency, History of. 12175
SS
Andrew Jackson, Life of. 184 B
SUNDERMANN, Herman
The wish. 10142 F
SUTRO, Emil
Basis law of vocal utterance. 11838
EE
SUTRO, Theodore
Sutro tunnel company and Sutro tun-
nel. 5786 H
SUTTON, J Bland
Evolution and disease. 7862 S
SUZOR, Renand
Hydrophobia; M Pasteur's system.
5185 S
SWAINE, S A
Turner, the artist. 7257 B
SWAITH, J C (ed)
Mistress Dorothy Marvin. 9896 F
SWAN, Annie S
Freedom's sword. 6264 J
SWEDENBORG, Emanuel
Works of, 20 vols. 1294 RE
SWETT, Sophie
Flying Hill farm. 12116 J
Mate of the Mary Ann. 12099 J
Tom Pickering of 'Scutney. 11923 J
SWETCHINE, Madam
Writings of. 950 E
SWIFT, Jonathan
Choice works of. 6632 F
Gulliver's travels. 10693 F
SWINBURNE, Algernon C
Atlanta in Calydon. 72 P
Essays and studies. 11201 E
Poems of. 63 P
SWING, David
Club essays. 5560 E
Motives of life. 11400 E
Truths for today. 11796 E
SWINTON, William
Language lessons. 8374 EE
Rambles among words. 451 EE
Twelve decisive battles of the war.
4156 H
SWINTON and Cathcart
Seven British classics. 8377 E
SYKES, Arthur Ashley
An essay on the truth of the Chris-
tian religion. 12543 RE

SYMONDS, Arthur
  Introduction to the study of Brown-
    ing. 68 EE
SYMONDS, Addington
  Blank verse. 9158 EE
  Greek poets, 2 vols. 8676 EE
  Italian byways. 9309 V
  Philip Sidney, Life of. 6685 B
  Religio Medici. 11538 E
  Renaissance in Italy, 5 vols. 4092 H
SYMONDS, J Addington and Margaret
  Our life in the Swiss highlands.
    11197 V
SYMONDS, Margaret
  Days spent on a Doge's farm. 11876V
  Recollections of a happy life, 2 vols.
    8501 B
SYMONDSON, F W H
  Two years abaft the mast. 865 F

TABOR, Eliza
  Pansie's flour bin. 6815 J
  When I was a little girl. 6795 J
  When papa comes home. 6800 J
TABB, John B
  Lyrics. 10740 P
TADEMA, Laurence Alma
  Wings of Icarus. 10140 F
TAINE, H A
  Ancient regime. 12244 H
  English literature, History of, 2 vols.
    4234 H
  French revolution, History of, 3 vols.
    11241 H
  Italy, Florence and Venice. 9299 H
  Lectures on art. 6499 A
  Modern regime, 2 vols. 11245 H
  Notes on England. 9120 H
  On intelligence, 2 vols. 613 EE
TAINSCH, E Campbell
  Study of the works of Alfred Lord
    Tennyson. 12651 EE
TALBOT, Th (ed)
  Enchiridion of Epictetus. 5088 P
  Tales from many sources, 4 vols.
    2571 F
TALMAGE, T De Witt
  Crumbs swept up. 6555 RE
  From manger to throne. 5747 V
TAPLEY, D J
  Amateur photography; a practical
    instructor. 6906 A
TARVER, Francis
  French stumbling-blocks and English
    stepping-stones. 11451 EE
TASMA (pseud)
  Not counting the cost. 11496 F

TASSO, Torquato
  Jerusalem delivered. 53 P
TAUSSIG, F W
  Wages and capital. 9806 SS
TAUPHOEUS, Baroness
  At odds. 11587 F
  Initials, The. 2902 F
  Quits. 2903 F
TAYLOR, Bayard (pseud of James
    Taylor)
  At home and abroad. 1641 V
  Central Africa. 1643 V
  Central America. 11734 V
  Central Asia. 9061 V
  Eldorado (California). 1629 V
  Hannah Thurston. 858 F
  India, China and Japan. 1643 V
  John Godfrey's fortunes. 4858 F .
  Lands of the Saracen. 1644 V
  Northern travel. 1645 V
  Story of Kennett. 4855 F
  Views afoot. 1640 V
TAYLOR, Bayard (ed)
  Cyclopaedia of modern travel, 2 vols.
    1638 V
  Travels in Arabia. 9060 V
  Travels in Central Asia. 9061 V
TAYLOR, Benjamin F
  Between the gates. 2564 V
  Oak openings. 344 F
  Poetical works of. 85 P
  Summer savory. 1127 E
  Theophilus Trent. 3203 F
TAYLOR, George B
  Man's friend, the dog. 7857 A
TAYLOR, H C Chatfield
  Two women and a fool. 9705 F
  Vice of fools. 10731 F
TAYLOR, Isaac
  Origin of the Aryans. 10589 H
TAYLOR, Jefferys
  Boy Crusoes; or Young islanders.
    6985 V
TAYLOR, J Traill
  Optics of photography and photo-
    graphic lenses. 9874 A
TAYLOR, M Imlay
  A Yankee volunteer. 12554 F
  On the red staircase. 10334 F
TAYLOR, Myra
  Bayard Taylor, Life and letters of.
    1351 B
TAYLOR, Shepherd Thomas
  Harz mountains and other essays.
    6637 E
TAYLOR, Winifred
  Violet Rivers, or Loyal to duty.
    11537 F

TEAL, F Horace
Punctuation. 11010 EE
TEGG, William
Knot tied; marriage ceremony of all
nations. 5075 L
Last act; funeral rites. 5073 L
TEGETMEIER, W B
Poultry book, The. 1797 A
TENNEY, W J
Military and naval history of the
rebellion. 8906 H
TENNYSON, Alfred Lord
Enoch Arden. 10 P
Handbook to works of. 11397 R
Harold. 802 P
Poems of. 8216 P
Queen Mary. 10695 P
TENNYSON, Hallam
Alfred Lord Tennyson, a memoir, 2
vols. 10915 B
TERHUNE, Mrs M H (see Harland,
Marion)
TETLOW, John
Progressive series of inductive les-
sons in latin. 8351 EE
THACKERAY, W M
Adventures of Philip. 1020 F
Burlesques.1026 F
Christmas books. 1023 F
Four Georges. 1025 H
Henry Esmond, History of. 2485 F
Newcomes, The.
Paris, Irish and Eastern sketches.
1022 V
Pendennis, History of. 2660 F
Poetical works of. 12169 P
Vanity Fair. 9107 F
THANET, Octave (pseud of Alice
French)
An adventure in photography. 8290 A
Best letters of Lady Montagu. 7243 E
Knitters in the sun. 3225 F
Missionary sheriff. 10437 F
Stories of a western town. 7815 F
THARAU, H
Fellow students. 2162 F
THAXTER, Celia
Drift-weed. 6503 P
Poems of. 11262 P
THAYER, T B
Theology of Universalism. 8503 RE
THAYER, William M
Poor boy and merchant prince.12488J
Turning points in successful careers.
11755 E
Youth's history of the rebellion.
4245 J

THAYER, William R
Dawn of Italian independence, 2 vols.
7762 H
THEAL, George M
South Africa. 9502 H
THEBAUD, August J
Gentilism religion previous to Chris-
tianity. 4269 RE
THEURIET, Andre
The Abbe Daniel. 9389 F
THICKNESS, Philip
A year's voyage thro' France and
Spain. 5027 V
THIEBLIN, N L
Spain and the Spaniards, 2 vols4333H
THIELMANN
Journey in Caucasus, Persia and
Turkey in Asia. 3349 V
THIERS, Louis A
Consulate and empire of Napoleon.
4031 H
French revolution, 3 vols. 4028 H
THOMAS, Bertha
House on the Scar. 6974 F
THOMAS, Chauncey
Crystal button, The. 6662 F
THOMAS, Edith M
Round year, The. 316 E
THOMAS, J
Universal pronouncing dictionary of
biography and mythology. 485 R
THOMES, William
Belle of Australia. 11332 F
Lewey and I. 11338 F
THOMPSON, Basil
Court intrigue. A. 10041 F
THOMPSON, Sir Benjamine
Memoirs of. 242 B
THOMPSON, Charles Miner
Nimble dollar and other stories.
10659 J
THOMPSON, Edward P
Roentgen rays and phenomena of the
anone and cathode rays. 11199 S
THOMPSON, Francis
New poems. 10746 P
THOMPSON, Maurice
Banker of Bankersville. 2554 F
Louisiana, Story of. 6364 H
Poems of. 7060 P
Witchery of archery. 12118 A
THOMPSON, Silvanus P
Dynamo-electric machinery. 7563 S
Elementary lessons in electricity
and magnetism. 9353 S
THOMPSON, W M
Land and the book, or Lebanon,
Damascus and beyond Jordan. 3371V

THOMSON, A (ed)
Poetical works of James Montgomery. 11704 P
THOMSON, C Wyville
Depths of the sea. 12469 S
THOMSON, James
Poetical works of, 2 vols. 6654 P
Seasons, The. 9129 E
THOREAU, H D
Cape Cod. 5752 E
Early spring in Massachusetts. 608E
Excursions. 2129 E
Familiar letters. 8817 E
Summer. 5833 E
Walden. 2128 E
Week on the Concord and Merrimac. 3317 E
Winter. 532 E
Yankee in Canada. 5774 E
THORNE, P (Mary Smith)
Jolly good times at school. 12091 J
THORNBURY, Walter
Life in Spain, past and present. 12193 H
THORNTON, J P
Training for health, strength and speed. 10992 S
THORVALDSEN
Life and works of. 1758 A
THORPE, T E
Humphrey Davy, poet and philosopher. 11151 B
THURBER, Francis B
Coffee from plantation to cup. 6385A
THURSFIELD, J R
Peel, Life of. 6780 B
THURSTON, Robert H
Growth of the steam engine. 1404 S
THWAITES, Reuben G
Afloat on the Ohio. 12010
Colonies, The (Epochs of American history). 9854 H
THWING, Charles F and Carrie F B
The family; an historical and social study. 481 SS
TICHE, Ambrose
Development of the Roman constitution. 9173 H
TICKNOR, George
Prescott, Life of. 6345 B
TICKNOR, Mary Agnes
Two coronets. 7227 F
TIEDEMAN, Christopher G
Unwritten constitution of the United States. 10698 H
TIFFANY, Nina Moore
From colony to commonwealth. 7704 H

TILLE, Alexander (ed)
Friedrick Nietzche, The works of. 10970 E
TILTON, Caroline
Holland ,History of. 3348 H
TILTON, Theodore
Tempest tossed. 11671 F
The sexton's tale, and other poems. 11846 P
TIMAYENSIS, T T
Greece, History of, 2 vols. 11252 H
Greece in the time of Homer. 11256H
TIMBS, John
Abbeys, castles and ancient halls of England and Wales, 3 vols. 8849 H
TINCKAM
Poet's year. 11552 P
TINCKER, Mary Agnes
San Salvador. 7153 F
TIREBUCK, W E
Meg of the scarlet foot. 12358 F
TOCQUEVILLE, Alexis de
Democracy in America, 2 vols. 9310H
TODD, C B
New York, Story of. 5629 H
Washington, Story of. 5630 H
TODD, Mabel Loomis
Corona and coronet. 12579 F
TOLSTOI, Count Leo
Anna Karenina. 3387 F
Christian teaching. 12337 RE
Invaders, etc. 792 F
Ivan Ilyitch, etc. 792 F
Kingdom of God is within you. 8330 RE
My religion. 790 RE
Russian proprietor, etc. 2757 F
Sebastopol. 3155 F
What is art. 12243 E
What to do? 788 F
TOMPKINS, Eliz Knight
An unlessoned girl. 9508 F
Broken ring. 11925 F
Her majesty. 9530 F
TOMKINSON, E M
Benjamine Franklin, Life of. 7320B
TOPELIUS, Z
Surgeons' stories, viz:
First cycle: Times of Gustaf Adolf. 5640 F
Second cycle: Times of battle and rest. 5641 F
Third cycle: Times of Charles XII. 5642 F
Fourth cycle: Times of Frederick I. 5643 F
Fifth cycle: Times of Linnaeus. 5644 F

Sixth cycle: Times of Alchemy.
5645 F
TOPINARD, Paul
Anthropology. 1454 S
TORREY, Bradford
Birds in the bush. 1119S E
Foot-path way. 1127S E
Rambler's lease. 11261 E
TOURGEE, Albion W
Appeal to Caesar. 2549 SS
Black ice. 7144 F
Bricks without straw. 2251 F
Button's inn. 1072 F
Figs and thistles. 11903 F
Fool's errand. 826 F
Guage and swallow. 5634 F
Hot plowshares. 1071 F
John Eax. 4998 F
Man who outlived himself. 12283 F
Out of the sunset sea. 8510 F
Royal gentleman. 2869 F
TOWLE, George M
Beaconsfield, Life of. 1252 B
Heroes and martyrs of invention.
5780 B
TOWNSEND, Edward W
Daughter of the tenements. 9407 F
Near a whole city full. 11414 F
TOWNSEND, Virginia F
But a Philistine. 2025 F
Darryll Gap. 9826 F
Deerings of Medbury. 5332 F
Dorothy Draycott's tomorrows. 10896
F
George Washington, Life of. 301 B
Hollands, The. 5333 F
Lenox Dare. 9900 F
Mills of Tuxbury. 5335 F
Mostly Marjorie Day. 8480 F
Only girls. 6273 F
Sirs, only seventeen. 9828 F
That queer girl. 8479 F
Woman's word. 6295 F
TRACY, Roger S
Handbook of sanitary information
for householders. 9501 A
TRAILL, H D
S T Coleridge, Life of. 218 B
William the Third. 6775 B
TRAIN, Elizabeth Phipps
Autobiography of a professional
beauty. 9594 F
TRASK, Kathrina
John Leighton, Jr. 11030 F
TRAVERS, Graham
Fellow travellers. 10363 F
TREADWELL, John H
Martin Luther, Life of. 5355 B

TREAT, Mary B
Home studies in nature. 1412 S
Injurious insects in garden and farm.
1808 S
TREGATHEN, Greville
Australasia. 9566 H
TRELAWNY, John Edward
Adventures of a younger son. 6556 F
TRENCH, Richard C
Select glossary of English words.
11708 EE
Study of words. 11843 EE
TRENCH, W Stewart
Realities of Irish life. 6968 H
TREVELYAN, George Otto
Cawnpore. 6805 H
Early history of Charles James Fox.
12487 B
Lord Macaulay, Life and letters of.
135 B
TRISTAM, H B
Great Sahara. 3441 V
Land of Moab. 3299 V
TROLLOPE, Anthony
Autobiography, 2 vols. 1354 B
Miss Mackenzie. 11676 F
Ralph, the heir. 11757 F
TROLLOPE, Francis
Michael Armstrong, Life and adven-
tures of. 5032 F
TROLLOPE, William
New Testament in Greek. 5173 RE
TROUESSART, E L
Microbes, ferments and moulds.1410S
TROUSSEAU, A
Therapeutics, Treatise of, 3 vols.
8705 SS
TROWBRIDGE, John T
Adventures of David Vane and David
Crane. 10982 J
Cudjo's cave. 5329 J
Drummer boy. 11907 J
Fortunes of Toby Trafford. 8177 J
Resolute Mr. Pansy. 10873 J
Scarlet tanager. 6916 J
Three boys on an electrical boat.
8779 J
Three scouts. 8179 J
TRUBNER and Co (ed)
Keys of the creeds. 8687 RE
TRUESDELL, Amelia Woodward
California pilgrimage. 10910 P
TRUMAN, Joseph
Afterthoughts. 6856
TRYON, George W
Structural and systematic conchology
1526 S

TSOUNTAS, Chrestos
Mycenacan age; a study of the monuments and culture of pre-homeric Greece. 1136S H
TUCKER, T de L Booth
Catherine Booth, mother of the Salvation army, 2 vols. 8147 B
TUCKER, George Fox
Quaker home. 7115 F
TUCKEY, J K
Narrative of an expedition to explore Taire river. 5922 V
TUCKEY, Janet
Joan of Arc, Life of. 5353 B
TUDELA, Benjamin of
His travels, 1160-73. 367 V
TULLOCH, John
Sundays at Balmoral (sermons preached before Queen Victoria). 332 RE
TULLOCH, W W
Queen Victoria, Story of life of. 1329 B
TUNISON, J S
Master Virgil. 11919 EE
TUPPER, M F
Proverbial philosophy. 2283 E
TURGENIEFF, Ivan
Fathers and sons. 2555 F
Lear of the Steppe. 7471 F
Liza. 2556 F
On the eve. 7476 F .
Spring flood. 7471 F
TURNER, Dawson W
Odes of Pindar. 9779 EE
TUSON, R V (ed)
Cooley's cyclopaedia of practical receipts, 2 vols. 1603 R
TUTTIET, M G (see Gray, Maxwell)
TUTTLE, Charles R
Border wars of the United States. History of. 5252 H
TUTTLE, Herbert
Prussia. History of, 1134-1740. 4407 H
Same, 1740-1756, 2 vols. 8084 H
TUTTLE, Hudson
Scenes in the spirit world. 9472 RE
TWAIN, Mark (pseud of S L Clemens)
American claimant. 7482 F
Following the equator. 10909 F
Huckleberry Finn. 539 J
Innocents abroad. 2529 F
Library of humor. 543 F
Life on the Mississippi. 2533 F
Merry tales. 7812 F
£1,000,000 bank note and other new stories. 7814 F

Personal recollections of Joan of Arc. 10387 F
Roughing it. 2531 F
Prince and pauper. 2532 F
Sketches. 2528 F
Stolen white elephant. 7813 F
Tom Sawyer. 2527 J
Tragedy of Pudd'nhead Wilson. 9524 F
Tramp abroad. 2534 F
Yankee in King Arthur's court. 7462 F
TWAIN, Mark and Warner, C D
Gilded age. 10908 F
TWEEDIE, W K
Environs of Jerusalem. 3319 V
TWISTLETON, E
Investigation of the handwriting of Junius. 1686 R
Tongue, The, not essential to speech. 1508 S
TYLER, Josiah
Livingston lost and found. 3439 V
TYLER, Moses C
Literary history of the American revolution. 10492 EE
Patrick Henry, Life of. 1244 B
TAYLOR, Edward B
Anthropology. 12531 S
Primitive culture, 2 vols. 12457 S
TYNAN, Katharine
Way of a maid. 9363 F
TYNDALL, John
Forms of water. 1380 S
Fragments of science, 2 vols. 1419 S
Heat as a mode of motion. 1489 S
Hours of exercise in the Alps. 5409V
New fragments. 7063 S
Sound. 9445 S
TYNER, Paul
The living Christ. 12328 RE
TYRRELL, J W
Across the sub-arctics of Canada. 11387 V
TYRRELL, R Y
Latin poetry. 11965 EE
TYTLER, Sarah (pseud of Henrietta Keddie)
Papers for thoughtful girls. 6887 EE

UHLHORN, Gerhard
Conflict of Christianity with heathenism. 11234 RE
UNDERWOOD, Francis H
Handbook of English literature. 11816 EE
Henry W Longfellow, Life of. 1317 B
J G Whittier, Life of. 1361 B

Lord of himself. 6232 F
Poet and the man. 8072 E
Quabbin. 7662 F
UNWIN, W Cawthorne
Elements of machine design. 7565 S
UPTON, George P
Standard cantatas. 340 A
Standard operas. 7574 A
Standard oratorios. 7576 A
Standard symphonies. 7575 A
Woman in music. 7643 A ,
UPTON, J K
Money in politics. 9512 SS
URE, Andrew
Dictionary of arts, manufactories
and mines. 1677 R

VACHELL, Horace Annesley
Romance of Judge Ketchum. 9352 F
VAILE, Charlotte M
Orcutt girls, The. 12302 J
Sue Orcutt. 12303 J
VALLARI, Pasquale
Savonarola, Life and times of. 10882B
VALREDRE, Adrian
At dusk. 5048 F
VAMBERG, Arminius
Hungary, Story of. 4349 H
Travels in central Asia. 3291 V
VAN BENEDEN, P J
Animal parasites and messmates.
1399 S
VAN BRUPSEL, E (trans)
Population of an old pear tree. 8142 J
VANCE, Clara
Andy Luttrell. 7209 J
VANCE-PHILLIPS, L
Book of the china painter. 10038 A
VANDEHOFF, George
Leaves from an actor's notebook.
655 B
VANDERGRIFT, Margaret
Queen's body guard. 2234 F
Rose Raymond's wards. 7195 F
VAN DYKE, Henry
Gospel for an age of doubt. 10167RE
VAN DYKE, John C
Art for art's sake. 7734 A
History of painting. 8847 A
How to judge a picture. 6752 A
Nature for its own sake. 11923 A
VAN DYKE, T S
Millionaires of a day. 6367 H
Still hunter, The. 6332 A
VAN HOLST, H
John C Calhoun, Life of. 180 B
VAN HORN, T B
George H Thomas, Life of. 156 B

VAN LAUN, Henri
French literature, History of, 3 vols.
4117 EE
VAN LENNEP, Henry J
Bible lands, their manners and cus-
toms. 4808 V
VAN NESS, Thomas
Coming religion, The. 7653 RE
VAN RENSSELAER, Mrs Schuyler
Art out of doors. Hints on good taste
in gardening. 11160 A
Handbook of English cathedrals.
11161 A
One man who was content, etc.
10366 F
VAN VORST, Frederick B
Without a compass. 9000 F
VASARI, Giorgio
Lives of seventy most eminent paint-
ers, sculptors and architects, 4 vols.
10888 B
VASEY, George
Philosophy of laughter. 5086 L
VASSAR, John Guy
Twenty years around the world.
6234 V
VAUX, Calvert
Villas and cottages. 8877 A
VAUX, W S W
Ancient history from the monuments
of Persia. 12454 H
Nineveh and Persipolis. 5046 H
VEEDER, Emily
Her brother Donnard. 7417 F
VEITCH, John
Hamilton, Life of. 7631 B
VERGA, Giovanni
House by the medlar tree. 5821 F
VERNE, Jules
American gun club. 2708 F
Around the world in eighty days.
2123 F
Desert of ice. 7386 F
Dick Sands.
Facing the flag. 10184 F
Famous travels and travelers.1047 V
Floating city, etc. 867 F
From the earth to the moon. 871 F
Giant raft. 878 F
Great explorers of the 19th century.
1646 V
Great navigators of the ... century.
1648 F
Hector Servadoc. 12442 F
Journey to the center of the earth.
870 F
Michael Strogoff, etc. 11303 F
Mysterious island. 886 F

Steam house. 2690 F
Twenty thousand leagues under the
  sea. 2116 F
VETROMILE, E
Travels in Europe, Egypt, Arabia,
  etc. 3365 V
VEYSEY, Arthur Henry
Cheque for three thousand. 10368 F
VIAND, L M J see Loti, Pierre)
VICKERS, Robert H
Martyrdoms of literature. 7655 EE
VICTOR, Orville J
Southern rebellion, History of.4010H
VICTORIA, Queen
Leaves from journal of our life in
  the highlands. 484 B
VIGNOLI, Tito
Myth and science. 11366 S
VILLARI, Pasquale
Machiavelli, Life and times of. 7705B
VINCENT, Benjamine
Hayden's dictionary of dates. 7994R
VINCENT, Frank
Animal world, The. 11791 S
Around and about South America.
  7717 V
Land of the white elephant. 3292 V
Through and through the tropics.
  3326 V
VINING, Edward P
An inglorious Columbus. 3392 H
VIZETELLY, Henry
History of champagne and other
  wines. 4879 R
VOLTAIRE, M de
Charles the twelfth. History of.
  10631 B
Famous romances of. 8788 F
VON HOLST, H
French revolution. 2 vols. 9101 H
John C Calhoun, Life of. 180 B
VOSMAER, Carl
Amazon, The. 2225 V
VOYNICH, E L
Gadfly, The. 10644 F

WACE, Henry
Sacrifice of Christ. 12351 RE
WADSWORTH, C
Sermons. 588 RE
William Wordsworth, Memoirs of.
  1358 B
WAGNER, Harr (ed)
Pacific history stories. 10701 J
Pacific nature stories. 10700 J
WAIT, Frona Eunice
Yermah, the Dorado. 10808 F

WAKE, C S
Serpent worship and other essays.
  5270 RE
WAKEMAN, Henry O (ed)
Essays; English constitutional his-
  tory. 12516 H
WALCOTT, C Doolittle
Fossil Medusae. 12650 S
WALDSTEIN, Louis
Subconscious self. 10857 EE
WALKER, Francis A
Second army corps, History of the.
  4361 H
WALKER, Hugh
Age of Tennyson. 12653 EE
WALKER, W S
Between the tides. 4772 L
WALLACE, Alfred R
Darwinism. 5414 S
Natural selection and tropical na-
  ture. 6804 S
WALLACE, Lew
Ben Hur. 8055 F
Fair god. 10194 F
Prince of India, 2 vols. 7926 F
WALLACE, Susan E
Along the Bosphorus and other
  sketches. 12546 V
Repose in Egypt. 10988 V
WALLACE, William
Correspondence of Robert Burns and
  Mrs Dunlop. 11352 E
Kant. 7632 B
WALLER, Horace
Last journals of Livingston. 3323 V
WALPOLE, F
Ansayrii, or assassins. 3372 F
Four years in the Pacific. 5008 V
WALPOLE, Spencer
England from conclusion of the war
  in 1815, 6 vols. 12133 H
WALSH, J H
Horse in the stable and field. 6432 A
WALTERS, John C
In Tennyson's land. 7611 V
WALTON, Isaac
Complete angler. 1817 A
WANDLE and Faulkner
Writers' reference handbook. 7299 R
WANTERS, A J
Stanley's Emin Pasha expedition.
  8146 V
WARBURTON, W
Edward the Third. 5482 B
WARD, Anna L (ed)
Dictionary of quotations from En-
  glish and American poets. 11250 R

Dictionary of quotations in prose. 11251 R

Quotations from English and American authors. 7487 R

Surf and wave as sung by the poets. 61 P

WARD, Artemus
Complete works of. 12559 F

WARD, E
Pair of originals. 6793 J

WARD, Herbert D
Captain of the Kittiewink. 7406 J
New senior at Andover. 6474 J
Republic without a president. 7851 F

WARD, Mrs H D (see Phelps, Elizabeth Stuart)

WARD, Mrs Humphrey
Amiel's journal ,2 vols. 8658 E
David Grieve, History of. 6849 F
Helbeck of Bannisdale, 2 vols. 9974 F
Marcella, 2 vols. 8427 F
Miss Bretherton. 8657 F
Robert Elsmere. 10624 F
Sir George Tressady, 2 vols. 9974 F
Story of Bessie Costrell. 9322 F

WARD, Lester F
Dynamic sociology, 2 vols. 5727 SS

WARD, Matt F
English items. 11748

WARD, May Alden
Dante; sketch of his life and works. 11275 B
Petrarch; sketch of his life and works. 12200 B

WARD, Samuel
Lyrical recreations. 11551 P

WARD, Thomas H (ed)
English poets. 6786 B
Milly and Olly. 6798 J

WARD, Wilfred
Cardinal Newman, Life and times of, 2 vols. 11962 B

WARD, William
Hindoos; manners and customs. 5920 H

WARDEN, Florence
Deldee, or the iron hand. 11864 F

WARE, William
Aurelian; or Rome in the third century
Zenobia, Queen of Palmyra.

WARING, George E
How to drain a house. 3144 A
Street cleaning. 11405 A
Whip and spur. 12338 F

WARINGTON, R
Chemistry of the farm. 12171 A

WARMAN, Cy
Tales of an engineer. 9437 F

WARNER, Anna B and Susan
Cross corners. 3187 F
Dollars and cents. 1136 F
My brother's keeper. 1139 F
Yours and mine. 7230 F

WARNER, Charles Dudley
Backlog studies. 5399 E
Being a boy. 721 J
Golden house. 9139 F
In the Levant. 3283 V
John Smith, Life of. 2002 B
Little journey in the world. 6079 F
My summer in a garden. 725 A
My winter on the Nile. 5400 V
On horseback; tour in Virginia, etc. 7041 V
Our Italy. 6058 V
Relation of literature to life. 10319 E
Saunterings. 957 V
Their pilgrimage. 8646 F
Washington Irving, Life of. 188 B

WARNER, Francis
Physical expression, its modes and principles. 11359 S

WARREN, Henry White
Bible in the world's education. 7749 RE

WARREN, S
Ten thousand a year. 2706 F
Passages from the diary of a late physician. 8912 F

WARTH, Julian
Full stature of a man. 7151 F

WASHBURNE, C A
Political evolution or from poverty to competence. 10468 SS

WASHBURNE, E B
Recollections of a minister to France. 2 vols. 4831 H

WASHINGTON, George
Accounts with the United States. 9046 R

WATSON, H B
Galloping Dick. 10144 F

WATSON, Henry C
Camp-fires of Napoleon. 7461 H

WATSON, J S (trans)
Histories of Sallust and Florus. 475 H

WATSON, J W
Beautiful snow and other poems. 11808 P

WATSON, Paul Barron
Aurelius Antoninus. 230 B

WATSON, Sereno
Botany of California. 1145 S

WATSON, William
Father of the forest and other poems.
9503 P
Hope of the world. 11020 RE
Poems of. 8261 P
WEBSTER, Augusta
Daffodil and the croaxicans. 6847 F
Housewife's opinions. 6870 A
WEEDEN, William B
Economic and social history of New
England, 2 vols. 12146 H
WEEKS, Clara S
Text-book on nursing. 6429 S
WEEKS, Lyman H
Among the Azores. 5416 V
WEISMAN, August
Essays on heredity. 4845 S
Germ-plasm. 7863 S
WELCH, Deshler
Bachelor and the chafing dish. 9527 A
WELD, Henry P
Fly-rod and fly-tackle. 1818 A
WELD, Kate
Miss Curtis. 3160 F
WELLDON, J E C
Hope of immortality. 12357 RE
WELLS, H G
Invisible man, The. 10734 F
Thirty strange stories. 10489 F
War of the worlds. 11083 F
Wheels of chance; a bicycling idyl.
10115 F
WELLS, James W
Three thousand miles thro' Brazil, 2
vols. 3359 V
WELSH, Alfred H
Development of English literature.
7073 EE
WENDELL, Barrett
English composition. 7241 EE
WENTWORTH, G A
Grammar school arithmetic. 8360EE
WENTWORTH, May
Fairy tales from gold lands. 9019 J
Poetry of the Pacific. 93 P
WESSELHOEFT, Lily F
Flipwing, the spy. 12093 J
Jerry, the blunderer. 10121 J
Old rough, the miser. 12092 J
Sparrow, the tramp. 12090 J
WESSELY, J E
Pocket dictionary.
English and French. 1660 R
English and Italian. 1658 R
English and Spanish. 1659 R
WETHERELL, Elizabeth (pseud of
Susan Warner)
Queechy. 8189 F

Wide, wide world. 9106 F
WEYMAN, Stanley J
Castle inn, The. 12345 F
From the memoirs of a minister of
France. (Short stories). 9331 F
Gentleman of France. 9284 F
House of the wolf. 12431 F
Man in black. 12430 F
My lady Rotha. 10712 F
Red cockade. 9406 F
Shrewsbury, a romance. 11064 F
Story of Francis Cludde. 7923 F
Under the red robe. 9984 F
WHARTON, Anne H
Martha Washington. 10386 B
Through colonial doorways. 7816 H
WHEATLEY, Henry B
How to catalog a library. 5496 EE
WHEELER, Charles G
Course of empire. 5735 H
WHEELER, G
Choice of a dwelling. 8914 A
WHEELER, Stephen
The Ameer Abdur Rahman. 9750 B
WHEELER, William A
Dictionary of noted names of fiction.
10469 R
Handbook of familiar allusions.
5249 R
WHEELER, Mrs W L
Washington symphony. 7984 F
WHEWELL, William
Inductive sciences, History of, 2 vols.
1421 S
WHIGMAN, H J
How to play golf. 11014 A
WHIPPLE, Edwin P
Great speeches and orations of Dan-
iel Webster. 10342 E
WHIPPLE, Edward P
American literature. 1205 EE
Recollections of eminent men. 1371 B
WHISHAW,. Fred J
Boris, the bear hunter. 12368 J
Out of doors in Tsar land. 8246 V
WHISTLER, J McNeill
Gentle art of making enemies.7443 E
WHISTON, William (trans)
Works of Josephus. 4209 H
WHITCHER, Frances M
Widow Bedott papers. 11832 F
WHITE, Adam
Popular history of birds. 11685 S
WHITE, Andrew Dickson
Warfare of science, 2 vols. 10388 RE
WHITE, Ellen
Great controversy between Christ
and Satan, 3 vols. 396 RE

Sketches from life of Paul. 1247 RE
WHITE, Gleeson (ed)
Practical designing. 12486 A
WHITE, Greenough
Matthew Arnold and the spirit of the age. 11875 E
WHITE, James (ed)
William Miller, Sketches of. 392 B
France, History of. 12187 H
WHITE, Richard Grant
England without and within. 11783V
Studies in Shakespeare. 458 E
Words and their uses. 255 EE
WHITE, Robert
Battle of Bannockburn. 4405 H
WHITE, Trumbull
Silver and gold. 9857 SS
WHITEHOUSE, H Remsen
Sacrifice of a throne. 11964 B
WHITEMARSH, H Phelps
Young pearl divers. 11084 J
WHITEHAM, J W B
Western wanderings. 5010 V
WHITING, Lilian
World beautiful, 3 series. 11904 RE
WHITTHAUS, R A
Medical chemistry. 8714 S
WHITMAN, Sarah W
Making of pictures. 8135 A
WHITMAN, Walt
November boughs. 390 P
Selected poems of. 7530 P
WHITNEY, Mrs A D T
Ascutney street. 5779 F
Bonnyborough. 2748 F
Boys at Chequasset. 1149 J
Faith Gartney's girlhood. 5794 F
Friendly letters to girl friends. 10108F
Gayworthys, The. 5336 F
Golden gossip. 7323 F
Hitherto. 2745 F
Homespun yarns. 2656 F
Leslie Goldthwaite's life, Summer in. 807 F
Mother goose for grown folks. 755 P
Odd or even? 2705 F
Open mystery. 10441 F
Other girls. 2751 F
Patience Strong's outings. 2747 F
Real folks. 2750 F
Sights and insights, 2 vols. 5337 F
We girls. 2744 F
WHITNEY, William Dwight
Essentials of English grammar. 11799 EE
Language and study of. 1495 EE
Life and growth of language. 1398 EE

WHITON, James Morris
Gloria Patri; or our talks about the Trinity. 11515 RE
WHITTAKER, Frederick
George A Custer, Life of. 8969 B
WHITTIER, John G
Poetical works of. 55 P
WHYMPER, Edward
Scrambles among the Alps down the Rhine. 5676 V
Travels among the Andes of the equator. 7364 V
WICKSON, E J
California fruits and how to grow them. 5544 A
WICKSTEED, Philip
Henry Ibsen. 6832 B
WIGGIN, Mrs Kate Douglas
Bird's Christmas carol. 7925 J
Cathedral courtship; Penelope's English experiences. 7784 F
Children's rights. 7440 EE
Marm Lisa. 10109 F
Patsy, The story of. 5339 J
Penelope's progress. 11289 F
Polly Oliver's problem. 8027 J
Summer in a canon. 5340 J
Timothy's quest. 8648 J
Village watch-tower. 9409 F
WIGLE, E
Prevailing prayer. 10881 RE
WIGMORE, John H
Australian ballot system. 5953 SS
WIKOFF, Henry
Four civilizations of the world. 4338 H
WILBERFORCE, H W W
Lawn tennis. 7545 A
WILBOR, Elsie M (ed)
Delsarte recitation and directory book. 7103 P
WILCOX, Ella Wheeler
An erring woman's love and other poems. 10524 P
Poems of passion. 10526 P
Poems of pleasure. 10525 P
WILDE, Lady J F S
Ancient cures, charms and usages of Ireland. 8226 H
Ancient legends, etc., of Ireland. 7114 F
WILDE, Oscar
Intentions. 10598 E
WILDER, Marshall P
People I have smiled with. 6362 B
WILDMAN, Rounsevelle
Panglima Muda. 8928 F

WILKIE, Franc B
Pen and powder. 6373 H
WILKINS, Mary E
Humble romance, etc. 10514 F
Jane Field. 7415 F
Jerome, a poor man. 10721 F
New England nun, etc. 10572 F
Once upon a time, and other child
verse. 11931 P
Pembroke. 10515 F
Silence and other stories. 12001 F
Young Lucretia and other stories.
7356 J
WILKINSON, J G
Ancient Egyptians, Popular account
of, 2 vols. 9312 H
Manners and customs of ancient
Egyptians, 3 vols. 11258 H
WILKINSON, William C
Preparatory latin course in English.
624 EE
WILLERS, P F
Henry of Navarre. 11188 H
WILLETT, Edward
Search of the Star. 7198 V
WILLEY, Samuel H
College of California, History of.
4368 H
Thirty years in California. 8594 H
WILLIAMS, Henry Ted
Window gardening. 11592 A
WILLIAMS, Sir Monier
Buddhism. 5540 RE
WILLIAMS, Samuel G
Modern education, History of.8000EE
WILLIAMS, S Wells
China, History of.
WILLING, Mrs Charles
Genevieve of Brabant. 11787 P
WILLIS, N P
Poetical works of. 31 P
Rural letters. 6202 E
WILMOT, S Eardley
Development of navies during the
last half-century. 7607 H
WILSON, Mrs Augusta J (Evans)
At the mercy of Tiberius
Beulah. 10957 F
Inez. 757 F
Infelice. 10958 F
St Elmo. 9324 F
Vashti. 10959 F
WILSON, Andrew
Abode of snow. 8183 F
WILSON, Sir Charles
Robert Olive, Life of. 12475 B
WILSON, Edward L
In scripture lands. 6343 V

Photographics. 9875 A
WILSON, Erasmus
Cleopatra's needle. 3048 A
WILSON, Francis
Eugene Field I knew, The. 11830 B
WILSON, F Mary
Primer on Browning. 11381 EE
WILSON, Henry
Reconstruction measures, History of.
5934 H
Rise and fall of slave power in Am-
erica, 3 vols. 10390 H
WILSON, Prof. J. (Christopher North)
Lights and shadows of Scottish life.
312 H
Noctes Ambrosianae, 5 vols. 306 E
Poetical works of. 313 P
WILSON, Woodrow
Congressional government. 8837 H
Division and re-union; epochs of
American history series. 9871 H
George Washington, Life of. 10110B
Mere literature and other essays.
11369 EE
State, The. 8274 SS
WINCHELL, Alexander
Geological excursions. 7132 S
Sketches of creation. 11613 S
Sparks from a geologist's hammer.
3019 S
World life. 2020 S
WINCKLEMAN, John
Ancient art, History of. 2 vols. 1755A
WINDELBAND, W
Philosophy,. History of. 9195 EE
WINDLE. Mary J
Washington, Life of. 5936 B
WINES, E C
State of prisons and child-saving in-
stitutions. 12521 SS
WINES. Frederic H
Liquor problem in its legislative as-
pects. 10436 SS
WINGATE, F R
Mahdiism and the Egyptian Sudan.
6803 H
WINSOR. Justin
Christopher Columbus, Life of. 7412B
Readers' handbook of the American
revolution. 1776-1783. 11280 H
WINSOR, Justin (ed)
Cartier to Frontenac. 8326 H
Mississippi basin. 11918 H
Narrative and critical history of
America. 8 vols. 6020 H
Western movement. 114 24H
WINTER, John Strange (pseud of Mrs
H E Stannard)

Aunt Johnnie. 7973 F
Bootle's baby. 8317 F
Only human. 7818 F
Other man's wife. 7849 F
Peacemakers. 11086 F
Strange story of my life. 12580 F
WINTER, William
Edwin Booth, Life and art of.7999 B
Gray days and gold. 6072 V
WINTHROP, Theodore
Cecil Dreeme. 11866 F
John Brent. 958 F
WISE, Daniel
Uncrowned kings. 11830 J
WISE, John Sergeant
Diomed; the life, travel sand obser-
vations of a dog. 12005 J
WISEMAN, Cardinal
Fabiola; or church of the catacombs.
2032 F
WISTER, Mrs. A. L.
See Heimburg, Marlitt, etc., all col-
lected on shelf under "German trans-
lation."
WISTER, Owen
Red men and white. 9492 F
WITHROW
Valerie, the martyr of the catacombs.
11570 F
WOLF, Emma
Joy of life. 9985 F
Other things being equal. 7413 F
Prodigal in love. 10502 F
WOLF, Lucy
Moses Montiflors, Life of. 194 B
WOLFF, Julius
Robber-count. 5832 F
WOOD, Alphonse
Introduction to botany. 1437 S
WOOD, Edward J
Wedding-day in all ages. 2676 L
WOOD, Mrs Henry
East Lynne. 8315 F
WOOD, Henry
Ideal suggestion thro' mental pho-
tography. 8156 EE
Natural law in the business world.
8150 EE
Political economy of natural law.
8259 SS
WOOD, H Trueman
Modern methods of illustrating
books. 7616 A
WOOD, J G
Homes without hands. 12155 S
Horse and man. 1800 A
Insects at home. 1528 S
Natural history, illustrated. 1504 S

Trespassers. 1500 S
Uncivilized races of man. 4095 S
WOOD, W M
Seas of India, China and Japan.
4732 V
WOODARD, B D
Racine Iphigenie. 11869 P
WOODARD, David
Narrative of. 6208 F
WOODARD, S P
Manual of the Mollusca. 12628 S
WOODBERRY, G E
Studies in letters and life. 11452 E
WOODBURY, C J
Talks with Emerson. 6517 E
WOODBURY, George
Edgar A Poe, Life of. 1239 B
WOODBURY, Walter E
Aristotypes and how to make them.
9862 A
Encyclopaedic dictionary of photog-
raphy. 12240 R
Photographic amusements. 10788 A
WOODHEAD, German Sims
Bacteria and their products. 7654 S
WOODHULL, Victoria C
Human body, the temple of God.
8096 RE
WOODMAN, Abby J
Picturesque Alaska. 6340 V
WOODS, Katharine Pearson
From dusk to dawn. 7580 F
John; a tale of the Messiah. 9986 F
Metzerott, shoemaker. 8639 F
Son of Hagar. 10777 F
WOODS, N A
Prince of Wales in the United States
and Canada. 415 V
WOODS, Virna
An elusive lover. 11038 F
WOODWARD, C M
Manual training school. 5672 EE
WOODWARD, George E
Architecture and rural art. 8939 A
Cottages and farm houses. 1791 A
WOOLLEY, Celia Parker
Girl graduate. 6282 F
Love and theology. 3179 F
WOOLSEY, S C (see Coolidge, Susan)
WOOLSEY, T D
Religion of the present and the fu-
ture. 330 RE
WOOLSEY, Theodore Dwight
International law. 7084 SS
WOOLSON, Constance F
Castle Nowhere. 6045 F
Dorothy and other Italian stories.
9412 F

East Angels. 8316 F
For the major. 1145 F
Horace Chase. 8168 F
Jupiter lights. 4995 F
Rodman, the keeper. 6044 F
WORCESTER, Dean C
Philippine islands and their people.
12597 H
WORDSWORTH, William
Memoirs of. 2 vols. 1358 B
Poetical works. 8943 P
WORMELL, R W
Electricity in the service of man.
1516 S
WORTHEN, W E (ed)
Appleton's cyclopaedia of drawing.
1551 A
WORTLEY, Lady Emmeline S
Travels in the United States, 3 vols.
5176 V
WRENCH, Frederick
Recollections of Naples, etc. 1781 V
WRENCH, Matilda
Visits to female prisoners at home
and abroad. 11826 SS
WRIGHT, G Frederick
Greenland icefields and life in North
America. 4836 S
Scientific aspects of Christian evi-
dence. 10969 RE
WRIGHT, Lewis
Practical pigeon keeper. 12662 A
Practical poultry keeper. 1795 A
WURTZ, Ad
Atomic theory. 11274 S
WYCKOFF, Walter A
The workers: an experiment in real-
ity (The East). 11026 SS
WYLIE, James Hamilton
England under Henry the Fourth.
History of. 12139 H
WYMANN, Gilbert (compiler)
Land and mining laws of Alaska.
10898 SS
WYSS, John Rudolph
Swiss Family Robinson. 10416 J

XENOS, Stephanos T
Andronike 10859. F

YAGGY, L W
Museum of antiquity. 5859 R
YALE, Leroy M
Nursery problems. 10860 S
YATES, Edmund
Broken to harness. 2201 S
Running the gauntlet. 2202 F

YEATS, S Levett
Chevalier a Auriac. 10653 F
YEATS, W B
Fairy and folk lore of Irish peas-
antry..11540 F
YECHTON, Barbara
Derick. 10775 J
We ten; or the story of the roses.
10655 F
YONGE, Charlotte M
Armourer's 'prentices. 2666 F
Beechcroft. 2662 F
Book of golden deeds. 5464 F
Book of worthies. 6532 F
Caged lion. 2664 F
Chaplet of pearls. 2658 F
Cameos from English history, 7 vols.
6822 H
Dove in the agle's nest. 2669 F
Hannah Moore, Life of. 6347 B
Heir of Redcliffe. 5690 F
Hopes and fears. 5691 F
Long vacation. 11502 F
Love and life. 9286 F
More bywords. 6137 F
My young Alcides. 5239 F
Nuttie's father. 2742 F
Reputed changeling. 7186 F
Scenes and characters. 3147 F
Three brides. 5693 F
Two guardians. 5692 F
Two penniless princesses. 6067 F
Two sides of the shield. 2588 F
Sentimental journey thro'France and
Italy. 5097 V
YOUATT, William
The dog. 1794 A
YOUMANS, E L
Classbook of chemistry. 8386 S
Culture demanded by modern life.
599 EE
YOUNG, Aleander
Netherlands; A concise history of.
4139 H
YOUNG, Andrew W
Government classbook. 8941 H
YOUNG, Charles
Last of the Vikings. 9533 J
YOUNG, Charles A
General astronomy. 7560 S
Lessons on astronomy. 7093 S
YOUNG, John Russell
Around the world with General
Grant, 2 vols. 3313 V

ZACK
Life is life, and other tales. 12351 F

ZAHM, J A
Sound and music. 7442 S
ZANGWILL, I
Children of the Ghetto. 9347 F
Dreams of the Ghetto. 11087 F
King of the Schnorrers. 9332 F
Master, The. 9329 F
Premier and the painter. 10855 F
ZANGWILL, Louis
Cleo, the magnificent. 11881 F
ZIELINSKA, Marie H de

Marie; a story of Russian love.
9009 F
ZIMMERN, Helen
Hansa towns, Story of. 5370 H
ZOGBAUM, Rufus F
Horse, foot and dragoons; sketches
of army life. 3383 F
ZOLA, Emile
Experimental novel and other essays.
11409 EE

Blessed Hope Church.

Elm Street,
West of the Y. M. C. A. Building.

Sunday Services:—
Preaching at 11 a. m.
Sunday School at 12:15 p. m.
Loyal Workers' meeting, 6:30 p. m.
Preaching at 7:30 p. m.

Mid-week services:—
Ladies' prayer meeting Tuesday at
2 p. m.
Regular prayer meeting Wednesday
evening at 7:30.

First Baptist Church.

Walnut Avenue.

REV. E. H. HAYDEN, Pastor.

Residence, 149 Locust Street.

Sunday Order:—
Preaching at 11 a. m. and 8 p. m.
(Nov. 1 to May 1, 7:30 p. m.)
Sunday School, 12:15 p. m.
Young People's Meeting, 7 p. m.
(Nov. 1 to May 1, 6:30 p m.)

Mid-week prayer meeting, Wednesday,
8 p. m. (Nov. 1 to May 1, 7:30 p.m.

Sentenial German M. E. Church.

Washington St., near Lincoln St.

REV. W. KOHLENBERGER,
No. 14 Elm Street.

Services as follows:—
Sunday School at 9:45 p. m.
Preaching at 11 a. m. and 7:30 p. m.
Epworth League Sundays at 6:45 p.
m., Fridays at 7:30 p. m.

Prayer meeting Wednesday, 7:30 p. m.
Instruction in German Saturday, 1:30
p. m.

First Christian Church.

Lincoln St., near Center.

ROBERT L. McHATTON, Minister.
Residence—See Directory on Church.

Services:—
Sunday, 11 a. m. and 7:30 p. m.
Bible school, Sunday, 10 a. m.
Christian Endeavor, 6:30 p. m.

Prayer meeting Wednesday evening.

No Creed But Christ.
No Name But Christian.
No Guide But His Word.

Congregational Church.

Corner of Lincoln and Center Sts.
REV. JAMES B. ORR, Pastor.

Public worship, 11 a. m. and 7:30 p. m.
Bible School, 12:15 p. m.
Chinese Bible Class, 5:30 p. m.
Y. P. S. C. E., 6:30 p. m. (6:45 in
summer.)
Mid-week service, Wednesday, 7:30
p. m. (7:45 in summer.)
Ladies' Society, Cheerful Workers, Little Helpers, Tuesday afternoon.
Chara Class, Thursday afternoon at 3:30.
The Woman's Foreign Missionary Society and the Woman's Home Missionary Society meet the last Tuesday afternoon of each alternate month.
The Congregational Association of Christian Chinese, cor. Berkenshire and Cooper Sts. School open every evening. In charge of Miss Eva Fikes.

Calvary (Episcopal) Church

Corner of Lincoln and Center Sts.

REV. C. O. TILLOTSON, Rector.

Services at 11 a. m. and 7:30 p. m.

Sunday School at 9:45 a. m.

Holy communion at 11 a. m., 1st and
3d Sundays of the month; other Sundays at 7:30 a. m.

Parochial Mission, St. John Baptist
at Capitola.

First Methodist Church.

Pastor, see Directory on Church.
Residence 90 Mission St.

Sunday School at 9:45 p. m.
Preaching at 11 a. m. and 7:30 p. m.
Class meeting at 12:30 p. m.
East Santa Cruz Sunday School at 3.
Epworth League meeting at 6:30.
Week-day services:—
Prayer meeting Wednesday evening;
East Santa Cruz Thursday evening.

Ladies' Working Band every Tuesday afternoon.

Willing Workers Circle, Thursday afternoon.

First Presbyterian Church.

REV. ALEX. EAKIN.
Residence, 33 Third St.

Preaching, 11 a. m. and 7:30 p. m.
Sunday School at 12:45 p. m.
Westminster League of Christian Endeavor at 6:30 p. m.

Week-day services:—
Prayer meeting Wednesday at 7:30 p. m.

Ladies' Missionary Society, the last Tuesday of each month.

"King's Daughter's Circles" at least once every two weeks.

Index to Advertisements.

Anderson. J. W.......................Merchant Tailor 77
Archibald, J. H......................Harness 31
Ball Optical Co......................Oculist. Cameras, etc............39
Bias & Towne........................Grocers 25
Bixby Bros..........................Druggists 23
Bixby & Otto........................Shoes 85
Brazer, John........................Stationery 83
Cascade Laundry.....................Morrison Bros 9
Central Lodging House...............Mrs. J. E. Pettit.................61
Charley's Cash Store................C. T. Johnson.....................55
Decorative Art Society..............Ladies' Exchange 81
Eastern Hotel.......................Mrs. H. R. Place 79
Electro Therapeutic Baths...........Dr. Charles Witney 43
Excelsior Stables...................D. H. Woods, Mgr..................21
Fagen's White Cyclery...............C. E. Fagen 5
Fay, Hamilton.......................Drugs 51
Firestein, A. M.....................New and Second Hand Furniture ...49
Gadsby, B. C. ....Artists' Materials 65
Gem Restaurant ....Mrs. Le 'Tellier..................59
Grand Central Bakery................F. Coates 19
Jonas, D. ....Clother and Gents' Furnisher 75
Klein, C. J. ....Jeweler, Watchmaker 37
Klingler, G.........................Planing Mill 33
La Bonbonniere ....A. S. Bagge, Confectionery 29
Lamb, W. H. ....Hardware 3
Leibbrandt & Lewis ....Grocers 13
Little Basin Lumber Co. ....Grover & Co. 35
Loma Prieta Lumber Co, ...Lumber. Tanks etc. 7
Michigan Stables ....E. G. Mosher......................69
Palmer, S. A. ....Drugs 87
Richards' Manse ....Mrs. Annie M. Richards 41
San Lorenzo Livery Stables ....A. G. Abbott 53
Seaside Store ....Samuel Leask, Dry Goods ..17-57-71-123
Struckmeier, L. F. ....Merchant Tailor 45
Tanner's Drug Store ....Kodaks, Photo Supplies 27
Union French Laundry ....C. Ticoulat 67
Walnut Ave. Wood Yard ....S. L. Welton 11
Warth, Sam ....New and Second Hand Furniture ...63
Whitney Bros. ....Rambler Bicycles 47
Williams Bros. ....Gents' Furnishers 15
Windsor House ....Lodgings 73

For Following Advertisements See Cover.

Chesnutwood's Business College   Santa Cruz Art Studio, Photos
Geo. Harris & Co, Painters   Santa Cruz Cyclery, R. L. Green
McKean, J. T., Photographer   Williamson & Garrett. Grocers
Monarch Grocery   W. R. Springer, Oculist
Mrs. Mary Beeson, Nurse   Y. M. C. A. Restaurant

Santa Cruz Church Directory, pp. 122-23.

www.ingramcontent.com/pod-product-compliance
Lightning Source LLC
Chambersburg PA
CBHW030622270326
41927CB00007B/1275